ART OF THE EXTREME

ART OF THE EXTREME

1905-1914

PHILIP HOOK

P

PROFILE BOOKS

First published in Great Britain in 2021 by
Profile Books Ltd
29 Cloth Fair
London
ECIA 7JQ

www.profilebooks.com

Printed and bound in Italy by
L.E.G.O. S.p.A.

A CIP catalogue record for this book is available from the British Library.

ISBN 978 1 78816 185 5
eISBN 978 1 78283 515 8

FSC
www.fsc.org
MIX
Paper from
responsible sources
FSC® C023419

Contents

Introduction: A Tumultuous Decade

On 22 March 1905 Paula Modersohn-Becker, a twenty-nine-year-old German artist on her second trip to Paris, visited the exhibition of the famously radical Salon des Indépendants. 'The walls are covered in burlap and there the pictures hang, with no jury in sight, alphabetically arranged in colourful confusion,' she reported. 'Nobody can quite put a finger on exactly where the screw is loose, but one has a strange feeling that something is wrong somewhere.' To the young German imagination, torn between innate orderliness and a guilty urge to experiment, the loosening screw is both an ominous and an exciting metaphor. Modersohn-Becker's artistic antennae have picked up a warning that a defence is about to give way. What would be unleashed? No one was quite prepared for the deluge that broke over the European art world through the next ten years, a deluge of modernist invention that would shake traditionalist convention to its foundations.

The year 1905 marks the beginning of a decade widely regarded as the most momentous in the history of modern art, quite possibly the most important in post-Renaissance art history. In quick succession, works of art were created that defined the direction of modernism. New movements poured out after each other with a chaotic volatility, like water gurgling in a bottleneck: Fauvism, Expressionism, Cubism, Futurism, Orphism, Rayonism, Vorticism, plus the breaching of the final frontier of Abstraction in 1913. But only in retrospect does their significance become clear. And it is easy to forget that these avant-garde movements, central to all the art history of the period written later, occupied only a small minority of painters operating at the time. There was a conventional majority, oblivious to modernism, who continued to paint pictures in the traditional manner to please rather than challenge the public.

The pace of life was perceived to have quickened in the new century. Trains, automobiles, telephones and the cinema all contributed to that acceleration. Advanced artists were responding to it, not least in the tempestuous way that they were applying paint to canvas. But there was an intensification of activity in other parts of the art world too. The ten years leading up to the First World War saw a huge boom in the market for old master pictures, as American moguls became rich to an unprecedented degree and found that what they wanted more than anything else was to surround themselves with trophies of the great European art of the past. This early form of money laundering, putting your new wealth into old art and thereby transforming it into old money, was a seductive and inflationary process. The highest price ever paid for an old master stood at £100,000 in 1905. In 1914 the world record had risen to £310,000. [Approximate Exchange Rates 1905–14: £1 = 5 US Dollars = 25 French Francs = 20 German Marks = 10.5 Austrian Crowns = 9 Russian Roubles] But as more and more impoverished European aristocrats waved goodbye to their treasures in exchange for comforting quantities of dollars, a threat was perceived to the cultural heritage of Europe. Pertinent new questions began to be asked about the role of museums and the importance of national collections.

What was the artistic temperature across Europe in the first days of 1905? At the latter end of the nineteenth century, there had been widespread reaction against the entrenched conservativism of the official academies and the traditional art that they encouraged. In France, Belgium, Germany, Austria and Scandinavia artists had set up their own breakaway organisations in order to provide outlets for exhibiting to the public (and selling) the more advanced art that they were producing. In the German-speaking world, these were known as Secessions. In France the

Salon des Indépendants, in opposition to the official Salon, had been established by the artists Georges Seurat and Odilon Redon in 1884. Membership was open to all, and a degree of anarchy prevailed. Funds were mercilessly raided by members wanting fishing rods for use on the nearby Seine. At one point the cashier had to defend himself with a revolver. More recently, in 1903, the radical Salon d'Automne had also come into existence as an alternative to the alternative. There was a selection jury, but that jury comprised artists of strong modernist persuasion. Thus at the Salon d'Automne there was a sharper and more intelligible focus on modernism.

Indeed one of the features of the new century in Europe was the increasing frequency and reach of art exhibitions. In the mid nineteenth century the only shows of contemporary art that people took seriously were the official ones, such as the Salon des Beaux Arts in Paris, the Royal Academy in London and the Academy in Berlin. The emergence of the 'alternative' Paris salons and the German Secessions at the turn of the century was followed by a proliferation of exhibitions of modern art. They were facilitated by the increasing efficiency of communication and transportation, and they came thick and fast, large, small, conventional, subversive, international, progressive, held not just in museums and official institutions, but in dealers' galleries and even in private houses. It should not be forgotten, however, that even in 1905 far more art lovers attended the official, conventional shows at the Salon and the Royal Academy than patronised the avant-garde. And of those who did venture, experimentally, into galleries showing advanced work, the reaction of the majority was still either derision or outrage.

So what, in 1905, did artists think a painting should be; what should it do? The majority, the traditionalists, still felt that its primary objective remained the creation of beauty, and that as far as possible it should tell an uplifting or at least amusing story. But the much smaller number of largely younger artists who comprised the European avant-garde were in rebellion against these ideas. They knew their priorities were different, that – in the words of Kandinsky – 'it couldn't go on like this'. At the beginning of the year 1905, however, they were having difficulty in formulating a coherent definition of the purpose of painting. Recent ideas that had driven artistic experiment were running out of steam. The Impressionist credo that a painting should be a perfect replication of the optical impression made on the eye had been pushed as far as it could go. It was now entering its final cul-de-sac in the shape of neo-Impressionism, which imposed on the picture surface a quasi-scientific divisionism of dots or dashes of unmixed colour. Plenty of artists were asserting their modernity by painting in a pointillist style, in Paris and across Europe: from Prague to Brussels, from Munich to Milan. But for the innovators on the most cutting edge of experiment, the search for a new direction was on. The Secessions were looking a little tired. In June 1905, a Whistler retrospective opened in Paris. It was attacked by critics as old-fashioned: Maurice Denis declared, 'Impressionism is finished; one has even come to doubt that it ever existed.' On his first visit to Paris that summer Paul Klee offered the following considered assessment of Renoir: 'Facile,' he called him in his diary, 'so close to trash and yet so significant.'

Observers spoke of a mood of stagnation. Where to turn now? One way forward was the expression of mood or emotion in a picture. Already in the 1890s some painters had been turning inwards, in reaction against the interminable surfaces of Impressionism, and seeking the subject matter of their dreams and the wilder shores of their imagination. For an artist such as the angst-ridden Edvard Munch, this meant nothing less than the pictorial dissection of the soul. The lessons to be learned from the great post-Impressionists, van Gogh, Gauguin and Cézanne, were also in the process of assimilation. Was it legitimate to paint trees red or horses blue? Was a picture best understood as primarily a decorative arrangement of coloured shapes? In what new directions might the analysis of form now be pursued?

Across Europe, new ideas were simmering and from 1905 onwards began to boil over. Thereafter an unprecedented succession of transformative innovations cascaded forth year by year, up to the First World War, against the backdrop of an increasingly baffled, outraged and unyielding conventional art. First came Matisse-led Fauvism in Paris, mirrored in Dresden and Berlin by the German Expressionists – Kirchner, Heckel, Schmidt-Rottluff and Pechstein – who called themselves Die Brücke and shared a Fauve desire to distort nature and exaggerate colour. In 1907 Paris felt the early stirrings of Picasso-led Cubism, which for the next seven years dominated European modernism with its revolutionary deconstruction of form. In 1910, the coming together in Munich of Kandinsky and Marc, Macke and Klee triggered the formation of Die Blaue Reiter group, a second wave of German Expressionism, whose colour and mysticism opened a route towards total abstraction. Meanwhile Kokoschka and Schiele were ratcheting up their own powerful and neurotic version of Expressionism in Vienna, and in Milan, Futurism, dreamed up by the poet Marinetti, was gathering pace; by 1912 Boccioni, Balla, Carra and Severini were spreading its message of conflict and energy across Europe. In 1913–14 invention intensified still further: there was Delaunay and Orphism in Paris, Larionov and Rayonism in Moscow, and Wyndham Lewis and Vorticism in London. For the frenzied avant-garde art world the Great War came as something of a respite.

To illustrate the gulf between modernism and conventional art in these years, and the huge changes undergone by modernism in the same period, here are four contrasting paintings, two from 1905 and two from 1913.

The first of the two painted in 1905 is by the popular Austrian painter Eugène de Blaas, and the second by Matisse. The de Blaas shows a pretty Venetian flower seller standing by a canal with an overflowing basket of choice blooms. Painted with great technical proficiency to a high degree of finish, the young woman is a pleasingly accessible image of youth and beauty. Like its subject, the painting will only answer back in an unthreateningly pert and charming way. It's an image to promote joy and well-being

1. Eugène de Blaas, *Venetian Flower Seller*, 1905

2. Matisse, *Woman with a Hat*, 1905

in the viewer, and would have delighted any number of conventional art lovers at the annual 'establishment' exhibitions. The Matisse, on the other hand, is a challenge. It is scratchy, ill-drawn, and painted in smears of violent and unrealistic colour. It shows a woman in a hat looking back at the spectator over her shoulder. She appears anxious, or downright cross. Most early twentieth-century spectators, offered a choice between the two to hang on the wall of their drawing room, would have opted unhesitatingly for the de Blaas. Matisse's *Woman with a Hat* was bought by a mad American recently arrived in Paris, Leo Stein, for 500 francs. De Blaas's *Venetian Flower Seller* would have sold for five times that amount.

Towards the end of 1913 Picasso painted his late Cubist masterpiece *Femme en Chemise*. It is immediately clear that something extraordinary has happened at the cutting edge of modern art in the nine years since Matisse's *Woman with a Hat*,

3. Émile Vernon, *Under the Lemon Tree*, 1913

4. Picasso, *Femme en Chemise*, 1913

the most advanced painting of 1905. Fauvism with its non-naturalistic colour has given way to Cubism and its even more radical formal upheavals. Picasso has in turn progressed through Analytical Cubism, a grey, ascetic style of painting bordering on the abstract, and emerged into the Synthetic phase of the movement, a more colourful, sensual regime. Indeed such was the sudden erotic charge that the critic Guillaume Apollinaire felt in front of *Femme en Chemise* that he said it made him want to take the subject's blouse off, which couldn't have been claimed of the Analytical Cubist portraits that had gone before. Émile Vernon's *Under the Lemon Tree* was also painted in 1913. The appeal of Vernon's girl to the artist's traditionalist admirers is much the same as that of Eugène de Blaas's saucy *Venetian Flower Seller* of 1905. Nothing has changed in the way pretty young women are depicted at the official Paris Salon, but it speaks volumes for the speed of change and innovation among the avant-garde that the

Picasso and the Matisse – also both portraits of women – look so different from each other. And while there would have been a similar demand in 1913 for an Émile Vernon as for a Eugène de Blaas in 1905, there had been significant developments in the market for modernism. Picasso had moved on, thanks to the artist's dealer Daniel-Henri Kahnweiler, who had been nudging his prices up. The small but growing international coterie of collectors of his work would have been asked to pay around 10,000 francs for *Femme en Chemise*.

What happened to art in the years 1905–14 is of immense importance. A generation of pioneers emerged to orchestrate modernism: not just artists themselves, but critics and proselytisers such as the poets Apollinaire and Marinetti, the art impresario Sergei Diaghilev and the lone British advocate Roger Fry; dealers such as Ambroise Vollard and Daniel-Henri Kahnweiler in Paris, and Paul Cassirer and Herwarth Walden in Berlin; and collectors such as the Americans Leo and Gertrude Stein and the Russian Sergei Shchukin. These are legendary figures. Their story occupies ground well and expertly trodden by historians, critics and museum curators ever since. Given the abundance of books, articles and exhibitions focused on these years, can there be anything new to say?

I believe there is. I have been lucky in that, through involvement in their sales, I have been able to study in depth a number of the works illustrated in this book. My art market experience – encompassing some great works of art of the period (and quite a few less great) – has given me some different angles on the story of the years 1905–14. For instance, I believe that the revolutionary art of the period must be seen in the context of the conventional art being created simultaneously; that what people were prepared to pay for both new and old art offers fresh insights into this fascinating decade, particularly in the way that rising demand for old art intensified issues of national heritage, and the way that national heritage in turn became weaponised by international tension; but above all, that this was a decade when artists changed, becoming more individualistic, more solipsistic, more temperamental, more in touch with their instincts. The twenty-first-century cry of 'Look at me, I'm an artist!' found its first expression a hundred years earlier. And finally, in among the extraordinary number of modernist masterpieces created in these years, I believe that there is a lighter side to all this striving. The art world – artists making art, critics criticising it, dealers selling it, collectors collecting it, museums acquiring it, the public misunderstanding it – has always been a rich source of material for the human comedy.

PART I

RELEASING CONTROL

Chapter One

Basic Instinct

What changed, to make so much happen in just ten years?

Some time towards the end of the nineteenth century a balance shifted. Up till that point most artists painted pictures whose primary aim was to give pleasure to other people. Then at the turn of the twentieth century there emerged a new group of young artists – the avant-garde – painting pictures whose primary aim was to give fulfilment to themselves. They were in touch with their instinct; and remaining true to that instinct transcended all other considerations. Intuitive improvisation was good; calculation and control was bad. If this produced art that was less immediately accessible to the public, then so be it. The public must adapt. And meanwhile the artist preserved his integrity. In other words, having been the servant of the public, the avant-garde artist reinvented himself as its master. 'I am an artist so I aim to delight your eye and your imagination' was replaced by 'I am an artist so you must be interested in the expression of my instincts and the motions of my soul'. The extent of the modern artist's self-obsession can be measured in Paul Klee's declaration: 'In creative moments I have the great privilege of feeling thoroughly calm, completely naked before myself, not the self of a day but the whole sum of self, totally a working instrument.' Is it possible to imagine Alma-Tadema, or Bouguereau, or Anton von Werner, or any other of the traditionalist academicians exulting in their nakedness before the whole sum of themselves?

In trying to uncover the thinking behind the new art, there is one man it is impossible to avoid. For the generation reaching intelligent adulthood at the turn of the century, and particularly for its artists, Friedrich Nietzsche set the agenda. Although he had died in 1898, and had been insane for ten years before that, Nietzsche's writing struck a powerful chord in the early twentieth century. God was dead. Human beings needed to adopt a Dionysian approach to life, to become supermen through engaging with the pure life force. His advocacy of the vitalistic power of nature as regenerator of art and society was an idea that swirled seductively through the studios of a number of young painters. It led in the following years to all sorts of nudism, sun-worship, and other acts of dotty-minded anarchism. But on one point Nietzsche was absolutely clear. 'Genius resides in instinct,' he wrote; 'goodness likewise. One acts perfectly only when one acts instinctively.'

The primacy of instinct was the belief underlying most modern art of 1905–14. It was understood to underlie all human experience. Its centrality was emphasised by Freud, who was in no doubt that 'the deepest essence of human nature consists of instinctual impulses, which are of an elementary nature, which are similar in all men and which aim at the satisfaction of certain primal needs'. For an artist, therefore, his first priority was to be true to his instinct. Where those instincts were sexual, Freud said, there was the potential for an artist to sublimate them into producing even greater art. The connection between the sex instinct and creativity was a constant fascination to all concerned.

Here is Matisse describing how he painted the revolutionary *Woman with a Hat* of 1905: 'I put down my colours without a preconceived plan. I discover the quality of colours in a purely instinctive way.' Francis Carco, a young writer friend of Picasso, commented perceptively in front of *Woman in a Hat*: 'You had the impression that the artist had been much more preoccupied by his own personality than he was with the model's.' Exactly. You had to be true to your temperament. In the Impressionist generation, Zola had described modern art as 'nature seen through a temperament'. This was now inverted, so that what was being painted was a temperament seen through nature. The artist became more important than his subject. This in turn opened the way to distortions of natural form and colour in order that the artist might more truthfully express himself.

The premium on the instinctive in the artistic process, on the artist remaining spontaneous, meant that creation must be uncontrived, uncalculated and unselfconscious. 'The quicker a painting is done, the better it is', decided Nolde. In a letter to his friend and patron Hans Fehr in 1909 he added: 'In art I fight for unconscious creation. Labour destroys painting.' This was not in itself a new idea: it echoed the artistic precepts of the Romantic era a century earlier. '*Posez, Laissez*', Baron Gérard instructed his pupils. Your first touch should not be reworked. It will be your best because it is the most spontaneous. What differentiated modernism at the beginning of the twentieth century from the Romanticism of the early nineteenth was the lengths to which it permitted instinct to be extended. 'Instinct' is a word that recurs in the statements of young artists. Its indulgence was the key to unlocking the mysteries of human behaviour and passion. Scribbled in the corner of one of Modigliani's early Parisian sketchbooks in the artist's hand are the words: 'What I am seeing is not the real and not the unreal but rather the unconscious, the mystery of the instinctive in the human race.'

The prioritising of instinct led to a reinterpretation of the art of the past. 'The art instinct is permanently primitive', declared Wyndham Lewis in his magazine *Blast*. The art of early civilisations and primitive peoples was prized for its simple directness. No one could get enough tribal masks from Africa, carvings from the south seas, Egyptian antiquities, or mosaics from Ravenna. There was a modernist reappraisal of the Italian Renaissance, too. After the Die Brücke exhibition in September 1907, Max Pechstein set out from Dresden to refresh his eye among the Italian masters. Like Matisse, who had been to Florence a few months earlier, he rejected the art of the High Renaissance in favour of Giotto, Mantegna and Botticelli. These earlier artists spoke to the new twentieth-century sensibility because they were more instinctive, less mired in mannerist artificialities.

Thus the evolving template for the avant-garde artist insisted that expression must be spontaneous, sincere and instinctive. This involved a release of control: Kokoschka, writing in Herwarth Walden's journal *Der Sturm* in 1912 declared: 'We must harken closely to our inner voice ... All that is required of us is to RELEASE CONTROL ... All laws are left behind. One's soul is a reverberation of the universe.' It was a template crossing boundaries between the arts: the composer Arnold Schoenberg, a close friend of Kandinsky, announced: 'Art belongs to the *unconscious*! One must express oneself! Express oneself *directly*! Not one's taste or one's upbringing, or one's intelligence, knowledge or skill. Not all these *acquired* characteristics, but that which is *unborn, instinctive*.' He took the words straight out of Kandinsky's mouth.

But there was understood to be a danger inherent in this pursuit of the instinctive. What must be avoided was the formulaic imitation of other people's spontaneity. It was no good trying to be primitive simply by reproducing the forms of tribal art, nor striving for instinctive self-expression by the mechanical replication of van Gogh's brushstroke. In 1906 Matisse painted *Le Bonheur de Vivre,* which took a step beyond the Fauvism that he had orchestrated with Derain in the previous summer. The human figure was now more prominent. It was a very large canvas, in which the colours of the landscape were flat and distorted and vibrant, and the brushwork had cast off all its neo-Impressionist moorings. The surface was more restful as a result, and Matisse achieved his declared ambition 'to make the colours sing'. It was of course greeted with public derision and incomprehension when exhibited at the Salon des Indépendants. Matisse accepted that, as he did most of the antagonistic reaction that his work provoked. But one criticism touched him on the quick and he reacted instantly to counter it.

The painter and theorist Maurice Denis denounced the work as formulaic and artificially constructed. Wrong, Matisse

5. Matisse, *Le Bonheur de Vivre*, 1906

told him. It was the product of instinct, not calculation. Instinct again: that most highly prized motivator of the avant-garde of the early twentieth century. To be formulaic and calculated and therefore artificial was the biggest sin you could commit, whether you were Matisse or Derain or Picasso, Kirchner, Munch or Heckel.

But Matisse – who was a brooder – went on pondering the question. In 1911 he wrote to his wife Amélie: 'I get worked up too easily. To give yourself completely to what you're doing while simultaneously watching yourself doing it – that's the hardest of all for those who work by instinct.' This admission is important: in the process of working by instinct a total surrender of control is to be avoided. 'Simultaneously watching yourself doing it' implies that some sort of stepping back from the maelstrom of instinct to exert surveillance and even direction is necessary in order to achieve the greatest art. This question was bothering Apollinaire too. Was unfettered instinct too random? In 1912 he decided, 'Kandinsky carries Matisse's theory on obeying one's instinct to an extreme, and ends up obeying no more than chance.' Apollinaire has reached the conclusion that there has to be some sort of editorial control on instinct for its expression to constitute a meaningful work of art.

As a touchstone by which to measure creativity, instinct was given further impetus by the French philosopher Henri Bergson in 1907. Bergson was the superstar of French philosophy, lecturing at the Collège de France to packed houses of intellectuals and society women (a distinctively Gallic combination: in Britain a society woman wouldn't have been seen dead in the same room as an intellectual, unless she was Lady Ottoline Morrell and the room was a bedroom). In this year Bergson published his *Creative Evolution* in which he asserts that evolution is not a purely mechanistic process; creativity is endowed with something that is not predictable in advance, 'an energised will, a force, an *élan vital*'. Mere knowledge does not penetrate to the instinctual stream of consciousness that surges beneath it. Intuition alone brings us into immediate contact with the true reality. Intuition, according to Bergson, is 'instinct that has become disinterested, self-conscious, capable of considering its aims'. Making contact with the movement of life was only to be achieved by intuition, and this was what constituted the 'aesthetic faculty'. 'You must take things by storm,' exhorted Bergson. 'You must thrust intelligence outside itself by an act of will.' 'To act freely is to recover possession of oneself, and to get back into pure duration.' Duration is an important Bergsonian concept, a recognition of the mobility of time which in turn frees up and enables creativity, particularly artistic creativity. 'Duration equals invention, creation of forms, continuous elaboration of the absolutely new,' said Bergson. The 'absolutely new' had become the holy grail of the modernist artist in the first decade of the twentieth century.

Bergson is prospecting in the same territory as Nietzsche, who charged his vitalism with the seductive idea (to artists) that superior individuals (often artists) could surpass themselves and become supermen, to the overall benefit of humanity. And

Bergson also shares ground with Freud and his basic instincts, those 'continuously flowing sources of stimulation', to which artists were particularly responsive, and whose sublimation when sexual – according to Freud – had the capacity to generate great art. This privileging of intuition over analysis, of instinct over intellect, was very exciting to progressive young artists and writers of the early twentieth century. 'Taking things by storm' gave them carte blanche to express themselves freely, to live eccentrically, rebelliously and self-indulgently, and generally behave rather badly. The battle cries of political anarchism were echoed in the artistic avant-garde.

Intuition, as Bergson made clear, was perception driven by instinct rather than intellect. To modern artists it took on a specific relevance to the challenge of portraiture. Kokoschka wrote that the aim of his method was 'to intuit from the face, from its play of expressions, and from gestures, the truth about a particular person, and to recreate in my own pictorial language the distillation of a living being that would survive in my memory'. This was a new kind of portraiture, as Carco had grasped in 1905 looking at Matisse's *Woman in a Hat*. It was less a record of the sitter than a record of the artist's instinctive response to that sitter.

Instinctive response was what mattered. The bicycle wheel that Marcel Duchamp attached to a stool in his studio in late 1913, thus creating the first 'ready-made', was a statement of his disenchantment with painting. It was also a gesture to underline that the modernist artist still had only one duty: to remain true to himself and his instinct. The same year Arnold Schoenberg conducted a new atonal piece. At its conclusion he bowed only to the musicians in the orchestra, not to the audience. If the public didn't get it, then that was their loss.

Chapter Two

The Guiding Lights: Van Gogh – Gauguin – Cézanne

A long tapering fuse smouldered through the 1890s, and as the twentieth century dawned it began setting off a series of increasingly incendiary bombshells among the new generation of modernists. It was called van Gogh. The first major explosion took place in the galleries of the Paris dealers Bernheim-Jeune in 1901, in the form of an exhibition of seventy-one works by the hitherto largely unknown Dutch artist. In fact it was the first ever show of his work in Paris, eleven years after his suicide in 1890. This was a significant moment in the artist's discovery, a discovery that had huge repercussions across Europe. What the young French painter Maurice Vlaminck wrote of his reaction to that exhibition reflects the excitement:

> Up to that date I had not known of Van Gogh. His work impressed me as final ... I was glad of the certainties that he brought me, but I had received a heavy blow! I found in him some of my own aspirations. The same Nordic affinities, perhaps. And with that a revolutionary feeling, an almost religious feeling for the interpretation of nature. My soul was in turmoil when I left that exhibition.[1]

Vlaminck brought along to the show a young fellow artist, André Derain, who was similarly impressed. The pure, unmixed colour of van Gogh and the vigour of its application was a revelation to both of them. Vlaminck goes on:

6. Vlaminck, *Wooded Landscape*, 1905

I heightened all my tone values and transposed into an
orchestration of pure colour every single thing I felt. I was
a tender barbarian, filled with violence. I translated what I
saw instinctively, without any method, and conveyed truth
not so much artistically as humanely. I squeezed and ruined
tubes of aquamarine and vermilion, which, incidentally,
cost quite a lot of money at the paint shop at the Pont de
Chatou where I used to be given credit.[2]

Here are the origins of the movement that later in 1905 would
become known as Fauvism, for Vlaminck and Derain also met
Matisse at the Bernheim-Jeune exhibition. Matisse remembered:
'I was moved to see that these very young men had certain
convictions similar to my own.' What hastened the advent
of Fauvism was the 'show within the show' at the Salon des

Indépendants in the spring of 1905 of a van Gogh retrospective, forty-five works assembled by Paul Signac with the help of Matisse; it was the first official exhibition of the artist held in Paris, and it reinforced the impact van Gogh had made at Bernheim in 1901. It prompted the man of letters Paul Léautaud to write in his diary on 24 March 1905:

> [Van Gogh is one of those] extraordinary people, a little mad, standing outside the social framework and all the mediocrity of everyday existence. They are none too common. When we meet one we must not grudge them our attention and our love. They jolt us out of the humdrum and inevitable routine and turn us away from the artists and writers who have become steeped in professionalism.[3]

Individualism, independence, standing outside the social framework: this was what the avant-garde of 1905 particularly prized in its artists; artists who had not become steeped in routine and the calculation of professionalism; artists, in a word, who were in touch with their instinct.

Van Gogh was making even more of an impact in Germany. For the members of Die Brücke, a crucial moment in their evolution was the arrival in Dresden on 26 October 1905 at the Gallery Arnold of a van Gogh show (fifty-four paintings which had come on from exhibition at Cassirer's Hamburg gallery). Revelation of a way forward had been brought to their doorsteps. Heckel went out and painted a view of the Elbe that was directly inspired by van Gogh. The water of the river is still handled in neo-Impressionist dabs; but the sky swirls away in dynamic gouges of pure pigment. It was intoxicating stuff.

The Berlin dealer Paul Cassirer was central to the discovery of van Gogh in Germany. He had entered into a commercial relationship with van Gogh's sister-in-law, the business-like Mrs Bonger in Holland, who was doing an excellent job of feeding the contents of Vincent's studio on to the art market at gradually increasing prices. At the beginning of 1905 Cassirer was

7. Gauguin, *Maternité (II)*, 1899

buying from van Bonger at about 1,500 marks per canvas, and aiming to sell on at prices between 2,000 and 3,000 marks. An exceptional example such as the *Portrait of Dr Gachet* (see p. 117) had been sold by Cassirer to the modernist pioneer Harry Kessler in July 1904 for a modest 2,000 marks. All in all, in 1905 Cassirer sold twenty works by van Gogh, almost all of them to German buyers. Besides a small but growing number of modernist collectors there was a generation of extraordinarily advanced young museum directors in Germany who were also eyeing van Gogh. The first example to enter a German public collection was in 1910.

On 7 July 1905 a Gauguin exhibition opened in Weimar organised by the indefatigable Harry Kessler, who was now director of the Weimar Museum. It lasted till 15 September, and one visitor on whom it made a big impact was Emil Nolde. Paintings, drawings and a wood sculpture were included from the south seas and Brittany periods. There were loans from the small band of Gauguin enthusiasts in France, collectors such as Gustave Fayet and Daniel de Monfried. Gauguin had died in 1903, a painter of instinct par excellence and a trailblazer for Primitivism, simplification, and the power of primary colours unleashed from their descriptive function and allowed to roam free to express emotion. In the last letter he wrote to the critic Charles Morrice, from the Marquesas Islands in April 1903, he declared 'I am a savage'. Why was it necessary to regress to such a state of nature? Because in recent years 'artists, having lost all of their savagery, having no more instincts, one could even say imagination, went astray on every path'. Gauguin, too, was in the process of discovery by the avant-garde, who were further seduced by the drama of his back story, the way he had thrown everything over in Europe for a new life in the liberating paradise of the south seas: there was a gathering appreciation in 1905 for artists who had lived 'outside society'. The Primitivist dream lingered on in Nolde's imagination, and he too set off to paint in the south seas in 1913. Max Pechstein departed on a similar mission a year later.

But it would be a mistake to assume that in 1905 the French post-Impressionists had conquered anyone except the most advanced critics and artists in Germany. The art journal *Die Kunst-Halle* announced, with ominously militaristic overtones: 'Warning! A collection of paintings by the ... obscure painter Paul Gauguin ... is advancing slowly towards – Berlin ... Following on the idiot van Gogh comes now – Gauguin.' On 15 July another exhibition devoted to 'the idiot van Gogh' opened in Amsterdam. It was the biggest yet, comprising 240 paintings and 200 drawings. In January 1906, a van Gogh exhibition reached Vienna; and that autumn in Paris it was Gauguin's turn for a major retrospective, at the Salon d'Automne.

By 1907 Die Brücke were being criticised for remaining too long in thrall to van Gogh. Writing of their group exhibition at the Galerie Emil Richter in Dresden in September, the critic Paul Fechter, generally sympathetic to the new art, took issue with what he saw as the slavish imitation of van Gogh's technique. 'All this wildness is not spontaneous means of expression,' he complained, 'but agenda, theory.' Emil Nolde, now allied with the group, saw the exhibition and had a change of heart, siding with Fechter in suggesting that Die Brücke should rechristen itself 'van Goghiana'. Fechter's word cut to the kernel of the issue: wildness that was not spontaneous, but deployed artificially in obedience to agenda or theory, betrayed a loss of contact with instinct. This, in 1907, was being recognised as a cardinal sin.

As a reminder of where conventional landscape painting was in 1907, here is a typical example by the popular Danish artist Peder Monsted. It shows a stream wending its gentle way through woodland, painted in a technique that is photographic in its realism and detail. Monsted was forty-seven and too old to adapt to modernism. Why should he? His was a winning formula: meticulous accuracy in the rendering of nature and the evocation of a mood of rural idyll, which were the elements that his many, mostly city-dwelling, admirers in Scandinavia and Germany particularly prized.

8. Peder Monsted, *River Landscape*, 1907

A second landscape from 1907, on the other hand, would have been comprehended and enjoyed by very few. It is by Georges Braque and was painted in the south of France that autumn. Braque's painting captures the moment when last year's modern art – Fauvism – yields to the initial stirrings of Cubism. Landscape is no longer seen in terms of pools of vibrant unmediated colour, but in blocky, simplified forms out of which the intensity of Fauvist colour starts to drain.

The change was precipitated by the momentous rediscovery in Paris of the third great harbinger of modernism, Paul Cézanne. He had died in 1906, and in 1907 a retrospective of his work was shown at the Salon d'Automne. It had a huge impact, refocusing a whole generation of young artists away from Fauvism into new investigations of form. Painters who had gorged themselves on colour in 1905–6 now looked for an antidote; they fell upon Cézanne. What attracted them? The

9. Braque, *Landscape*, 1907

greater formalist rigour and discipline of his approach; the restrained colouring, applied in delicate patches; the multiple viewpoints in the same composition, precipitating vertiginous distortions that in turn pointed the way forward to Cubism. You had to work hard to understand Cézanne. Rilke memorably described the process of his conversion to Cézanne at this show: 'The puzzlement and insecurity of one's own first confrontation with [Cézanne's] work, along with his name which was just as new. And then for a long time nothing and suddenly one has the right eyes.' Cézanne was indeed a jump. One dealer had made it earlier than most: for the wily Vollard, who had been stock-piling Cézannes for the past ten years, the years of plenty were just beginning.

For Picasso and Braque the revelation of Cézanne that they received at the Salon d'Automne was a crucial stepping stone in their invention of Cubism. In June there had been an exhibition

10. Cézanne, *Grandes Baigneuses*, 1902–1906

of seventy-nine of Cézanne's watercolours at Bernheim-Jeune, a kind of warm-up for the autumn show. Picasso had already been impressed by these watercolours, which awakened him to what he called Cézanne's 'palpability', the way that the veils of colour make 'palpable' the light and space. Would Cubism have been invented without Picasso? Yes, probably, although it would have been a more anodyne phenomenon. Would it have been invented without Cézanne? Almost certainly not.

Art history sometimes takes lasting shape through the catalyst of a major exhibition. In 1912 the Sonderbund, a group of artists, collectors, and museum curators from the west of Germany, assembled in Cologne a mammoth show of 577 works by 160 international artists in what was intended as an up-to-date and comprehensive survey of the European avant-garde.

There were sections devoted to the contemporary art of Austria, Holland, Norway, France and Germany. The exhibition drew a large attendance: through the summer visitors flocked in not just from all over Germany, but also from abroad. They came to learn, to wonder and to deplore; and they came to smoke. A special Sonderbund cigarette was marketed and achieved record sales. There was no doubt about the artists now understood to be the presiding geniuses of modern art: the first five galleries of the exhibition were filled with 125 works by van Gogh. Gauguin and Cézanne were also substantially represented with around thirty apiece. Thus these three emerged as the fathers of the new art, and – through the cigarette smoke – the direct ancestry of modernism was set in stone.

Chapter Three

Colour and Fauvism

Colour was most spectacularly unshackled in 1905, and its liberation can be charted in the progress of Matisse through the year. These were arguably the most important twelve months of his career. He was not as young as the others in the vanguard of advanced art in Paris: at thirty-six he was half a generation older than Vlaminck or Derain or Picasso. He was not an easy man, either. He was fiercely serious about his art. Gertrude Stein, who could be perceptive about people despite her idiocies and eccentricities, later identified in him a 'brutal egotism'. Artistically he started 1905 still mired in a kind of Pointillism, still trying to adapt the discipline of painting in dots of pure colour to his own personal vision. He had spent the summer of 1904 painting in St Tropez with his friend Paul Signac, excited by the light but struggling to express it within Pointillist constraints. There were subversive politics at work here too, but different from the subversions that stimulated Picasso. Picasso focused at this time on down-and-outs, on beggars, on frugal meals, on people who lived beyond the constraints of society. The political message of Signac's art was an ideal of anarchistic society played out in unlikely Arcadian landscapes delineated in dots and populated by languorous nymphs.

Matisse's own very personal take on all this was his *Luxe, Calme et Volupté*, painted in autumn 1904 and first exhibited in the Salon des Indépendants in March 1905. It was a strange, hybrid painting; transitional out of neo-Impressionism, still bearing traces of Pointillist technique, but with an odd new decorative outlining; and infused with that spirit of Arcadian sensuality that

11. Matisse, *Luxe, Calme et Volupté*, 1905

to Signac at least carried a radical political message. Signac and Matisse were never closer than at this point. They had worked together on the van Gogh retrospective. And now Signac came forward to buy *Luxe, Calme et Volupté* for a generous 1,000 francs. Perhaps it was one of the pictures whose colourful confusion disconcerted Paula Modersohn-Becker on her visit to the exhibition. But to certain other artists it pointed a significant new direction. Raoul Dufy saw it at the Salon des Indépendants where he records he 'contemplated this miracle of the imagination introduced into design and colour. I immediately understood the new pictorial mechanics.'

Dufy was in a very small minority. Most of the Parisian public did not understand the new pictorial mechanics at all. The point about the Salon des Indépendants was that it was open to everyone, so there was a massive amount of painting on view. The writer Jules Renard compared it to a huge bookshop whose stock comprised only self-published titles: some good, some bad, some conventional, some daring and some apparently unhinged. Spectators came in numbers to visit the show, some driven by genuine curiosity and others by the sort of prurient pleasure that people derive from witnessing car crashes. Every now and then you might catch a glimpse of something shocking; a Marquet or a Maillol or a van Dongen, or a *Luxe, Calme et Volupté*. The conservative press would deride the dots and the exaggerated colour and the simplified forms. Certainly almost no one would buy them. Most people went home gratifyingly outraged.

'I cannot and will not look upon drawing and colour as anything except *means of expression,*' wrote Andre Gidé in May 1905. 'The line or the colour that expresses nothing is useless; and in art everything that is useless is harmful.' Gide has his finger on the pulse of advanced visual art at this point. Decoration alone is not enough. Expressing inner meaning is now what counts. Expression through colour; expression through line; and expression through brushstroke, through the tempestuous way paint is applied to canvas. That summer, Matisse headed off to the south of France in search of expression. Here he invented Fauvism, which in retrospect can be seen as French Expressionism, or German Expressionism without the angst.

He had good memories of St Tropez the previous year, whose sun and colour had inspired *Luxe, Calme et Volupté*, but now he went to Collioure, a fishing village on the Mediterranean much closer to Spain. It was suitably primitive. There was only one hotel, where he stayed, but he rented a separate room above a café in which to work. There were acute money worries. He was down to his last fifty francs, and would not have managed had his wife and children not been put up by her relations nearby. But none of that mattered, because three influences came together in Collioure that summer to transform Matisse's painting. First, there was the renewed impact of van Gogh, sustained through the exhibition he had helped Signac put on

12. Matisse, *Open Window, Collioure*, 1905

at the Indépendants. Second, there was his discovery of the full
force of Gauguin. Matisse had already been impressed by seeing
Fayet's Gauguins that year, which had opened his eyes to the aesthetic and Expressionist potential of flat planes of colour. Now,
through the sculptor Maillol who had a house near Collioure,
he was introduced to Daniel Monfried, whose Gauguin collection included sculptures of an extraordinary primitive power.
And third, the summer light of the Mediterranean unleashed
a new relish of colour in him. It was an explosive mixture and
led to the collapse of divisionism in his work, and its evolution
into something quite different, 'a tumbling mass of coloured
brushstrokes' rather than the mosaicised discipline of Pointillism. The view he painted through the window at Collioure, of
the glittering vision of the Mediterranean glimpsed outside, is

symbolic of his breaking free from the constrictions of the dot. 'I couldn't resist taking risks,' he remembered of that summer.

There was something alarming to Matisse in this cataclysm of colour that he had unleashed, an element of ordeal. 'Ah, how wretched I was down there,' he claimed later. There may have been a touch of retrospective self-mockery in this statement, but he recognised that he was on to something momentous, and his immediate reaction was of loneliness, of the need for a colleague with whom to share the audacity that he seemed to be orchestrating single-handed. So he sent for André Derain.

Derain joined Matisse in Collioure on 7 or 8 July. He was instantly overwhelmed by the power of the southern light and the impact of its colour, now heightened through Matisse's eyes. By the end of July, Derain had eradicated the orderliness of divisionism from his work. 'I am becoming coarser and coarser,' he wrote to Vlaminck. The power of pure colour came as a revelation as awesome to Derain as it had been to Matisse. As he described it later, 'colours became sticks of dynamite. They were primed to discharge light.' Matisse explained: 'We were at that point like children before nature, and we let our temperaments speak … I spoiled everything on principle, and worked as I felt, only by colour.' On 14 August a postcard from Signac arrived in answer to a request from Matisse to remind him of the lines of Cézanne he had read the previous summer in St Tropez. The postcard was inscribed with Cézanne's words: 'Line and colour are not distinct … when colour is at its richest, form takes on its fullest expression.' So the three midwives of modernism, van Gogh, Gauguin, and Cézanne were all in attendance at the birth of Fauvism that summer.

At the end of August Derain took the train back to Paris with thirty finished canvases and seventy more drawings and sketches. Matisse returned with fifteen canvases and 140 drawings and watercolours. One of Derain's paintings was the view of trees at Collioure illustrated here. Vollard bought it from him later in the year, and it remained in the dealer's possession until his death in 1939. Thereafter Vollard's estate was entangled in a

13. Derain, *Collioure*, 1905

protracted legal dispute, and the painting wasn't seen again till the case's resolution in 2010. At that point it was dug out from a sealed bank vault and offered for sale at auction. Preserved in darkness for more than half its life, the painting's colours were a revelation to the twenty-first-century spectator. Here was a glimpse of the 'sticks of dynamite primed to discharge light', as explosive as when they were painted.

Matisse's accounts of the summer of 1905 communicate the excitement and the emancipation of 'using colour in a purely instinctive way'. But the results of his new method were shocking. If anyone needed evidence that the artistic avant-garde was pursuing a course totally at variance with the sympathies and aesthetic preferences of the general public, he or she had only to attend the momentous exhibition of the Salon d'Automne that opened in Paris on 18 October. Cézanne was still alive and working in Provence: ten works that he had submitted were hanging, to trouble spectators or intrigue them, depending on their point of view. But Cézanne was a mild indoor firework by comparison with what was to come in the notorious Room 7, where spectators found themselves in a war zone. Here Matisse (who was on the selection committee) and sympathisers detonated the sticks of dynamite that had been primed in Collioure. Georges Desvallières, the vice president of the Salon d'Automne, was responsible for the grouping in the same room of the submissions of Matisse and Derain, together with those of their followers, who included Vlaminck, Albert Marquet, Henri Manguin, Charles Camoin and the Dutchman Kees van Dongen, recently arrived in Paris from Holland. What was new and explosive about the paintings in Room 7 was their colour, their roughness, their primitivism, and the emotion that the viewer sensed was communicated through them. It was the critic Louis Vauxcelles who called them fauves, wild beasts, in his review of the show. 'Fauve suited us admirably', said Matisse later. The imagery of the wild beast absolutely chimed with the sacrosanctity of instinct, purest and most accessible in its animal manifestation.

One painting that Matisse included in the exhibition had been produced between his return from the south and the opening of the show: this was *Woman in a Hat*, the notorious portrait of Madame Matisse. Frantz Jourdain, the vice president of the Salon d'Automne, tried to have it refused as being too modern even for his organisation's exhibition. Certainly very few people understood it. Even those prepared to take Matisse seriously – Maurice Denis, or André Gide, for instance – were wary about this new development. But at the end of the exhibition Denis at least acknowledged that 'the school of Matisse is the most alive, the newest, and the most disputed'.

The next year, 1906, the dealer Ambroise Vollard sent Derain to London to paint views of the city in the new and controversial high-colour Fauvist style. He was despatched in the hope that he would create something to rival the Monet series of views of the

Thames of 1901–4 that had recently been exhibited, to considerable acclaim, at Durand-Ruel. Monet, now a great and fêted name, had stayed at the Savoy. Derain, a penurious young man with his way still to make, could only afford a boarding house in Notting Hill. Still, out of two trips to London, in March/April 1906 and January/February 1907, he produced an extraordinary series of Fauvist paintings of the British capital. These represent a high point of Fauvism, yet simultaneously signal its demise.

What did Vollard expect from the series, and what did Derain? Vollard was probably satisfied: he took twenty-nine canvases in all, which appealed to his eye for vibrant, subversive colour and yet were topographically recognisable views of a reasonably commercial subject, the alien but (even to a Frenchman) important city of London. He felt confident he could sell them. Derain, on the other hand, was more ambivalent about the project. He claimed he was in pursuit of something he called 'the Absolute'. Whatever that was, he wasn't sure he achieved it in London. The light was very different from the visual revelation triggered by the Mediterranean sun that he had experienced the previous summer with Matisse in Collioure. He said he wished there had been more fog, but while that had been a bonus for Monet, it's hard to see how it would have helped Derain, breaking free from a residual neo-Impressionism into flat planes of pure colour. There is no doubt that he found painting his impressions directly on to canvas in England more difficult than he had expected. Returning to Paris, he told Matisse he had produced '*quelques toiles qui me font horreur*'. The existence of sketchbooks which contain drawings done on the spot of the views he ultimately created as paintings suggests that most of his oils were finished or actually executed later, possibly even back in Paris. But one thing happened to him in London that pointed a new direction in his pursuit of the Absolute. That was his discovery of primitive sculptures in the British Museum.

What was the Absolute? 'My dream would be to find a balance between my thinking and my unthinking,' Derain explained, 'between what my reason dictates and what my inclination

leads me to'. In other words, he was enmeshed in the fashionable struggle between intellect and instinct. Was colour, freed
from its descriptive function, the key to this? When he arrived in
London he believed so; he was possibly even set on a path that
would lead logically to total abstraction, to pure painting which
is 'no longer the image of objects but the image of feelings' as
he wrote to a friend he made in London, the Italian Bartolomeo
Savona. By the end of the year he wasn't so sure. The revelation
of Primitivism in the British Museum upset his balance. Now he
was torn between the seductions of colour and a reawakened
interest in the plastic potential of the human form.

What brought Derain back to Paris for a few days in late
March 1906 were two exhibitions: the Salon des Indépendants,
in which Matisse showed an extraordinary new painting called
Le Bonheur de Vivre, and Matisse's solo exhibition at Galerie
Druet which Derain helped to hang. It was also an opportunity
to show off one trophy of his British experience. When he came
back to Paris, newly kitted out by a horrified London tailor, he
was dressed like a Fauve painting: 'A green suit,' remembered
Derain later with some pride, 'a red waistcoat, and the yellowest
of yellow shoes.'

In *Le Bonheur de Vivre* (p. 17) Matisse had taken steps beyond
the Fauvism that he orchestrated with Derain in the summer
of 1905. Signac, his old ally, shook his head when he first saw
the work in January and said Matisse had 'gone to the dogs'. He
wasn't the only one to receive the painting with hostility. Mirth
and derision greeted its exhibition at the Indépendants. The
figures are the thing now, unexpectedly arabesque in outline,
looming ever larger in importance in the artist's conception. In
the same way that decoration alone had not been enough in
1905, now landscape alone, even animated by Fauvist fireworks,
was found wanting. The challenge for Matisse this year – as it
would be for Derain – was to re-engage with the human figure.

It was a challenge that Derain didn't much enjoy. On 2
August he wrote to Matisse, 'Everything I do seems frivolous
to me, for I should so like to produce something stable, fixed

and precise.' That was what pure Fauvist landscape was now in danger of becoming as far as he was concerned: frivolous. He must recalibrate the balance between artifice and spontaneity, between intellect and instinct in his art. That summer of 1906, in their different ways, Matisse, Picasso and Derain were all trying to define a post-Fauvist territory into which to move forward.

One artist who managed to make Fauvism continue to work for him was van Dongen. He was never a pure landscapist, so there was no heart-searching about reintegrating the figure back into his painting. He had mastered early on the knack of combining the wilder extremes of Fauvist colouring and technique with the exciting subject matter offered by the Parisian demi-monde. He wasn't hamstrung by the sort of doubt about the relationship between colour and form that was now beginning to weigh heavily on Derain and Vlaminck. By 1908 van Dongen had moved out of his studio in the Bateau-Lavoir. It was symbolic of a new direction: he was leaving the front line of the avant-garde as manned by Picasso and his gang, and following a path that would lead him ultimately into the embrace of society portraiture. Van Dongen was unmoved by Cézanne, and his style remained colourfully Fauvist. His work was still deeply attractive to the artists of Die Brücke, who continued to ply him with invitations to exhibit in Germany; but at the same time there was an increasing modishness to his Fauvism. The sitters in his portraits grow from now on ever more fashionable and rich. The recipe for his success was simple and enduring: sex and colour.

Another artist who in 1906 embraced Fauvism fervently was the young Georges Braque. But by autumn 1907 the exaltation of sheer colour had left him: 'with time the enchantment faded, and it was then I realised that one had to find something more profound, more lasting … I saw there was something further. I had to cast around for another means of self-expression more in keeping with my nature.' He found it in Cézanne. Indeed the retrospective of Cézanne's work held at the Salon d'Automne in 1907 sounded the death knell of classic Fauvism. Braque learned

lessons about form and landscape that moved him on productively to Cubism. Vlaminck and Derain were not so lucky. It is
hard to avoid the conclusion that the Cézanne show did these two
serious damage. From now on Vlaminck descends into a consti-
pated colour range, trapped in a Cézannesque mesh of trees and
water. Colour drains from his landscapes from 1907 onwards, as
it does from those of Derain. But at this point Derain was less
concerned with the lessons to be learned from Cézanne's landscapes than from his figures, particularly his *Grandes Baigneuses*.
He struggled to absorb into his own work these prototypes of
the modern nude. Perhaps Derain should have been physically
restrained from visiting the exhibitions at the Salon d'Automne
in these years: in 1906 he had been sidetracked by the Gauguin
retrospective into a temporary obsession with arabesque fantasy
involving Primitivistic figures in heavily stylised exotic settings,
and then came Cézanne in 1907. 'I'm going through a crisis,' he
wrote to Vlaminck that year. 'Impossible to do anything of my
own. Very weary physically and in terms of morale ... I'm doing
almost nothing but sketches. And I have several large paintings
in my head. But it's nothing.' For the rest of their lives Derain
and Vlaminck were looking for the inspiration that they had
found in the heady rush of peak Fauvism but never quite captured again.

In its purest, most intense form, Fauvism was a very brief
movement, but one whose repercussions reverberated for
the next few years throughout Europe. Second-wave Fauvists
responded in places as widespread as Prague, Amsterdam and
Moscow, seduced by the hot, rebellious colours. Fauvism was
a sensation to the Scandinavian avant-garde, who by 1908 were
arriving in Paris in numbers to worship at the shrine of Matisse.
One of them, the young Swede Isaac Grunewald, reported:
'Suddenly I stood before a wall singing – no, shrieking – with
colour and radiated light ... All of the rules I had previously
learned and used were abandoned. It was a completely new language which spoke in these canvases. But strangely enough I
felt I understood this language.' In the same year J. D. Fergusson

14. Vlaminck, *Wooded Landscape*, 1907

even blazed a trail to Paris from his native Glasgow to become that most alarming of combinations, a Fauve Scotsman. But very soon after Apollinaire was reading the last rites on the movement. 'The Fauvist kingdom,' he wrote, 'whose civilisation had seemed so new, so powerful, so bright, suddenly resembled a ghost town.'

Chapter Four

Expressionism and Angst

'What is art?' wrote Edvard Munch in 1905. 'Art emerges from joy and pain. Mostly from pain.' Opening yourself up to your instincts was now an essential part of being an artist, but it was by no means a guarantee of happiness. Instincts stimulated desires. Desires could be frustrated. Not getting what you were striving for bred suffering. But at least suffering was a powerful stimulus to creativity, as Munch had been demonstrating most of his life. Again, Nietzsche had views on this. Even if you never quite got to where you were aiming, the virtue was in the striving. 'Possession usually diminishes the Possession,' Nietzsche had laid down, an idea which was underlined by Thomas Mann in *Tonio Kröger* (1903) when he wrote, 'One may not possess. Yearning is Giant power, possession unmans ... ' A work of art should be the record of an ordeal. It was the journey that counted, not the destination.

As a tortured young painter, Munch had already made a scandalous impact in Germany when he lived and exhibited in Berlin in the 1890s. He was an accomplished purveyor of anxiety, not a happy man at the best of times. At least he recognised one consolation in his professional life. Unlike some painters, he was not concerned by the threat of photography to his art. 'The camera will replace the artist only when it can visit heaven and hell,' he declared. Still, it was a grim business.

You could argue that by 1905 his greatest days were actually behind him. *The Scream* still sounded out plangently, but having been painted ten years earlier its echo was receding. What is not always recognised about Munch's most famous painting

15. Munch, *The Scream*, 1895

is that it is the outside world that is doing the screaming. The tortured face is hearing the noise, not making it. In a poem in Munch's hand, attached to the frame of a version of the subject sold in 2012, he makes it clear that the central figure is himself, and describes how 'shivering with anxiety, I felt the great Scream in Nature'. Nature is screaming at the inner man rather than the inner man screaming at the outside world. It is a turning in rather than a bursting out.

But in 1905 Munch found himself something of a hero to a new generation of advanced painters in central Europe. The

16. Emil Filla, *A Reader of Dostoievsky*, 1907

artists of Die Brücke, who first got together in Dresden that summer, idolised him. They put him on the same level as van Gogh, which was the ultimate tribute. Although Munch spent much of 1905 on the edge of a nervous breakdown, suffering acute mood swings and indulging in regular alcoholic binges, there were occasional moments of sunshine in the gloom. In January and February his work was exhibited to considerable fanfare in Vienna and Prague. Munch visited these shows, and was fêted. 'Munch's work exploded in our hearts like a hand-grenade,' recalled Emil Filla, a young painter in Prague. 'It shook us to the very foundations; all our hopes and longings were suddenly realised. We were delirious with the feeling ... that an *artist* had arrived in our midst. An artist of our time and our mind.' No matter how depressed you are feeling, concerted adulation and having beautiful young women dance attendance on you will provide a measure of relief. Yet Munch acknowledged the enthusiasm with which he was received in a somewhat curmudgeonly manner: 'In Prague there was a lot of glory, but little money.'

But Munch's exhibition and visit set something off in Prague. In the early years of the twentieth century the Czech avant-garde was tenaciously absorbent of new developments in France and Germany as soon as it got wind of them. On artists like Emil Filla, Bohumil Kubista and Vaclav Spala the effect was immediate. Paintings expressing tortured agonies of the spirit proliferated in strange and expressive new ranges of colour. It was as if Munch had triggered a mass nervous reaction in the Czech soul, which resulted in paintings like Emil Filla's *A Reader of Dostoievsky*. Here the anguished subject lays aside his book and closes his eyes, unable to take any more suffering. He is quintessentially Munchian, turning in on himself rather than bursting out.

Van Gogh and Munch remained the key influences as the ideal of spontaneous expression of instinctive emotion spread among modernist artists in Germany and Austria. Munch continued to be in demand with the artists of Die Brücke. In February 1906 they issued the first of their many invitations to him to join them, if not as a fully fledged member of the group then at least to exhibit with them. Given their youth and inexperience, it was a bit like a provincial amateur dramatic society asking Sarah Bernhardt to star in their next production. Munch, still oppressed by existence, remained aloof. Instead he went to Weimar that summer at the invitation of Harry Kessler, to paint a posthumous portrait of Nietzsche. 'I have depicted him as the poet of Zarathustra, in his mountain lair,' explained Munch. 'He is standing on his verandah and, looking down over a deep valley, a radiant sun rises over the mountains.' It is a composition of large and colourful rhythms, the undulations of the landscape expressing a Nietzschean vitalism (and echoing the undulations of the great philosopher's distinctive moustache). It is also an

17. Munch, *Portrait of Nietzsche*, 1906

image emblematic of the age: the painter whose angst-ridden style inspired a generation of young artists portraying the philosopher whose radical thinking enthralled them. It's wonderful cultural history, but less good art; its slightly wooden quality and metallic colours are a reminder of how difficult it is to paint a successful portrait of a sitter you have never met.

Munch's Expressionist technique intensified in the years 1907–8. On the beach at Warnemunde in the summer of 1907, he painted a large canvas of naked men splashing in the Baltic Sea, perhaps protesting their health and vitality a little too vigorously. Given Munch's own concurrent alcoholism and mental problems, it is possible to catch in their cavortings the echo of a cry for help. At this point he began to re-emphasise gestural Expressionism in the way he applied paint to canvas. He wrote: 'I felt compelled to break up the flat areas ... with broad distinct lines, sometimes a metre long, or brushstrokes that went

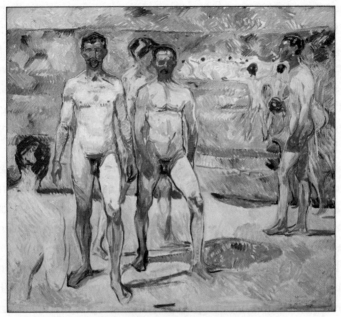

18. Munch, *Men Bathing*, 1907

vertically, diagonally, horizontally.' Later that year he painted another work in this style, *The Death of Marat* (see p. 140). It seethed with angst. The vertical naked woman standing in front of the horizontal corpse has just murdered her lover. It harks back to Munch's tumultuous affair with Tulla Larsen that began nine years earlier and ended with Munch firing a bullet into his own fingers.

In January 1906 the van Gogh exhibition which had made such a compelling impact on the young artists of Die Brücke in Dresden in late 1905 moved on to the Galerie Miethke in Vienna, with similar results. Klimt – the leader of the Austrian avant-garde – was too old a dog to be receptive to the sort of gestural Expressionism that van Gogh inspired, but for some younger Austrian painters it was transformative. Richard Gerstl, just twenty-two and dangerously passionate, had recently learned Pointillism from Signac and Vuillard, whose work had been exhibited in Vienna the previous year. Now van Gogh's handling of paint and power of emotional expression were a revelation. Gerstl, still at art school, was a difficult and self-regarding young man. He was only willing to join Professor Lefler's class at the Vienna Academy on the condition that he was given his own studio. And something else ominous was on the horizon: Gerstl moved in musical circles, and that spring he met the then struggling modernist composer Arnold Schoenberg, to whose wife Mathilde he started giving painting lessons. The scene was set for the subsequent unfolding of the sort of artistic tragedy that the highly charged neuroticism of early twentieth-century Vienna seemed actively to encourage, particularly when the inflammatory extra ingredient of angst-ridden, van Gogh-inspired Expressionism was thrown into the mix.

The Vienna Kunstschau, an annual summer exhibition, was now the focus for Austrian modernism. Klimt was still in charge, but by 1908 the elaborate Jugendstil decoration that characterised Klimt's work was being challenged by a younger generation who were increasingly obsessed with angst and self-torture. Klimt invited the twenty-two-year-old Oskar Kokoschka to exhibit, but his submissions were felt to be so outlandish that the committee was minded to reject them. Only the intervention of Klimt himself kept them in: 'Our duty is to give an artist of outstanding talent the opportunity of expressing himself,' said Klimt generously. 'Oskar Kokoschka is the greatest talent among the younger generation. Even if we run the risk of sinking our own exhibition, then it will just have to sink.' And, putting his finger on the elements of anarchic rebellion and masochistic self-torture so dear to the hearts of artists like Kokoschka, he added caustically: 'Let the press tear him limb from limb, if that's what he wants.' The press were indeed highly critical, but – against expectation – most of Kokoschka's work sold and the exhibition enhanced his reputation. His drawings were bought by other artists, including Kolo Moser and Emil Orlik. Perhaps his most controversial exhibit was a painted bust entitled *Warrior*, but actually, in Kokoschka's words 'a self-portrait with open mouth, the expression of a wild cry ... In the mouth were daily to be found bits of chocolate or whatever; in this way, presumably, the ladies of Vienna expressed their scorn at the work of this "super-Fauve", as the critic Ludwig Hevesi called me.' A buyer was even found for the bust: the modernist architect Adolf Loos. It was the beginning of a friendship between Kokoschka and Loos, who became his most important patron.

In 1909, to show his readiness to meet any new challenge that art or life might throw at him, Kokoschka shaved his head. Klimt, on the other hand, took to wearing what looked very much like a dress. Doubtless Freud, had he been consulted, would have had an opinion on both these developments. In 1910 it was now the turn of Egon Schiele – only twenty, four years younger than Kokoschka – to pit himself precociously against Klimt. Schiele dated his own final breakaway from Klimt's decorative influence to that same year, 1910. Looking back from the vantage point of November, the precocious young artist wrote: 'I went through Klimt until March. Today I believe I am quite different.' He was different in that he was now deploying his sublime line as a draughtsman to express an extraordinary intensity of emotion. The livid, elongated expressiveness of the fingers of the figures painted by Kokoschka and Schiele become the outward emblems of inner turmoil.

Teutonic painterly angst, which underlay classic German Expressionism, reached an apogee in the tortured production of Ludwig Meidner. In November 1912 Meidner's work was exhibited publicly for the first time. It was in a group exhibition with fellow Expressionists Jakob Steinhardt and Richard Janthur at Herwarth Walden's Galerie Der Sturm in Berlin. The three of them announced themselves as Die Pathetiker, exponents of 'the new pathos'. The pathos in question here was defined by the poet Kurt Hiller (writing of the Der Sturm exhibition) as 'the painterly expression of a feeling, of an experience, of the needs of the soul'.

Meidner's 'feelings', 'experiences', and 'needs of the soul' weren't exactly light-hearted, to judge by the titles of his pictures:

19. Ludwig Meidner, *Apocalyptic Landscape*, 1912

they included *Lamenting Women*, *Burned-Out House* and *Cholera*. And here for the first time the public was confronted with Meidner's apocalyptic landscapes. His subject matter is the city, but the city depicted ruined and devastated in explosions and conflagrations while comets and shafts of lightning blaze in the sky and human beings scurry about in the hopeless quest for safety. It is troubling stuff. The way that cities wobble and fragment might reflect some Futurist influence, particularly in view of the Futurist exhibition in Berlin from April to May that year; but Meidner's work is underpinned less by the excitement of Futurist dynamism than by profound despair. It should come as no surprise that Meidner was another artist who had been reading a lot of Nietzsche. No doubt Zarathrustra's words percolated through his imagination as he painted: 'I am nauseated by this great city ... Woe unto this great city! And I wish I already saw the pillar of fire in which it will be burned. For such pillars of fire must precede the great noon.'

Meidner's landscapes are often interpreted as uncannily accurate presentiments of the First World War. But they are more relevant as expressions of a turmoil that was already seething in the minds and imaginations of many young artists across Europe. Meidner's scenes of urban conflagration and destruction are a continuation of Munch's Scream of Nature theme. 'The sky turned a bloody red ... and over the blue-black fjord and city hung Blood and Tongues of Fire,' Munch had written in his poem on the frame of *The Scream*. Thereafter, the early years of the twentieth century had provided regular reminders of man's insignificance and impotence in the face of the power of nature; there had been the Messina earthquake of 1908, Halley's Comet in 1910, and in 1912 a rogue iceberg had sunk the Titanic. On top of that, the summer of 1912 was a freakish one in Berlin: a heatwave afflicted the city from April to August, and Meidner, sweltering in his small studio, turned out his anguished apocalyptic landscapes as a kind of visual manifestation of sunstroke. Meidner is one of those rare artists whose writing is as graphic and powerful as his painting. He recorded:

> I trembled, all that high summer through, in front of can-
> vases that seethed with all the fuming anguish of earth, in
> every patch of colour, in every scrap of cloud ... My brain
> bled dreadful visions. I could see nothing but a thousand
> skeletons dancing in a row. Many graves and burned cities
> writhed across the plains ... July had beaten my brains to
> a froth with its implacable brightness and the white, noise-
> less heatstroke. But August pinioned me like a bird of prey,
> hacking at me with its beak ... August has a stale, sour
> smell of diarrhoea and dead bodies.

He added a memorable description of the act of painting:

> Teeming Paris blue on white chalk grounds; cynical, cackling zinc yellow; white and ivory black, the colour of bedridden old people; permanent green next to screaming cinnabar; umber, bright cadmium, and fiery ultramarine – existence absolutely must be trapped between firm fat tubes of oil paint.[4]

Expressionism was about ordeal, but there were moments of creative pleasure in the experience, too. Finding materials to give physical form to strong emotion was part of the challenge. The artists of Die Brücke became enthusiasts for direct carving: Kirchner elaborated on its appeal in a letter to the collector Gustav Schiefler on 27 June 1911: 'It is good for painting and drawing to carve figures. It gives drawing more determination and it is a sensual pleasure, when blow for blow the figure grows out of the tree trunk. In every trunk a figure is to be found, you only need to pare away the wood.' That sensual element, taken in conjunction with Meidner's pleasure in 'trapping existence between firm fat tubes of oil paint' articulates the energy pulsating at the heart of German Expressionism in the years leading up to the First World War.

CHAPTER FIVE

Primitivism: the Wisdom of Savages

The Dionysian new regime of modern art encouraged an anarchistic disregard for petty regulations. Indulging your instinct trumped obeying the law. On 27 February 1907, Apollinaire brought along to supper at the Bateau-Lavoir a disreputable friend called Géry Pieret, who listened to Picasso waxing lyrical about the Iberian sculptures in the Louvre and decided to steal a couple for him. Pieret's motives were not so much to give a helping hand to modernism as to make a quick profit. Picasso paid Pieret fifty francs for the stolen loot and bore them off into his studio where they exerted an important influence on his painting. What made these examples of primitive art so desirable to Picasso, pieces that a generation earlier would have been dismissed as crude native artefacts of interest only to anthropologists?

In the first years of the twentieth century there had been an awakening to non-western or prehistoric art. It was driven by a reaction against industrialisation and the advances of science, by a desire to reject the artificialities of 'civilisation' and recapture a natural state which gave free play to instinct. Out went the certainties and sophistications of traditional Renaissance art, its flagrant calculation and rationality. In came subjectivism and a desire to reconnect with the innocence of primitive societies and the spontaneity of their artistic expression. As a young European artist, how could you find out about primitive art? You could study it in ethnographic museums; you could see it in the examples of tribal art that people brought back from the colonies; or, like Gauguin (and later Nolde and Pechstein), you could travel halfway round the world in search of remote places where the primitive survived and renew your own art under its stimulus. Or, if you were Picasso, you could have it stolen for you and brought to your studio.

The burlap that Modersohn-Becker noticed covering the walls at the Salon des Indépendants in 1905 was itself a statement of the primitive, the rough and ready in preference to the silk or damask of the museum or the traditional dealer's gallery (although the fact that burlap was cheap may have had something to do with it too). There was a pervasive desire among the avant-garde to pare down to basics, to cut out the inessential. Rousseau's ideal of the *bon sauvage* was dusted down and redeployed, the belief that if you stripped man of all his affectations and left him only with his natural instincts, his innate nobility would be revealed. Vlaminck describes himself in the first flush of Fauvism as 'a tender barbarian, filled with violence. I translated what I saw instinctively, without any method, and conveyed truth less as an artist than as a human being.' Having cast himself in the role of the noble savage, Vlaminck was one of the first to go digging in Parisian bric-a-brac shops for tribal art. Derain's conversion to Primitivism came soon after, in the ethnographic department of the British Museum during his trip to London in 1906.

Matisse, too, was moving in the same direction. In that miraculous summer of 1905 at Collioure, the sculptor Maillol introduced him to Daniel Monfried, whose Gauguin collection included sculptures created in Tahiti which made a deep impact with their extraordinary primitive power. Back in Paris, Matisse began looking at the sort of tribal art that had been Gauguin's original inspiration. So did Picasso. His discovery of Primitivism was perhaps the most dramatic of all in terms of what it precipitated. Picasso was prodigiously talented and highly self-confident. His blue period and his pink period produced a succession of very beautiful paintings of human figures – down-and-outs, street urchins, circus folk – and already constituted an extraordinary body of work for a man who was still only twenty-five. But he had not yet made any revolutionary change in the history of art. What triggered in him something new and shocking, leading on to his eccentric and outrageous *Demoiselles d'Avignon* in 1907, was the impact of primitive art.

Picasso and his girlfriend Fernande Olivier spent the summer of 1906 in the Pyrenees. They stayed in the village of Gosol, 5,000 feet up, in a primitive peasant community. Here Picasso's art changed. The final throes of blue period compassion and rose period charm were being worked out of his system. The human figure remained central, and his eye continued to focus on the female nude; but something more primitive emerged, and something more sculptural as he too started experimenting in woodcarving. Gradually he also began to challenge the laws of perspective that had held good since the Renaissance. Fernande – whose diaries remain the chief source of day-to-day information about Picasso's activities – also remained his main model, but his pictorial treatment of her changed: Picasso was now presenting her, in the words of John Richardson, as 'a flat-footed, bull-necked, banana-fingered earth mother'. His *Two Nudes* of that autumn comprises the same female figure seen from two angles. The space around the figures is growing shallower. His compositions are gradually being drained of colour and sentiment, and his forms are being pared down to the essential. The short legs and squat dimensions of the figures attest to the influence of African statues, like the Congolese Vili figure that Matisse had just bought when he exposed it to Picasso's envious gaze at the Steins' studio that same autumn. Picasso was fascinated by it. A new world was opening up for him.

The testimony of Picasso about himself is not always the most reliable, but his later description of his first encounter with African Art in the Museum of Ethnography around this time has the ring of truth:

The masks weren't like other kinds of sculpture. Not at all. They were magical things ... I understood what the purpose of the sculpture was for the negroes ... all the

20. Picasso, *Two Nudes*, 1906

fetishes were used for the same thing. They were weapons. To help people stop being dominated by spirits, to become independent. Tools. If we give form to the spirits, we become independent of them. The spirits, the unconscious (which wasn't yet much spoken of then), emotion, it's the same thing. I understood why I was a painter.[5]

The mask became one of modern art's key themes in the first part of the twentieth century. Avant-garde artists used masks in a variety of ways: as emblems of primitive, more instinctive cultures; as symbols of human emotion; as protective surfaces beneath which deeper feelings run; and, in the hands of Picasso, as instruments of magic.

Modernists responded to the strong sculptural element in primitive art. As Derain thrashed about for a post-Fauve identity in 1907, he did come up with one exceptional and powerful piece which owed something to the lingering influence of Gauguin. His *Crouching Figure* is carved from a block of stone with a powerful primitive expressiveness. But it didn't lead Derain much further, and by the autumn of 1907 he was back with his painting, grappling with Cézanne's bathers. This sort of Primitivist carving was the direction in which Brancusi was now moving, too, as he entrenched his reputation as the rough-hewn Balkan. After his brief experience in Rodin's studio, he moved into the complex of cheap studios called La Ruche, a place of refuge for penurious young artists arriving in Paris from abroad. First, Brancusi carved his *Sleep*, a beautiful piece of Rodinesque lyricism; and then he produced something distinctly un-Rodinesque, a first version of *The Kiss*, carved directly not out of marble but of stone. *The Kiss* is an elemental piece, dredged from Romanian folkoric memories and a new awareness of tribal art. The block remains the block, animated by the primitivism of the features of the two mirror-imaged figures locked in an embrace.

It is a simple and oddly touching image, and it had an immediate reincarnation in tragically romantic circumstances. In

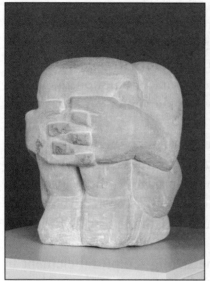

21. Derain, *Crouching Figure*, 1907   22. Brancusi, *The Kiss*, 1908

November 1910 a young Romanian woman, Tatiana Rachewsky, committed suicide in Paris as result of an unhappy love affair. Her family commissioned a monument for her grave from Brancusi, who carved another version of *The Kiss* which was installed in Montparnasse cemetery in April 1911. Walking through the same cemetery a hundred years later I was amazed to see it still there, an unlikely modernist intrusion among a jumble of more traditional tomb design. Its survival, unstolen up to that point, was testament either to the innate decency of the thieving fraternity in Paris, or its art-historical ignorance.

In its essence, direct carving was profoundly Primitivist and profoundly Expressionist. Brancusi was thus part of a movement that had modernist adherents across Europe, linking him to Kirchner and the artists of Die Brücke. What Brancusi was doing had an influence on his friend Modigliani, too. In the years 1910–12 Modigliani operated primarily as a sculptor, and shared Brancusi's pleasure in the primitive, elemental immediacy of working in stone. He was strongly influenced by African art, particularly tribal masks, and by ancient Egyptian prototypes (see p. 157).

While Modigliani's Primitivism was externally triggered in that its catalyst was contact with the art of primitive cultures, there was a new awe of art produced by the untutored artist directly in touch with his own instinct. Henri Rousseau – who rose to unexpected fame as a painter in the first years of the twentieth century – was both by character and painting style a genuine naif. He had spent most of his career working as a customs officer, hence his nickname 'the Douanier'. By 1900 he had given up his day job to concentrate on the hobby that obsessed him: his painting. His work caught the excited attention of various members of the Parisian avant-garde, Picasso included. A simpleton artist had an impact in the first ten years of the twentieth century – when Primitivism was being prized – out of all proportion to the impact he would have made in the first ten years of, say, the nineteenth century. It underlines how important in the history of art it is to be operating in the right place at the right time. Even Picasso might not have flourished quite so spectacularly had he been born in 1781 rather than 1881. The same with Rousseau: had he been painting in Budapest rather than Paris, would he have become as admired and influential as he did? His works had a strange and mesmerising quality, but so did those of certain other primitive painters of the time, whose fate it was to be overlooked. Take the case of the Hungarian Mihaly Tivadar Kosztka Csontvary (1853–1919). He was a mystic, one of the great 'loners' of art history. He suffered from schizophrenia. His paintings, naive, dreamlike compositions sometimes on a megalomaniac scale, possess a Rousseauesque intensity. He even exhibited in Paris in 1907, but no one noticed him. He is celebrated today in Hungary; but he is not known on the international stage in the way that he would be if, say, Apollinaire had spotted him and taken him up.

In December 1907, Rousseau got himself into trouble with a cheque presented to him by one of his pupils (in order to support

23. Henri Rousseau, *Exotic Landscape*, 1907

24. Csontvary, *The Solitary Cedar*, 1907

himself Rousseau also gave music lessons). When Rousseau – unaware that it was forged – tried to cash it, he was arrested and imprisoned. The case came to court, and the outcome was in the balance. The argument that finally inclined the judge towards clemency was the defending counsel's submission of one of Rousseau's paintings as evidence. 'Can you still doubt that my client is an innocent?' the lawyer asked. In the vexed history of the relationship between art and law, this is a rare instance of a work of art being accepted in court as evidence of anything, let alone positive affirmation of the artist's character.

The banquet in honour of Henri Rousseau that was held at Picasso's studio on 21 November 1908 has taken on the status of legend. As such, it is difficult to separate fact from fiction in the later accounts of it, written either by those who had been there but couldn't remember very clearly what had actually happened, or by those who thought they had been there but probably weren't and wrote even more unreliable reports of proceedings. What is certain is that Picasso genuinely admired the simplicity and intensity of Rousseau's pictorial vision and owned works by him. The invitation to a dinner at the Bateau-Lavoir as guest of honour was not entirely a joke. Rousseau was seated on an imitation throne, a chair elevated on packing cases. Fernande cooked paella, so she was there. So were the Steins and Alice B. Toklas. Also Picasso's poet friends, Apollinaire and André Salmon. Braque and Juan Gris were there, plus Sonia Delaunay, at this point sailing under a flag of convenience as Mrs Wilhelm von Uhde. Marie Laurencin was there, and in the course of an inebriated dance, fell into a tray of jam tarts. Was Brancusi there? He later claimed to have been. There were toasts and songs, and Rousseau became rather emotional, played his fiddle, then dropped off to sleep. The guests got extremely drunk and fell about laughing. Most of the mirth was directed at Rousseau. Even among the avant-garde, his naivety both as an artist and as a man provoked amusement. And what did Picasso really feel? He no doubt enjoyed the absurdist spectacle of it all. The truth is that Picasso was perfectly capable of simultaneously admiring an artist's work and mocking him cruelly. It was the way he was made.

Naivety was of growing fascination to artists. Where could you find it in its purest form? The first gallery to which the visitor came on entering the radical Kunstschau in Vienna in 1908 was a whole room of children's art. Matisse would have approved: he felt that he benefited from studying the paintings of his own young offspring. Their innocence was inspiring. And why stop there? If you could learn from children, then why not from animals? While it might not be possible to persuade animals actually to make art themselves, the challenge was on for modernist artists to paint pictures that captured the essence of animal instinct. What Franz Marc was looking for by 1911 was 'a feeling for organic rhythm in all things, a pantheistic empathy into the shaking and flowing of the blood in nature, in trees, in animals, in the air ... I see no happier means to the *animalisation* of art, as I would call it, than the animal picture.'

Another aspect of the worship of the primitive was the cult of nudism that gathered momentum in Germany in the early years of the twentieth century. It contained echoes from earlier in the nineteenth century of Friedrich Ludwig Jahn's Gymnastics movement, whose motto *Frisch, fromm, frohlich, frei* (Brisk, devout, joyful, free), brought a note of suitably Germanic high-mindedness to the shedding of clothes. But its popularity now was driven by a desire to recapture innocence, to counter the pace and stress of modern urban life, which was perceived to trigger excessive 'excitation of the nerves'. Bathing and getting close to nature were identified as calming antidotes. Nude beaches, on which consenting men and women might bathe and sun themselves '*textil-frei*', were set up behind regulation 2.5-metre-high fences which had been carefully checked for knot-holes. Inspired by a Nietzschean faith in the beneficence of the sun's rays, Die Brücke artists took to the rural open air in order to 'sketch, bathe, paint, rest, play ball games, shoot bow and arrows, throw boomerangs, toss reed spears' unconstrained by clothing.

Their pursuit of a Gauguinesque Tahitian idyll was stimulated by frequent visits in 1910 to the newly reopened Dresden
ethnological museum. The experience prompted Kirchner
to a renewed spate of woodcarving. He also attended the
'ethnographic displays' at Dresden zoological gardens, where
primitive people specially shipped over from Samoa were put
on show, penned into enclosures like exotic animals in a zoo for
the Europeans to ogle. Kirchner's quest for ethnic diversity in his
models led him to the Dresden cabarets, where among the per-
formers he met the strikingly beautiful Africans, Sam and Milli,
who were invited back to his apartment to model. They feature
in a number of paintings of this time, and apparently entered
with amused tolerance into the easy-going and unconventional
atmosphere of Die Brücke studio life. *Milli Telling a Story* shows
the model relaxing on a sofa among Kirchner's bric-a-brac. That
summer, Kirchner, Heckel, Schmidt-Rottluff, Pechstein and
their friends felt the time had come to take the German capital
by storm, and exhibited their work at the radical Neue Secession
in Berlin. All the Die Brücke artists were concentrated in one
room, penned in rather like the Samoans. Public reaction was
predictably outraged: one Berlin critic summarised Die Brücke's
offerings as 'the mutiny of primitive, inward instincts against
civilisation, culture and taste in art'. The irony was that the Die
Brücke artists would have agreed with every word of this assessment. It was an accurate definition of early twentieth-century
Primitivism.

The Italian critic Giovanni Papini wrote in January 1913 of the
rational straitjacket that was holding back modern art, and identified five types that were outside that straitjacket: 'the savage,
the child, the delinquent, the insane, the genius ... these are the
last remains of primary and original man, of true man.' It was
in search of primary and original man that Emil Nolde turned
his back on Europe in 1913 and set off on a journey that would
last more than a year and take him via Russia, China and Japan
to the South Sea Islands, specifically the colony of German New
Guinea. But he was too late. 'We live in times in which entire

original states and original peoples are perishing,' he reported. 'Everything is being discovered and Europeanised. Not even a small area with unspoilt nature and original peoples will remain for posterity.' It was a conclusion that Pechstein reached too, on his trip to the Far East and beyond in search of the same thing a year later.

The most obvious consequence of Primitivism in the work of the avant-garde was the distortion of natural form. Its justification was the subject of serious and careful analysis. Leo Stein likened Matisse's 'distorted drawing' to the way 'a dissonance is used in music or as vinegar and lemons are used in cooking'. But only a minority had Stein's ear or palate for such things. In January 1914 Vanessa Bell was still grappling with the question of why distortion in art was so difficult for the public to accept, and wrote to Duncan Grant: 'I believe distortion is like Sodomy. People are simply blindly prejudiced against it because they think it abnormal.'

Over the previous ten years international modernism had reached the following broad consensus on distortion. The sort of distortion that emerged as an expression of unfettered instinct was a declaration of artistic freedom and a legitimate, indeed praiseworthy, creative device. There was, however, an uneasy distinction to be made between this creative distortion and the distortion that resulted from sheer artistic incompetence. It was a distinction complicated by the proviso that, where apparent incompetence was actually an expression of naivety, it regained its legitimacy.

By comparison, sodomy was pretty straightforward.

CHAPTER SIX

Sex and Sublimation: Exciting the Whole Machine

Like it or not – and many avant-garde artists did rather like it, in fact – the most basic instinct of all was the sexual one. There was considerable appeal in the idea that in embracing instinct they also embraced sexual liberty. Throwing off the shackles of deadening convention led to an identification of their creative urge with their sexual one. On 6 July 1909 Pechstein rhapsodised:

> Into the cold sea, floundered about, bathed and then ... painted, and the dear sun is laughing heartily above, [it] is worth living ... I could chop my paintings with an axe like wood, that's how strong I feel ... so let's dance ... and jump, everything now is copulating, the roebuck is after the doe, and above our window the cock pigeon is crowing, on the street the rooster is strutting amongst his harem, so why not we humans, after all it is the sensuality within us that creates.[6]

Paul Klee, with a disconcertingly Swiss precision and economy, described the genesis of a work of art: 'In the beginning the motif, insertion of energy, sperm.' And in an abrasive show of creative independence Vlaminck maintained: 'I try to paint with my heart and my loins, not bothering with style. I never ask a friend how he makes love to his wife in order to love mine.' Even the elderly and arthritic Renoir, who was occupying his old age in the south of France with painting a series of ever more pneumatic and lobsterised naked women frolicking in

Mediterranean landscapes, felt moved to contribute his views. An earnest American journalist came to interview him, and was taken aback by the extent of his debility. 'But with such arthritic hands, Monsieur Renoir, how do you manage to paint?' 'With my prick,' replied Renoir rudely. It was an answer that would have interested Freud, several hundred miles away in Vienna.

What was the relationship between art and sex? It was a question that exercised distinguished minds throughout Europe, and particularly in the German-speaking world, where earnestness and eroticism often walked hand in hand. Some, like the philosopher and politician Walter Rathenau, concluded that they were two experiences ultimately beyond the scope of words. On 15 November 1906 Rathenau told Harry Kessler that 'an art critic who analyses a picture is like a man who during coition suddenly comes up with observations about love'. The year before, in Vienna, Sigmund Freud had published his revolutionary *Three Essays on Sexuality*. Freud defined instinct – which he agreed was at the root of all human behaviour – as 'the psychical representative of an endosomatic, continuously flowing source of stimulation'. He too confirmed that the most powerful human instinct was the sexual one. But the new idea that Freud introduced was what he called 'sublimation'. Sublimation 'enables excessively strong excitations arising from particular sources of sexuality to find an outlet and use in other fields, so that a not inconsiderable increase in psychical efficiency results from a disposition that in itself is perilous. Here we have one of the origins of artistic activity.'

This, of course, put artists such as Gustav Klimt, who led active sex lives, in a dilemma. On the one hand, as an artist, he was identified as the sort of being thrillingly in touch with his instinct, and following that instinct involved a considerable degree of sexual licence. One of his sitters, Anna Beer, remarked that Klimt 'always smelt like an animal', an observation that would have delighted Freud, who strongly maintained the importance of the sense of smell to sexuality, even marking similarities between the structure of the nose and of the female sex organs. In proof of his instinctual energy, Klimt left a string of illegitimate children across Austria. But on the other hand he was being told by Freud that if he wanted to maximise his artistic achievement, he must deploy sublimation. 'Excessively strong excitations' should be 'enabled to find an outlet and use in other fields': thus a bit of sexual urge must be left unsatisfied, for rechannelling into his work. It was a dilemma that resonated through the twentieth century. According to George Melly, Piet Mondrian worked in a spirit of feverish sexual abstinence, convinced that 'every drop of sperm spilled was a masterpiece lost'.

As so often, Nietzsche had prepared the way for these conclusions. In 1889, he had written in *Twilight of the Gods*:

> If there is to be any aesthetic doing and seeing, one physiological condition is indispensable: frenzy. Frenzy must first have enhanced the excitability of the whole machine; else there is no art. All kinds of frenzy, however diversely conditioned, have the strength to accomplish this: above all, the frenzy of sexual excitement, this most ancient and original form of frenzy.[7]

Nietzsche identifies the potency of sexual excitement as a component in the creation of art. It is Freud who refines the process by positing the necessity of a measure of sublimation, a rechannelling of sensual energy, in order to produce art. Without sublimation, the logical consequence will be a mass of etiolated artists who have achieved repeated sexual satisfaction but no works of art. *Ars longa, coitus brevis*.

In 1909 Freud wrote a short book about Leonardo da Vinci. By his own admission Freud was not an aesthetician; he left the analysis of the formal aspects of Leonardo's oeuvre to others. His approach mined biographical details of Leonardo's life to give weight to his theories about how art is made, specifically that art is the result of the sublimation of excessive sexual libido in those who create it. He fell joyfully upon historical evidence of Leonardo's homosexual inclinations, whose early repression and redirection into art added a thrilling extra factor to da Vinci's creative mix. He seized with relish the recollection that Leonardo has left us of his infancy: when he was in his cradle, a large bird opened his young mouth with its tail and beat it against his lips. The sexual imagery is clear to Freud: the tail is a penis substitute and the memory is a fantasy, an expression of passive homosexuality.

'Conventionality is deadness,' Lady Ottoline Morrell decided in her diary in 1907. 'Your life must break bounds set by the world.' What she was expressing was Nietzsche filtered through the English philosopher G. E. Moore, whose *Principia Ethica* had been published in 1903. Here Moore contended that 'personal affections and aesthetic enjoyments include *all* the greatest and *by far* the greatest goods we can imagine'. 'Personal affections' and 'aesthetic enjoyments': it's sex and art again. To that element of the English avant-garde constituted by the Bloomsbury group, who seized upon Moore's words with enthusiasm, the one essential was integrity. In art you could break bounds galore provided you did it with integrity. It didn't matter how many different people you slept with provided you did that with integrity too. It was a credo that resonated across 'modern' Europe: the artists of Die Brücke, for instance, would also have identified strongly with its message of enlightened promiscuity.

The Die Brücke team put free love at the centre of their artistic practice. In the summer they repaired to the Moritzburg lakes in force, to paint the landscape, each other, and their female models as they all shed their clothes and frolicked in the water and the woods. From mid July to the end of August 1910, for example, Heckel and Kirchner were joined by Pechstein in this idyll of open-air Primitivism. The south seas were being recreated just a few miles out of Dresden, in a kind of adult themepark. Who were the women in the party, and what exactly was their role, beyond doing the cooking and the washing-up? It is difficult to be sure of their identities, but Kirchner's long-suffering girlfriend Dodo was certainly there, as was Franzi, the

25. Kirchner, *Bathers at Moritzburg*, 1910

daughter of a local circus family, who was very young, no more than eleven. That, of course, was Franzi's appeal. Here is Kirchner writing to Heckel that summer on what Franzi had to offer:

> There is great charm residing in such a pure female creature. Intimations that can drive one crazy. More fantastic than in older girls. More free, without which of course the older woman loses. Perhaps some things here are more complete than among the more mature ones and then wither away. Certainly there is greater richness here now.[8]

If sex was a natural instinct, then why shackle its expression by arbitrary limitations of age? In some accounts we read of a girl called Marcella, apparently an older sister. A convenient confusion exists here between Franzi and Marcella, and the theory has been proposed that they were in fact one and the same girl: Franzi the eleven-year-old when childlike Primitivism was to be evoked, and the rather older Marcella when something more adult came into play.

The artists produced a series of sketchy, spontaneous paintings of themselves and the *textil-frei* girls. Their jagged and angular figures show the influence of the tribal art from Palau in the south seas that they had just seen in the Dresden ethnological museum. One particular carved beam in particular captured their imagination: its decoration showed a local inhabitant with such a massive erection that it stretched out across the sea, an item of considerable interest and curiosity to those on the adjacent island where it made landfall. That phallus symbolised the whole Moritzburg summer.

Advanced medical opinion was coming round to the view that sex was good for you. The highly talented and neurotic young Polish sculptor Henri Gaudier-Brzeska moved from Paris to settle in London in 1911. He arrived poverty-stricken, but nursing the recommendation from his doctor in Paris that he should as regularly as possible employ the services of prostitutes. It is not clear whether this was to promote his productivity as an artist or his physical health; possibly both, but it was a very Gallic medical prescription. As it turned out the *filles de joie* to whom Gaudier-Brzeska had access in London were a disappointment. Having engaged one, he found he couldn't go through with it. Being an honourable man he still paid her fee of five shillings, an expenditure which he could ill afford.

Perhaps he should have consulted Vienna for a second opinion. There he could have compared notes with Egon Schiele, an artist who most spectacularly combined sex and angst in both his life and his work. Schiele depicts himself sitting astride a stool anxiously contemplating his own erection; indeed, most of his more intimate self-portraits, the drawings showing tortured and twisted contortions of his body and the guilty severing of his hands and limbs, can be interpreted as images of masturbation. Schiele wrote a poem in 1910 which is a graphic reflection of the confused instincts and emotions that were gurgling in the bottleneck of his mind:

> An eternal dreaming full of the sweetest excess of life
> Restless, with frightening pains inside, in the soul
> Flares, flames, grows after struggle
> Heartfelt struggle. Resulting and madly active with
>   excited lust ...[9]

Herr Schiele, won't you come through? Professor Freud is waiting for you in the consulting room. He wants to talk to you about sublimation.

The Futurists were as energetic as anyone in their enthusiasm for the instinct of sex. Being Futurists, their angle on it was often tinged with violence. In 1912 Valentine de St Point, multi-talented activist, poet, dancer and feminist sex-bomb, produced her own *Manifesto of Futurist Woman*. Severini described her admiringly as capable of 'a full night of carnal play, and then spending an hour the following morning in fencing practice'. She gave a public reading of her manifesto in the Salle Gaveau in Paris on 27 June 1912. Even though it took issue with Marinetti's 'scorn for women', she enlisted Marinetti, together with Severini and Boccioni, to act as her bodyguards when things got out of hand (as was indeed the measure of success for any Futurist gathering). Once mounted on the podium, de St Point – wearing a plumed hat 'as wide as an umbrella' – soon got into her stride. Women needed to reassert their virility, she declared. Sentimentalism must be kicked out. 'Let woman once more find her cruelty and her violence ... Woman, become sublimely unjust once more, like all the forces of nature!' She went on, 'Lust is a strength, because it destroys the weak, excites the strong to exert their energies, thus to renew themselves. Every heroic people is sensual.' Reeling from this onslaught, one elderly gentleman in the audience asked gamely, 'At what age, Madame, should we teach lust to our daughters?' He was exhorted to 'bring them along and we'll give you the answer afterwards'.

A year later Valentine de St Point came out with the *Futurist Manifesto of Lust*. 'Flesh creates in the way that the spirit creates,' she declared. 'A strong man must realise his full carnal and spiritual potentiality.' The pursuit of 'sensual pleasures, in which their constantly battling energies can be unwound and renewed' was the right of soldiers. And artists. 'The artist, that great universal medium, has the same need,' she decreed, with a nod to Nietzsche. To illustrate the way that lust was the progenitor of what she called 'the art of the flesh', she invented '*la Métachorie*', or 'Beyond Dance', a performance of which was staged in Paris in 1913. This involved an assault on all the senses: de St Point danced a solo, veiled and all but naked, while words from her own *Poems of War and Love* were read out, mathematical equations were projected on a screen and perfumes were pumped into the auditorium. To complete the experience, the musical accompaniment was intentionally disconnected from the movements of the dancer. The great joy of de St Point's theory was her view that artists produced their greatest art only when their 'constantly battling energies' had been 'unwound and renewed' in 'sensual pleasures'. No nonsense about sublimation here.

One question remains to be answered on this subject. Why did no advanced artist in the febrile five years from 1910 to 1914 – maybe some particularly synaesthetic Expressionist in the circle of Kandinsky, or a really radical Futurist determined to grapple with 'dynamic sensation itself' – attempt to paint the orgasm? Or perhaps they did, but without putting a specific name to their abstractions; thus the significance of the climactic explosions of line and colour evident in various contemporary 'improvisations', 'compositions', 'fugues' and 'lines of force' has so far eluded scholars. In fact, one of the most impressive and sexually powerful images of the time was made in Britain: Jacob Epstein's sculpture *Rock Drill*. It consisted of a real drill, a 'ready-made' purloined from some building site, surmounted by a plaster figure riding it in a powerful display of phallic energy. It was first put on public exhibition at Brighton City Art Gallery from December 1913 to January 1914. Wyndham Lewis paid homage to it in his Vorticist magazine *Blast* in 1915: 'The nerve-like figure perched on the machinery, with its straining to one purpose, is a vivid illustration of the greatest function of life.' It is a telling image of how far sex had taken art, or art had taken sex, in the frenetic years before the war.

CHAPTER SEVEN

Anarchism

An anarchic society offered a reversion to the state of nature, promising human beings a life in harmony with their instinct, uncompromised by the petty restrictions of an over-developed civilisation. Anarchism was revolutionary, in that it advocated the overthrow of the existing social and political order – indeed the overthrow of all social and political order. It was espoused by a wide variety of people who had become disaffected with the status quo in the late nineteenth and early twentieth century, including many avant-garde artists. There were degrees of adherence: in its mildest form it manifested itself in a relish for the ridiculous and the illogical, in acts of absurdist subversion; and in its most extreme form it generated terrorist bombs in fashionable restaurants and political assassinations. The end justified the means.

The term 'avant-garde' applied to modernist artists is a piece of military imagery that lends drama to those artists' perception of themselves as freedom fighters. But as a metaphor it's not quite accurate. In the theatre of war, an army's avant-garde is its front line. Although its 'arrière-garde' is some way behind it, that rearguard is marching in the same direction, supporting the efforts of the men ahead. But in the theatre of art, the avant-garde is more likely to be comprised of mutineers, their guns trained on their own arrière-garde. The commanding officers at the rear are the enemy. In 1890 the kaiser emphasised the total obedience and loyalty that he expected from new recruits to the German army when he told them 'with recent socialist turnovers, it is entirely possible that I will order you to shoot your own relatives, brothers, even parents.' In 1904, an Anti-Militarist Congress was held in Amsterdam, attended by anarchist sympathisers from across Europe. In words that would have resonated in the most advanced artistic circles of the time, this 'Affiche aux Conscrits' was issued: 'When they command you to fire your guns on your brothers in misery ... workers, soldiers of tomorrow, you will not hesitate, you will not obey. You will fire, but not on your comrades. You will fire on the gold-braided old troopers who dare to give you such orders.' For advanced artists, the gold-braided old troopers at the back were the academicians, the conservatives, the indulgers of bourgeois taste, issuing orders in direct opposition to the ideals of the avant-garde. There could be no anarchy without mutiny.

The ten years leading up to the First World War were particularly turbulent. The faultline in Russian society shifted and widened ominously as workers took to the streets in pursuit of their rights. There were frequent strikes in France and Spain, and a general strike in Vienna. In London, too, there were disturbing signs that the status quo might not hold for ever. The Conservatives were voted out in the 1906 General Election in favour of a Liberal administration prepared to listen to some of the demands of the emerging Labour Party. Anarchism, allied to the incendiary vitalism of Nietzsche, inflamed many young imaginations across the continent, not least those of painters. 'The artist is related to the lovers of his art as a heavy cannon is to a flock of sparrows,' Nietzsche had declared with his accustomed forthrightness. The metaphor of the explosive impact of new art – an extension of the military one – was widely deployed.

In 1905 there were 452 separate anarchist publications appearing in France. That year, the Paris police opened a file on one 'Pablo Ruiz dit Picasso' as a known Spanish anarchist. Had Picasso (who often talked bigger than he acted) been aware of the authorities' interest in him, he would have been scared out of his wits. But meanwhile all sorts of exciting political posturings were possible in the relative security of the Bateau-Lavoir and its surrounding hostelries. As summer turned to autumn in 1905, Picasso's girlfriend Fernande became an enthusiastic participant. She writes:

> Since I have come to understand Picasso and his friends, I think like this. I'd like to wave a banner with the inscription: 'Make way for artists, the only people with the right to live outside society.' What an awful word, 'society': it's black, it's grey, dusty, sticky. Ugh! I don't like society![10]

Hostility to the conventional norms of behaviour and to bourgeois values was not new among avant-garde artists, but it seems to take on a peculiar intensity in the early years of the twentieth century. Zola had already noted the tendency in the previous decade. He recorded seeing in Paris

> a strange procession of men with big beards and wide felt hats. At first these men looked to me like conspirators; with their darkened brows, furious eyes, and ironic lips, they watched passers-by with contained rage and an obvious longing to leap at their throats. Then I realised these men were painters.[11]

Picasso had moved into the Bateau-Lavoir in Montmartre in 1904. This labyrinthine wooden shack was home to a number of young painters, and writers such as the poet Max Jacob and André Salmon. An anarchist tradition pervaded the place; out of the camaraderie of material poverty, rebellion, and huge artistic ambition, the *bande à Picasso*, the 'Picasso Gang', came into being. Their style was anarchic, iconoclast and absurdist. The writer André Salmon described the nature of the gang at this time: 'Apollinaire, Jacob, myself and the others frequently played a rather burlesque role. We made continual fun of everything … We invented an artificial world with countless jokes, rites and expressions.' Apollinaire's contribution was to introduce Picasso to 'black humour, paganism, and the wilder shore of sex'; he

26. Picasso, *Family of Saltimbanques*, 1905

may also have introduced him to the Marquis de Sade. If so, he had a lot to answer for. Artistically, Apollinaire encouraged Picasso away from the 'blues' of the Blue Period into something strange, lyrical and other-worldly. Emblematic of the new mood in Picasso's art was the saltimbanque, the strolling player, the circus performer, a subject increasingly dear to his heart, combining as it did agility, independence, artistry and a life lived outside the constraints of society. At the beginning of 1905 he started a monumental composition on the subject. It was to occupy him off and on through the rest of the year, much redesigned and reworked. And it was to play an important part in the development of the contemporary art market in the ten years to come.

Another of Picasso's literary friends in these early years was the absurdist writer Alfred Jarry, who enhanced Picasso's relish of subversion and his pleasure in shocking people. Picasso knew him from the gatherings of writers and artists that he sometimes joined at the Closerie des Lilas restaurant. He relished Jarry's parodic approach to life and art which elevated 'anti-reason' and mocked the old standards of beauty and good taste, embracing reversals of logic and alternative realities. Like Picasso, Jarry also enjoyed brandishing a gun; indeed he is said to have bequeathed his revolver to the painter. A favourite cry of Jarry after some particularly subversive or outrageous jape was: 'N'est-ce pas beau comme la littérature?' He was perhaps the first, but not the last in the twentieth century, to turn his life into one long piece of performance art. A Jarry-esque subversion was thus part of Picasso's creative process; and a movement as radically revolutionary as the Cubism that Picasso would shortly bring into being could only have been conceived in a climate that was already highly charged with anarchical ideas.

Subversive social and political tendencies were widespread in advanced artistic circles. Matisse's anarchistic instincts were different from those that stimulated Picasso, but they were also strongly felt. Under the influence of Paul Signac, the Pointillist to whom he was close in 1904, Matisse subscribed to an ideal of anarchistic society operating beyond rules and set – rather conveniently – on the Côte d'Azure. Matisse's own personal contribution was his *Luxe, Calm et Volupté* exhibited at the Salon des Indépendants in March 1905. It can be read as something of an anarchist manifesto; indeed much of Matisse's pre-war art is a dream of how a society might work in which people lived solely according to their instinct. Just so long as the sun kept shining.

Then there was van Dongen. He had recently arrived in Paris as a young man with impeccable anarchist credentials, and moved into the neighbouring apartment to Picasso in the Bateau-Lavoir in 1905. Back in Holland he had illustrated the cover of a Dutch translation from the Russian of Peter Kropotkin's classic text *Anarchy*. In autumn 1906 the anarchistically inclined Félix Fénéon was taken on by Bernheim-Jeune to run its contemporary art department and one of his first initiatives was to buy five paintings and fifteen drawings by van Dongen. None of this escaped the jealous eye of Picasso, who, smelling capitalist compromise, took to mocking van Dongen as 'the inspired Kropotkin of the Bateau-Lavoir'. Indeed the trajectory of van Dongen's subsequent career took him away from anarchism and into the embrace of society portraiture. But artists as they get older learn that while rebellion is all very well, they also have to provide for their families. The pram in the hall is a powerful neutraliser of revolutionary instincts.

Across Europe, the bourgeoisie were the prime target of derision for those young artists who wanted change. At the Munich Secession in 1905 the youthful Paul Klee showed his etchings for the first time. Among them was his *Two Men Bow, Each Thinking the Other is of a Higher Rank*. The figures contort their bodies in agonies of mutual subservience, locked in an apparently eternal dance of social aspiration and bourgeois insecurity. Absurdly each has lost his clothes, and thus his means of identifying to what class the other belongs. It is a telling critique of the unyielding social code against which the new generation of German artists was rebelling.

There was a taste for anarchic subversion in Vienna too. In 1908 Adolf Loos, the architect and early patron of Kokoschka, published a treatise entitled 'Ornament and Crime' which set out a modernist agenda for design. 'As there is no longer any organic connection between ornament and our culture, ornament is no longer an expression of our culture,' Loos declared. 'Lack of ornamentation is a sign of intellectual strength.' But it is a mistake to take Loos too literally. There is a larding of absurdist irony to his protestations. Loos homes in on the tattoo as a bodily manifestation of pernicious over-decoration. 'In certain prisons as many as eighty per cent of the inmates are tattooed', he writes. 'People who wear tattoos and are not in prison are merely latent criminals or degenerate aristocrats. When someone with a tattoo dies a free man, it is simply the case that he passed away several years before committing a murder.' These are Loos's words; but they could just as well have been written by Jarry.

The sort of anarchy practised among iconoclastic young artists had its comic side. You could still have fun as a painter in Paris. In a moment of hilarity at the Lapin Agile in 1910, a group of artists tied a paintbrush to the tail of a donkey that belonged to the proprietor and encouraged the donkey to swish it across a canvas. The painting that resulted was put on show in the Salon des Indépendants that spring as by an unknown painter called Boronali (a play on the French word for jackass). Had he been aware of it, Franz Marc in Munich might profitably have studied it as an example of pure animal instinct translated directly on to canvas. Still, as a piquant symbol of artistic subversion, it lingered in the imagination of the European avant-garde. Two years later in Moscow, when a group of rebel artists including Gontcharova and Larionov were looking for a suitable name for themselves, they settled on 'The Donkey's Tail'.

Anarchy was an artistic statement. It spread throughout the arts in the form of a deliberate sinning against conventional norms and standards. Arrhythmia in ballet, and dissonance and atonality in music were assertions of the same anti-traditionalist instinct as the distortion of nature in art. This was particularly so in Russia as 1917 approached. Russian rebels took to anarchy and subversion in art as part of the broader movement to political revolution. Exulting in the sheer pace of change, Malevich urged his public, 'Hurry, for tomorrow you will not recognise us'. With a red wooden spoon attached to his lapel, Malevich announced at an evening organised by the Jack of Diamonds group on 19 February 1914 that he too 'renounced reason'. The last word in subversive absurdism had been an interview given on 1 January 1914 to the editor of *Teatr v karrikaturakh* in Moscow by Larionov – now a self-proclaimed Rayonist, but prepared to march under the broader Futurist banner – and the painter Ilia Zdanevich. It was a despatch from the front line in the war on logic and bourgeois complacency, a war being waged with gusto by the Russian avant-garde in all its anarchic splendour:

> Are you Futurists? *Yes, we are.* Do you deny Futurism? *Yes, we do. May it disappear from the face of the earth.* But aren't you contradicting yourselves? *Yes, our task is to contradict ourselves.* Are you charlatans? *Yes, we are.* Are you devoid of talent? *Yes, we are.* Can you be talked to? *No, we can't.* But what are your new year's resolutions? *To be true to ourselves.*[12]

CHAPTER EIGHT

Violence, War and Guns

Marinetti was a poet and a professional wild man. He wanted to make Italy great again and he knew how to do it. War, like sex, was a basic human instinct. 'We wish to glorify War,' he wrote in his *Manifesto of Futurism* in 1909, 'the only health-giver of the world – militarism, patriotism, the destructive arm of the Anarchist, the beautiful Ideas that kill, the contempt for women.' Scorning women seems a shade gratuitous, but when you were waging all-out war there would inevitably be collateral damage. And after all, women could be dangerous bloodsuckers of male virility, as Munch and Kokoschka were prepared to testify. It was heady stuff.

Harry Kessler, an eyewitness, describes a talk Marinetti gave at the Futurist exhibition in Paris in February 1912. The gallery was packed with 'a half-elegant, half bohemian public, the heat and the crush of the bodies inhuman'. When Marinetti advocated 'bombs and petroleum' as 'weapons against museums', the audience 'stormed the podium and began to beat him with canes and umbrellas. Marinetti's friends then attacked the public, all shouting at each other.' Proceedings ended when the police were called and some sort of order restored. This kind of physical manifestation of conflict and energy was an inseparable part of the Futurist message, an early example of performance art. It was all brewing up nicely as far as Marinetti was concerned. He proclaimed 'the hour is nigh when men with broad temples and steel chins will give birth magnificently, with a single thrust of their bulging wills, to giants with flawless gestures'.

Guns in the hands of creatures of instinct – modernist artists – could be a threat to health and safety regulations. Yet for those artists who harboured fantasies about themselves as men of action, firearms exerted a dangerous attraction. In Norway, in the summer 1905, Munch undertook a portrait of his fellow painter Ludwig Karsten. It was a good portrait, but towards the end of the sittings Munch took sudden exception to his sitter. There was a fearful row. Accounts are muddled, but Munch had a gun and fired shots at Karsten. Fortunately he missed. Three years earlier he had drawn a gun on his then lover Tulla Larssen, which had resulted in Munch firing a bullet through his own fingers. The recurring pain in his left hand was a constant reminder that, in the grasp of a passionate artist, a brush was a safer weapon than a firearm. But who wanted always to be safe? Not Munch; nor Picasso either, although in Picasso's hands the gun was an instrument of subversion rather than of passion. Picasso enjoyed possession of a gun; it was a Browning, the one allegedly given to him by the absurdist poet Alfred Jarry. He would fire it off (into the air) in order to silence boring German artists spouting incomprehensible theories, or anyone who voiced criticism of Cézanne.

Of course you could always challenge someone to a duel, and many people in the art world did. Duels stood in the same relation to homicide as waltzing did to sexual intercourse. Very few people were actually killed: honour was satisfied by the token drawing of blood. It was 'a reconciliation of [man's] brutal instincts and his ideal of justice', said Anatole France. The number of artistic disagreements that led to such challenges seems to have grown dramatically in the feverish years 1905–14.

An example of this was an exhibition that Kessler opened at his museum in Weimar in January 1906, of drawings and watercolours by Rodin. The locals didn't like it. One particular work was the focus of unease, even outrage. It showed a squatting nude female figure apparently in the act of relieving herself. It didn't help that Rodin, under the misapprehension that the Grand Duke of Weimar was as much of an admirer of his work as Kessler, had inscribed this very drawing with a dedication '*à son Altesse Royale*'. Kessler tried to hide the dedication under the mount, but it was no good. Kessler was vilified by his enemies at court and, in a reversion to traditional type that sits piquantly with his immaculate modernist credentials, attempted to settle the issue by a duel with the ducal chief of staff, General von Palezieux. Palezieux died before the duel could take place and Kessler, thwarted, resigned from the post of director on 13 July.

It is no surprise that Marinetti fought duels. On 16 April 1909 he took time from his busy schedule to undertake one with the critic Charles Henri Hirsch, who had not been flattering about Marinetti's Futurist play *Le Roi Bombance*, which had just had its debut in Paris. The duel was fought at the Parc des Princes, the sports stadium which was the location of choice for the settling of disputes of honour. Presumably there was some sort of reservation system operated by the stadium to avoid double-bookings. On this occasion both combatants emerged physically unscathed. On 12 June 1914 the Parc des Princes was the scene of another duel, this time between a German Expressionist called Gottlieb and Modigliani's friend, the young Polish painter Moise Kisling. Blood was shed, although there was no loss of life. Word had got around in advance so the press was there. Newspapers had to decide whether to send their crime, sport or art correspondents. Why were the two men fighting? 'It was a matter of honour,' reported *Le Miroir*. 'They did not think about art in the same way.'

CHAPTER NINE

Journeys Inwards: the Symbolist Strand

It is not possible to understand the art of Europe in the early years of the twentieth century if it is studied simply as a breathless progression of avant-garde developments, each one more revolutionary than the last. Yes, it is true that Fauvism was followed in quick succession by Expressionism and Cubism, with Futurism and Abstraction heady episodes to follow. But there were other currents flowing too. Besides the pretentious rhetoric and saccharine sentimentalities of late academicism, and the beguiling slickness of fashionable portraitists such as Sargent, Boldini, Sorolla and Zorn, there was also what can best be described as a powerful residual strand of Symbolism. The artistic Symbolism of the 1880s and 1890s had been in part a reaction against the superficiality of Impressionism, a turning inwards into dreams and the imagination after such an intense focus on outer surfaces. Here was a subject matter – the dissection of the soul – beyond the reach of photography. 'The camera will replace the artist only when it can visit heaven and hell', Munch had declared.

This Symbolist strand persisted in the artistic imagination of the early twentieth century and contained several threads. One comprised painters like Redon and Kubin, who created imaginary worlds of fantastic monsters and occult mystery. Another was the representation of what were variously called 'absolute truths' or 'primordial ideals' in a symbolic, highly imaginative visual language. The French poet Jean Moréas, in his Symbolist Manifesto of 1886, said that the function of Symbolism was to 'clothe the ideal in perceptible form', by deploying real-world phenomena as 'perceptible surfaces created to represent their esoteric affinities with the primordial ideals'. In artists' hands this led to a lot of allegorical nudity, the naked human body being an easily perceptible, real-world form eminently bendable into the expression of primordial ideals. And something subtler also emerged, a mood of strangeness, of dreamlike other-worldliness that artists began to evoke in their treatments of everyday reality, a process of rendering the ostensibly familiar suddenly unfamiliar. All these strands involved a retreat from reason that created common ground with those avant-garde artists whose aim was to paint in accordance only with their instinct. The release of restraint advocated by modernists was similarly implicit in Symbolism's wholesale embrace of the imagination.

Painters of primordial ideals were particularly thick on the ground in the Alpine triangle of Switzerland, Austria and Bavaria at the end of the nineteenth century. Was it something to do with mountains? In Geneva the highly regarded Ferdinand Hodler was preoccupied with Symbolist themes, particularly death: the subject cast an obsessive shadow over his imagination. Early on in life he had lost not just both his parents, but also all five of his siblings to tuberculosis. By 1900 he was the most famous artist in Switzerland, revered for his large-scale pictorial engagements with momentous, faintly depressing subjects with titles like *Communion with the Universe; Sacred Hour; View to Infinity; Eurhythmy; Day; Night; Dialogue with Nature.* The human body, either nude or clad in flimsy, vaguely classical costume and set in timeless often rocky landscapes, was the vehicle for the expression of these ideas. To the modern eye his deployment of the then-fashionable 'language of dance' to animate his figures teeters on the verge of absurdity, but his contemporaries revered him as an institution. Indeed his powerful earlier work *Night* (1889–90), in which a menacing black shape disturbs the sleep of the artist, was particularly influential on the imaginations of both Klimt and Schiele. As Paul Klee put it in 1911, Hodler 'knows how to portray the soul by means of the body like few others do'.

'More than one,' wrote Hodler gloomily on the frame of *Night*, 'who lies down peacefully in the evening will not wake up the next morning.' That just about summed up his attitude to existence. But then, in 1908, he had a life-changing experience. He met Valentine Gode-Darel, an attractive and vivacious French woman in her thirties, with a very noble and distinctive Roman nose. She had moved to Geneva following the break-up of her marriage to a professor at the Sorbonne in Paris. Short of money, she became Hodler's model. Alma Mahler, something of a connoisseur of amorous men, had an insight to offer about Hodler. She met him in Vienna and described him as 'like a tree, uncouth and gigantic. There was not a woman he did not deem his prey, without prelude or postscript.' So it was not long before Valentine Gode-Darel became his lover.

Under the inspiration of his new girlfriend, Hodler began a series of more upbeat works in which she features as a life force in communion with nature, with titles like *Cheerful Woman* (Gode-Darel dancing in a thin dress), and *Splendour of Lines* (Gode-Darel dancing naked). To sum it all up, Hodler finished a painting called *Love* in 1908. The naked, horizontally entwined lovers are a reflection of Hodler's more positive mood under Gode-Darel's revitalising influence. As originally conceived, the project was to be a large-scale depiction of multiple pairs of lovers, all horizontal, to give the impression, in Hodler's words, 'of a sea of human passion, eternally moving in low tide and high tide, in a movement that has neither beginning nor end'.

The second most famous Swiss painter of the early twentieth century was Félix Vallotton. Vallotton had settled in Paris in 1882 and established his reputation in the Nabi circle working alongside Bonnard and Vuillard. His was a highly individual vision, making use of flat planes of colour, decoratively deployed in striking compositions that translated well into woodcuts. Vallotton, too, experimented with Hodleresque Symbolism. In 1908, while Hodler came up with *Love*, Vallotton painted his curious picture *Hate* as an emblem of strained relations between the sexes. It shows a nude man and woman in vertical full length,

27. Hodler, *Love*, 1908

their faces distorted in expressions of mutual hostility. There are many lessons to be learned from this image. Perhaps the most salient is that, as a rule of thumb, a moustache on any male nude intended to symbolise an eternal truth is a distraction and probably a mistake.

At the turn of the century the leading painter in Austria, Gustav Klimt, had been commissioned by the ministry of education to paint three large allegories – of philosophy, medicine, and jurisprudence – for the university of Vienna. These proved a turning point in his career: the vertiginous, more than faintly erotic Jugendstil compositions that he came up with alarmed the authorities, so in 1905 he withdrew from the arrangement. He also resigned from the Vienna Secession, where he was president. It was a declaration of independence and determination to follow his own instincts. There followed a continuing sequence of Hodleresque Jugendstil paintings on primordial themes including *The Three Ages of Woman* (1905), *The Tree of Life* (1905–9), *Death and Life* (1908–11) and possibly his most famous work, *The Kiss* (1907–8). Classical myth was also a good vehicle for the expression of primordial ideals: in 1908 Klimt exhibited his deeply Freudian *Danae* as a powerful symbol of passionate love. The varied metamorphoses of Zeus for the purpose of

28. Vallotton, *Hate*, 1908

seduction have always been a stimulus to painters, but the depiction of a naked woman having sexual relations with a quantity of gold coins – which was how Zeus decided to manifest himself to Danae – presents a particular challenge to artistic ingenuity. Klimt rises to the occasion, depicting a naked woman with a lot of thigh and buttock curled up round the coinage. It is a telling image of the relationship between art, money and sex in early twentieth-century Austria.

In neighbouring Bavaria, the most famous living painter was Franz von Stuck. He had been one of the founders of the Munich Secession in 1892 and was now highly regarded as a teacher, as an authority, as an all-round eminence whose treatment of big subjects – OK, primordial ideals – managed to combine high camp melodrama with an exciting sensuality. In some respects von Stuck was a Bavarian Klimt: a purveyor of sultry symbolism in the language of art nouveau. But von Stuck

29. Klimt, *Danae and the Shower of Gold*, 1908

30. Von Stuck, *Inferno*, 1908

was more worldly and reaped the rewards of rank and celebrity, even being ennobled in 1906 when he became Franz Ritter von Stuck. In 1908 von Stuck made the journey to the place where Munch said no camera could penetrate, painting his macabre and deeply Freudian *Inferno*, a tempestuous mixture of writhing naked bodies and lapping flames with a few snakes thrown in. It is no surprise to discover that Carl Jung was an admirer of von Stuck, and noted with considerable professional interest that his pictures expressed a 'mixture of anxiety and lust'.

In the first years of the twentieth century Klimt also produced a series of Symbolist landscapes the moodiness and melancholy of which elicited sympathetic responses across Europe when shown in various international exhibitions. As far afield as Helsinki, the Finnish artist Akseli Gallen-Kallela – an early member of Die Brücke – paid tribute to Klimt with his lake landscape *Keitele*, painted in 1905. The sort of interiors being painted by the Dane Vilhelm Hammershoi, while not directly influenced by Klimt, nonetheless partook of a similar mood. Up till 1905 Hammershoi had mainly showed his silent, grey, hauntingly beautiful empty rooms in the Free Exhibition (founded in 1891), Copenhagen's equivalent of a Secession. In that year Rilke 'discovered' him and contemplated writing a book about him. A major exhibition of his work followed in the Eduard Schulte Gallery in Berlin that summer (it went on to Hamburg and Cologne). But Rilke's book never appeared and the internationalisation of Hammershoi never quite happened. He remained a largely Scandinavian taste for another hundred years until his rediscovery by the international art market in the early twenty-first century.

Another Symbolist taking everyday landscapes and endowing them with strangeness and mystery was the Belgian Léon Spilliaert, holed up in Ostend where he worked, largely immune to the latest developments of international modernism. In 1908 he painted *Digue d'Ostende aux Réverbères*, a night scene in which the lights of the harbour shaft mesmerisingly deep into the blackness of the water. A few streets away in the same town,

31. Hammershoi, *Interior*, 1904

James Ensor was experimenting with compositions involving skulls and masks. From 1880 to 1917 Ensor's studio was the attic in his parents' house. His most famous painting is a Symbolist masterpiece, the vast *Christ's Entry into Brussels in 1889*. It remained for many years in that Ostend attic and was not publicly exhibited till 1929.

Symbolism, and the wilder flights of the imagination, flourished in odd, unexpected places across Europe. Ostend was one. Another was the small castle in Zwickledt, Upper Austria, where Alfred Kubin lived an increasingly reclusive life, painting and drawing his macabre, ghostly fantasies. He also wrote a novel, *Die andere Seite (The Other Side)*, published in 1907. Needless to say it was deeply Kafkaesque. But Kubin's extraordinary blend of fantasy and nightmare was recognised

32. Spilliaert, *Digue d'Ostende aux Réverbères*, 1908

and admired by the artists of the Blaue Reiter group, and he was an early exhibitor with them in Munich, adding his own individual thread to the strand of mysticism running through the group's activities.

What is best described as a mood of strangeness descended upon a number of different artists in 1908, as they developed a taste for the piquancy of the everyday reinterpreted as the extraordinary; of reality so intensely observed that it assumed the quality of a dream. Giacomo Balla was thirty-seven in 1908. Like many of the progressive Italian artists of his generation, he had engaged with divisionism – the Italian version of Pointillism – and was now emerging into something beyond that. In this year he painted *Salutando (Waving)*, a startlingly novel composition whose dynamism sows the seeds of what in the

33. Balla, *Waving*, 1908

34. Monet, *Doge's Palace, Venice*, 1908

next few years would grow into full-blown Futurism. From an unusual and vertiginous viewpoint, at the top of a curving stair-well that apparently descends into infinity, we see three women negotiating their way down. They pause to look back up and are frozen into a moment of eternity. It is the stairwell of a smart apartment block, such as you might find in any number of pros-perous European cities in the early twentieth century. But by the cropping of the composition and his emphasis on the flow of the stairs Balla endows the painting with an extraordinary force and movement, and at the same time evokes an unsettling, dreamlike atmosphere. There are strange echoes of Piranesi: do the steps go on for ever?

Even the elderly Monet was affected by 'mood'. Having vege-tated for long tracts of time in his garden at Giverny, he chose the autumn of 1908 temporarily to break free from his en-tanglement with the waterlilies and make the last of his painting forays abroad. In a stroke of commercial genius he decided to go to Venice: so the master of light engaged with the city of light. It was a project possibly thought up and certainly encouraged by the dealers Bernheim-Jeune, who ultimately held a profitable exhibition of the series. Monet and his wife arrived in Venice on 1 October and stayed until 7 December, and in those nine weeks Monet produced thirty-seven canvases, many painted from the vantage point of a boat anchored on the lagoon. This created extraordinary effects of light reflected on water, a haze of colour that Monet called the 'envelope'. In Monet's hands it had the effect of dissolving the architecture into something timeless and dreamlike, a mood of trance oddly not dissimilar to the atmosphere evoked by Balla's stairwell. It is one that pre-figures the strangeness of the townscapes of Giorgio de Chirico.

It was in the autumn of 1910 that the young de Chirico, sitting on a bench in the Piazza Santa Croce in Florence, under-went a moment of revelation. He records,

> At the centre of the square stands a statue of Dante wearing
> a long tunic … The hot, strong autumn sun brightened the

statue and the façade of the church. Then I had the strange impression that I was looking at these things for the first time, and the composition of the painting revealed itself to my mind's eye.[13]

The picture that he painted commemorates the experience in deliberate distortions of what he saw. The space is compressed, the figure of Dante has become a piece of antique statuary, the church is a classical temple, the rigging of a sailing vessel is visible beyond. He called it *Enigma of an Autumn Afternoon*. Afterwards he said: 'Now every time I look at this picture I see that moment once again. Nevertheless the moment is an enigma for me, in that it is inexplicable.' This is the beginning of the metaphysical movement that de Chirico pioneered. He has gone beyond the physical reality to an alternative reality, a strange, dreamlike place whose mood was to be glimpsed earlier in Balla's staircase and Monet's Venice of 1908.

Nietzsche lurked in the margin of the minds of many artists in the first years of the twentieth century, but in the imagination of de Chirico he seems to have taken up full-time occupation. On 26 December de Chirico wrote to his friend Fritz Gartz: 'I am the only man who has understood Nietzsche – all of my paintings demonstrate this.' On 5 January 1911 he was even more specific about his debt to the German philosopher:

It is only with Nietzsche that I can say I have begun a real life … the whole world appears totally changed – the autumn afternoon has arrived, the long shadows, the clear air, the serene sky: in a word Zarathrustra has arrived, do you understand? Do you understand the enigma this world holds – the great cantor has arrived, he who speaks of the eternal return, he whose song has the sound of eternity.[14]

If you believed with Nietzsche in the Eternal Return, that the world was fated to go on repeating the same identical life cycle ad infinitum, then it would indeed impart an enigmatic and

35. De Chirico, *Melancholy of an Afternoon*, 1913

potentially disturbing charge to existence, one which de Chirico sets out to express pictorially.

In 1913 Apollinaire picked out de Chirico as an artist to watch. Picasso agreed that the Italian had originality, and it was on the recommendation of the two of them that the young dealer Paul Guillaume took on de Chirico and started paying him a monthly stipend of 100 francs. Apollinaire identified the unique quality of his art:

It possesses nothing of Matisse, nor of Picasso, it does not come from the Impressionists ... Monsieur de Chirico's very sharp and very modern perceptions generally assume an architectural form. There are railroad stations adorned with clocks, there are towers, statues, large deserted squares; railroad trains go by on the horizon.[15]

And, he might have added, that this year exotic greengrocery begins to appear in the foreground: artichokes, bananas, and every now and then a pineapple.

Like Nietzsche, de Chirico was fascinated by the Ariadne myth and produced a cycle of paintings on the theme which feature Ariadne as a sculpture positioned in architectural settings at challenging angles. De Chirico summed up what he was striving for in a letter to his new dealer: it was a very rare sort of intelligence, 'Nietzschean intelligence, the kind of intelligence that has to do with God and the acrobat, the hero and the beast.' Central to de Chirico's imagination was the Nietzschean sequence of surprise, discovery and revelation, which in turn went back to what Schopenhauer had written in 1851:

> To have original, extraordinary, and perhaps even immortal ideas, one has but to isolate oneself from the world for a few moments so completely that the most commonplace happenings appear to be new and unfamiliar, and in this way reveal their true essence.[16]

De Chirico's pictorial mission was the exploration of this process. In later 1913 and early 1914 his compositions grew even fuller of foreboding, anxiety, and long, ominous shadows, of illogical perspectives and light effects, of interiors that seeped into exteriors and vice versa. He expanded his repertoire of the 'odd everyday' to occasional rubber gloves, and he started populating his macabre stage sets with faceless troubadours, the 'animated mannequins' that became his later trademark. What he was doing now would have a major influence on the art of the inter-war years. We are on the verge of Surrealist territory.

Part II

PARIS, CAPITAL OF THE MODERN ART WORLD

CHAPTER TEN

The Artistic Mecca

The undisputed capital of modern art in the years leading up to the First World War was Paris. Its position as the centre of experiment and innovation had been established in the nineteenth century and confirmed by the Impressionist revolution. Now, more than any other city in Europe, Paris offered artistic freedom: freedom to be individual, to break rules, to indulge invention over convention, expression over imitation, instinct over intellect. The avant-garde was experimenting elsewhere, of course: in Berlin, in Dresden, in Munich, in Vienna, in Prague, in Moscow, in Milan, even in London. But few innovations were made in these places that did not keep one eye anxiously trained on what was going on in Paris. Advances in Paris, on the other hand, happened without reference to anywhere else, which outside France caused periodic resentment. But as long as the most cutting-edge artists from across Europe kept flocking to Paris to learn and to work, there was not much anyone could do about it.

And flock they did in 1905–14. A list of young artists from abroad who spent significant time in the city or even settled there for good includes Picasso and Gris (from Spain); Modigliani, Severini, Boccioni, Carra, Balla and de Chirico (from Italy); Brancusi (who walked quite a lot of the way from his native Romania); Larionov, Gontcharova, Chagall, Archipenko, Sonia Delaunay, Lipchitz, Exter, Popova, Jawlensky, and Kandinsky (from Russia and Eastern Europe); van Dongen and Mondrian (from Holland); Vallotton and Klee (from Switzerland); Kupka (from Czechoslovakia); Pechstein, Macke, Marc, and Feininger (from Germany); and Sickert, Epstein and Augustus John (from Britain). In most cases they would have been different and lesser artists without their Parisian experience.

What was Paris like? Umberto Boccioni first visited the city as a twenty-three-year-old in 1906. He was overwhelmed by precisely those dynamic aspects of big city life that four years later would generate Futurism. He wrote to his family in April:

> Think of the thousands of carriages and the hundreds of omnibuses, horse-drawn, electric and steam-driven trams, all double-deckers, and the motorized taxi-cabs in the streets; think of the Metropolitan, an electrified railway that runs under all of Paris and the tickets are bought by going down into great underground places entirely illuminated by electric light ... in the midst of all this movement put thousands of bicycles, lorries, carts and waggons, private automobiles ... [and] three million souls who rush about wildly, run, laugh and work out deals.[17]

And the place was costive with artists. 'There are as many painters here as there are grains of sand on the beach,' Paula Modersohn-Becker wrote in wonder when she first arrived in Paris from Germany in 1900.

CHAPTER ELEVEN

Paris and Germany

Paris was the city where in Modersohn-Becker's words 'we Germans have much to learn'. She wasn't the only German to feel this way: Nietzsche acknowledged it too, declaring in his autobiographical *Ecce Homo*: 'As an artist one has no home in Europe but in Paris.' But despite being eager to adapt, not every visiting German quite got the hang of the place. Writing in 1914, Wyndham Lewis rather unkindly mocks the way the German artist is irresistibly drawn to the bohemianism and innovation of Paris but when he gets there, instead of renting a romantic garret, 'occupies a sensible apartment on the second floor'.

Paris gave German artists an inferiority complex. Underlying everything was the nagging suspicion that German art would never be as good as French art. In 1905 Harry Kessler proposed the mounting of an exhibition of German art in London to build cultural and political bridges between Germany and Britain. But Max Liebermann, the leading German Impressionist painter and one of the founders of the Berlin Secession, vetoed the idea on the grounds that his own work and that of his fellow Germans wasn't worth the trouble of showing abroad. 'Honestly, what are we supposed to do after these giants Monet, Renoir, Manet, etc.?' Kessler reports him as saying. 'These are people that come round once in two hundred years. What should we little people do next to them?' In other words, the artistic relationship between Britain and Germany was a mere sideshow by comparison with the main business of modern art, which happened in Paris. The poet Stefan George took an even more pessimistic view: 'It would be no great tragedy if war did break out and

36. Munch, *Portrait of Harry Kessler*, 1906

Germany suffered a defeat,' he told Kessler. 'Then the people here would be taken down a peg and once again could produce some art and culture.'

Other German artists approached Paris in a more critical and aggressive frame of mind. In 1906 the young Expressionist painter Ludwig Meidner arrived there and took up residence in Montmartre. By the beginning of 1907 he was on his way home again. He found the 'decaying cultural milieu' 'distasteful'; 'Paris (like France in general) borders on sickliness,' he reported. 'Today the French are no longer productive ... Berlin – how different! Berlin is a struggling, earnest, burgeoning city ... Berlin has become the world's intellectual and moral capital.' Before he left, Meidner was painted by a fellow art student and the portrait was exhibited at the Salon d'Automne later in the year. The art student was Modigliani. Here was a further example of the internationalism that the city uniquely fostered, despite Meidner's strictures: a German Expressionist painted by an Italian modernist in a Parisian studio.

Max Pechstein, too, although he admired the Fauvism of van Dongen, was ambivalent about Paris, where he spent the early months of 1908. At the Salon des Indépendants he found the sheer volume of art of varying degrees of quality overwhelming. 'I consider myself to be modern,' he reported, 'but what my eyes got to see there was simply unbearable ... too much chaff to be separated from the wheat, [but] then again one sees some quite fantastic stuff as well.'

No one split advanced German opinion more dramatically than Matisse. At the beginning of January 1909 a big show of his work opened in the gallery of Paul Cassirer. This was an event, an opportunity for Germans interested in modernism to get a handle on the man understood to be at the forefront of the avant-garde in Paris. Matisse himself travelled to Berlin for the opening. He must have wished he hadn't: local reaction was distinctly hostile. Max Beckmann, a highly independent young painter, was among those not impressed. Here is his diary entry for 7 January:

> Got up late *à cause de champagne*. Then in the afternoon to the Cassirer gallery where I met Schocken. I disliked the Matisse paintings intensely. One piece of brazen impudence after another. 'Why don't these people just design cigarette posters,' I said to Schocken, who fully shared my opinion. Curious that these Frenchmen – otherwise so intelligent – can't say to themselves that after the simplification practised by van Gogh and Gauguin it's time to go back to multiplicity. There is no way beyond those two: you have to take what they have achieved, turn back, and look for a new path from some earlier point on the route.[18]

It was predictable that the mass of the German public would find Matisse's exhibition at Cassirer incomprehensible. A burgeoning anti-French feeling in Berlin, which was as much political as aesthetic, did not help. A handful of visitors, however, were very impressed indeed by what they saw, notably the members of Die Brücke. For them it was still Matisse's Fauvism that struck a chord, lending authority to their own vivid colours and violent disfigurations. Van Dongen had already been recruited to their group as an exhibiting member, but they immediately fired off an invitation to Matisse to join them (plus the annual unsuccessful attempt to persuade Munch to send something).

Exhilarated, they hurried back to their studios to paint Fauvist pictures for the annual exhibition of Die Brücke which opened at the Richter Gallery in Dresden in June. There they were ambushed by the critics on the grounds that they had succumbed to excessive French influence. Richard Stiller of the *Dresdner Anzeiger* identified Gauguin and van Gogh as the main culprits, 'creating a hazardous disturbance in the lineage of the Brücke painters'. Stiller felt that these two post-Impressionists had 'individuality too sharply stamped, too much the expression of particular eccentric temperaments, for other worthy painters to be able lightly to appropriate their manner.' Stiller is echoing the reservations expressed by Beckmann after his visit to the Matisse show: the paths beaten by van Gogh and Gauguin were now too well worn to be of service for the next generation. There was nowhere to go beyond them, only the imitation of their style. The implication was that German painters must turn away from Paris and come up with something more German.

Unfortunately for those critics trying to promote a distinctively Germanic modern art, free of unhealthy French influence, the artists of the Blaue Reiter Group were orientated towards Paris too. Having studied there, both August Macke and Franz Marc were clear-eyed about the merits of the French way of doing things. 'In Germany,' wrote Macke to his patron Bernhard Koehler in April 1910, 'we take care to ensure that great talents are nipped in the bud. In France, where there is a tradition of risk-taking, the boldest experiments of young painters have success on their side. Our experiments are failures, carried out by muddleheaded people who can't speak the language properly.'

This sort of Francophile talk from Germany's avant-garde intensified the silent majority's resentment, which found particularly bitter expression in 1911 in the Vinnen protest. Carl Vinnen was a second-rate German landscape painter, but his diatribe against foreign – specifically French – infiltration into

German national art touched a chord at home. The publication of his protest drew the support of a large number of conservative artists, critics and museum directors. 'A great powerfully upward-striving culture and people like ours cannot forever tolerate spiritual usurpation by an alien force,' he declared. 'German and French art dealers work hand in glove, and under the guise of supporting art flood Germany with great masses of French pictures.' Furthermore, art critics had been recruited to join the conspiracy: 'Our able writers are in the hands of the Paris–Berlin speculators.'

Vinnen's quarrel with the French Impressionists was no longer that they were artistically inadequate. That battle had been largely fought and lost. It was rather that the examples of their work which the deplorable French were allowing the gullible Germans to get their hands on were of inferior quality. 'On the whole we are granted only left-overs, only those paintings not bought by the French themselves or by the great American princes of finance.' And of course prices for these 'old studio remnants by Monet, Sisley, Pissarro, etc.' were 'far too high and sure to decline'. This line of argument was enough to persuade even an artist of such modernist sympathies as the painter and printmaker Kathe Kollwitz to add her signature to the protest.

Once it came to the post-Impressionists, Vinnen let rip with particular fervour. 'The French despise us to such an extent that their arrogance is turning into insolence. The most pathological paintings of van Gogh's insane period, the rejected experiments and barely prepared canvases from Cézanne's estate, have been acquired with pleasure by the good German Simpletons.' As for those Germans who had actually bought Matisse and Picasso, they were guilty of a lamentable surrender not just to Parisian sensuality but – even worse – to the values of Africa.

Kollwitz, for one, had rethought her position by the summer of 1911. On 20 May she was in Berlin and recorded in her diary:

> I told myself I'd run over to the National Gallery and see something really good for a change ... I went up to the

French artists, and in the very first room ... I began to
regret my having signed Vinnen's protest. For here I saw
French art once again represented with really good works
and I said to myself that come what may, German art needs
the fructifying Romance element. It is simply that the sensuous nature of the French makes them that much more
gifted at painting; the Germans lack any colour-sense and
left to herself Germany would produce the type of painting represented by the Dresden School, which I despise.[19]

The Dresden School, roundly condemned for their lack of colour
sense, were the artists of Die Brücke. There was not much
they could do about it, according to the despairing Kollwitz:
as unsensuous Germans they were simply irredeemable. Pechstein would not have agreed. He visited Paris again in 1911 and
by now his attitude to the French had hardened. He reported:
'Everything ... is on the decline.' He sensed an opportunity for
Germany: 'We are still raw, but we strive towards perfection
whereas the Roman people are brutally oversimplifying. Our
blood is fresher!'

But influential modernist dealers such as the energetic Herwarth Walden of Der Sturm Gallery in Berlin, or Thannhauser
in Munich, continued to put on exhibitions featuring the latest
French art from Paris. Delaunay, who exhibited at Der Sturm
Gallery in January 1913, wrote enthusiastically to Franz Marc
of the experience: 'People of different countries get to like one
another by seeing. In Berlin I felt out of place only in terms of
the language spoken there.' But he would have looked in vain
for reciprocal exhibitions in Paris featuring examples of the
latest German art. French critics showed little enthusiasm for
what Die Brücke and the Blaue Reiter produced. The abstractions that Kandinsky was painting in Munich, according to
Apollinaire, took blind obedience to your instinct much too far.

Artistic relations between Berlin and Paris became more
highly charged as the war approached. Tensions rose in the
world of traditional art as well. In the conventional Berlin

Salon of 1913, still going strong for the pleasure of the silent majority of conservative Berliners, a retrospective tribute was planned for the grand old man of German academicism, the emperor's favourite artist, Anton von Werner. Von Werner had first come to prominence as a military painter, a visual chronicler of German heroism in the Franco-Prussian war. But at the last moment, nameless 'high authorities' demanded that those works which focused on that war should be withdrawn from the exhibition for fear of upsetting French sensibilities. In the fervid atmosphere of summer 1913, you had to tread delicately. Indeed, there was a brief brake on militarism in Berlin: large-scale celebrations of the centenary of the Battle of Leipzig (1813) were orchestrated, but instead of the display of troops and martial might, they involved the more aesthetic choreography of many thousands of gymnasts. Perhaps it was a last-ditch attempt to uncover the sensuous side of the German character.

Daniel-Henri Kahnweiler – a German in Paris – was distracted by the gathering success of his international promotion of French modernism from grasping how close Europe was slipping towards war, and how totally destructive to his own operation European hostilities would prove to be. He might have understood its imminence had he paid more attention to the French press's reporting of the Peau d'Ours sale in the spring of 1914. This was the first public auction of a collection of cutting-edge modern art and it had been highly successful. But the anti-German tone adopted by the Paris newspapers in analysing it echoed the anti-French rancour of the Vinnen protest in Germany two years earlier. In an article ominously entitled 'Avant l'Invasion', the critic Maurice Delcourt wrote in *Paris-Midi* on 3 March:

> High prices were paid by undesirable foreigners for grotesque and misshapen works, and it is the Germans as we have always rightly warned who in two weeks paid and raised these prices. They have a clear strategy: naïve young painters will be caught in the trap. They will start imitating

the imitator Picasso, who made a pastiche of everything and, running out of material to imitate, sank to the cubist bluff. Thus the qualities of balance and order that are characteristic of our national art will gradually disappear, much to the great joy of M. Thannhauser and his fellow countrymen, who will one day suddenly stop buying Picassos and by then will move everything from the Louvre gratis, without any protest, because our blind snobs and intellectual anarchists are their unwitting accomplices.[20]

The Germans were blaming the French, and the French were blaming the Germans. Each stood accused of corrupting the other's national art in acts of massive and calculated subversion. In each case it was the purchase by Germans of avant-garde work by artists like Picasso and Matisse that was seen as the problem. The Germans viewed it as a conspiracy by the French to foist on them worthless modern pictures, thus facilitating the 'spiritual usurpation by an alien force' of German culture; the French saw the purchase of these worthless modern pictures and the driving up of their prices by the Germans as a conspiracy to destroy 'the qualities of balance and order that characterise [French] art'. Thus modern art became one more element in the chasm of mutual misunderstanding that was opening up between France and Germany.

Chapter Twelve

Paris and London

In London French Impressionism was still controversial in 1905. Whereas elsewhere in Europe all but the most conservative art lovers had come to terms with it, in Britain it continued to be viewed with suspicion. So the large exhibition of the Impressionists at the Grafton Gallery that opened in January was considered daring in offering a platform to dangerously modern Parisian art. But the political mood was changing, and rapprochement with France was in the air. Showing French Impressionist pictures in London was thus an expression of the recently agreed Entente Cordiale.

One spectator who responded positively was the instinctively subversive Lytton Strachey. In a letter to Leonard Woolf of 20 January he called the paintings on show wonderful. 'There are millions of them, and all worth looking at. The general effect is one of dazzling beauty – sheer physical pleasure to the eye. It's quite clear, after looking at them, that no-one knew how to do colour before.' Strachey noted that it was the collection of 'a person called Durand-Ruel who bought all these pictures for tuppence ha'penny when they were first painted'.

The 'person called Durand-Ruel' was the great Parisian art dealer and pioneer of the Impressionists, Paul Durand-Ruel, who was responsible not just for assembling the collection but also for its exhibition in London. Thanks to his promotion, the Impressionists had long since conquered America, and found favour in Germany. The time was right, Durand-Ruel calculated, to make another attempt on Britain. He brought 315 pictures to show in the Grafton Gallery, including works by Boudin, Cézanne, Degas, Manet, Monet, Berthe Morisot, Renoir and Sisley. Such masterpieces as Renoir's *La Loge* and Manet's *Bar at the Folies Bergère* were highlights. Some 11,000 people attended, many still to scoff, but some to weep. One lady artist 'was seated on a settee in the big gallery and the tears were streaming down her face … "the pictures are so beautiful," she sobbed.' But she was still in a minority. Only ten works were sold, one to the Irish dealer and collector Hugh Lane, who was just beginning his heroic project to found a National Gallery of Modern Art in Dublin.

'He may not succeed, but at least he has come formidably armed,' wrote *The Times* on 17 January of Durand-Ruel and his show. The reviewer went on to find fault with Degas, Manet and Renoir on the grounds of ugliness, but called Monet a genius. On 22 January, the *Sunday Times* art critic Frank Rutter launched an appeal to buy an Impressionist painting for the nation. He raised £160, just about enough to buy a Monet, but encountered obstruction at the National Gallery, who announced regretfully that their charter did not permit them to accept the work of a living artist. He then approached the Tate Gallery, who turned the idea down on the grounds that, while they could accept the work of a living artist, that artist had to be British. In the end Rutter arranged for the purchase and donation to the National Gallery of a work by Boudin; it was less impressive than the Monet, but Boudin was a less controversial artist, and at least had the merit of being incontrovertibly dead. 'Except among a few hundreds of artists, art students and enthusiasts,' recalled Rutter sadly in his autobiography, 'the Impressionist exhibition made very little impression on London or England. The general public was hardly aware of its existence.'

Monet wrote to Durand-Ruel on 13 February 1905 commiserating on his lack of success at the Grafton Gallery. He put it down to the jealousy of 'a group of painters in London hostile to French art and to your exhibition projects and also to mine'. Monet's own exhibition project was a London show of his foggily atmospheric Thames views, executed largely from a balcony at the Savoy Hotel between 1901 and 1903, and exhibited to considerable acclaim in Paris in 1904. Unnerved, Monet abandoned his plans for a London show of them in 1905. He withdrew to Giverny and spent the ensuing years sequestered in his garden, painting very little except his lily pond.

A year later another French artist – the Fauve André Derain, sent by Vollard – came to London to paint the Thames. London was pretty much oblivious to this incursion into its midst of something far more radical than Monet's Impressionism. Underlying London's periodic attempts to acquaint itself with Parisian modern art over the next ten years, there was a rich tradition of profound Anglo-French misunderstanding. Eighty years earlier, Delacroix had arrived in the British capital and professed himself amazed by the absence, in such a large city, of anything that his fellow countrymen would call architecture. Derain found himself similarly knocked off balance by London. 'I hate the English spirit, sad, hypocritical and mocking,' he reported in a letter home, but added: 'The women are very curious in their hypocrisy and most of them admirably beautiful.' From which it could be deduced that among Derain's London experiences was an affair with an English girl who first led him on and then let him down.

In the decade that separated Durand-Ruel's Grafton Gallery exhibition from the outbreak of the First World War, Paris paid very little attention to modern art in Britain. An exhibition in Paris of work by modern British artists was even less likely than one of modern German art. But intrepid Englishmen occasionally visited the French capital and attended exhibitions at the Salon des Indépendants, with its total freedom from any sort of control by jury, and the Salon d'Automne, with its determination to showcase the most radical new art. Most were shocked beyond words by what they saw, but not the young Scotsman James Duncan Fergusson, who arrived in Paris in 1907 from the dank northern mists and became a convert to Fauvism. So Scottish Colourism was born, a minor outgrowth in the

Parisian hothouse but a glorious effulgence in the otherwise gloomy firmament of contemporary British painting.

Back in London Frank Rutter continued his efforts to drag British art into the twentieth century by opening its eyes to what was going on in Paris. In 1909 Rutter instituted something called the Allied Artists Association and commandeered the Royal Albert Hall for its first exhibition in the summer. It was modelled on the Salon des Indépendants and intended to provide a platform for British modernism, with modernist contributions from abroad, too. When it opened in July, the first show included 3,000 exhibits and proved difficult to navigate because of its lack of selection. It included such home-grown independents as Steer, Pryde, Lucien Pissarro, Theodore Roussel and Sickert; and younger names such as Bevan, Fergusson, Peploe, Ginner and Gilman. It also featured a special Russian section which comprised nothing very revolutionary beyond some large decorative paintings by Nicholas Roerich, but at least reminded a British audience that art was being made in other parts of Europe beyond France.

The second of Rutter's Allied Artists exhibitions was held in the Royal Albert Hall the following year. This time new exhibitors included Augustus John and, a little unexpectedly, Wassily Kandinsky, who even sold a work. The buyer was the university don Michael Sadleir. Rutter had also discovered Cézanne: he speaks of being 'stunned and knocked over, as by cannon balls, with the pears and apples of Cézanne'. It is Nietzsche's imagery that he is quoting, and just to underline that he has grasped the cross-currents of advanced continental aesthetics, Rutter hails Cézanne as 'a sort of Nietzsche of painting'. There were not many people in Britain in 1910 who would have been able to quote the two names in the same sentence.

But in December 1910 came something genuinely transformative. Roger Fry, critic, painter, occasional dealer in old masters, and impresario and advocate of the new, mounted his exhibition of the latest French art, entitled 'Manet and the post-Impressionists'. It was intended to open the eyes of his fellow countrymen – whom Fry called 'the custard islanders' – to the newest French art. Fry had spent the summer scouring Paris for suitable exhibits. The main emphasis was on van Gogh, Gauguin (the most extensively represented artist in the show with thirty-seven works) and Cézanne. Seurat, Signac and Cross were also included. There was Picasso, but nothing Cubist. There was Vlaminck, but only more recent post-Fauvist examples. There was Matisse. Where did Fry trawl to gather together the exhibition? There were a few loans from private collectors like the Steins, and Mrs Bonger was persuaded to send a fair number of van Goghs, but the majority of the works were consigned by dealers. Kahnweiler, Bernheim-Jeune, Druet and Vollard all contributed in the hope that, just as German demand for avant-garde French art had surged, so the lucrative British market might be opened up as well.

Virginia Woolf has left us a memorable description of Roger Fry in the process of hanging the exhibition. He had set up a number of Cézannes, Gauguins and van Goghs on chairs in the Grafton Gallery beneath a very old-fashioned-looking portrait by George Frederick Watts:

> And there was Roger Fry, gazing at them, plunging his eyes into them as if he were a humming bird hawk-moth hanging over a flower, quivering yet still. And then drawing a deep breath of satisfaction, he would turn to who ever it might be, eager for sympathy. Were you puzzled? But why? And he would explain that it was quite easy to make the transition from Watts to Picasso; there was no break, only a continuation. They were only pushing things a little further. He demonstrated; he persuaded; he argued. The argument rose and soared. It vanished into the clouds. Then back it swooped to the picture.[21]

That exhibition was a *succès de scandale* in London. The majority of visitors were either horrified or prompted to ridicule by it; a small minority were impressed; but everyone talked about it.

One of the most striking and controversial paintings in the show was a Matisse, *Girl with Green Eyes*, of 1909. It was dismissed by the Observer critic P. G. Konody as 'an intentionally childish daub'. Augustus John, torn between first-hand experience of what was going on in Paris and his own indomitable self-regard, called the painting 'a vulgar and spurious work' and the artist 'a charlatan, but an ingenious one'. For most spectators, even informed ones, Matisse was a step too far; his name became synonymous with outrageous artistic behaviour, not so much legitimate experiment but intentional 'fumisterie', a practical joke at the expense of the viewer. There was also the factor of art's political weaponisation in the gathering tension of these pre-war days. The German weakness for the French avant-garde was there to be mocked, and Konody went on: 'the majority of the pictures at the Grafton Gallery are not things to live with. Germany is welcome to them.'

The writer Robert Ross was unequivocal about van Gogh: he called his work 'the visualised ravings of an adult maniac'. Under the circumstances it was hardly surprising that almost nothing in the exhibition actually sold, but the prices asked shed light on the market for van Gogh in 1910. Mrs Bonger, who still enjoyed a large holding of the works of her illustrious brother-in-law, was apparently asking around £120 for an individual painting. On the other hand, the French dealer Druet lent to the Fry exhibition the outstanding *Portrait of Dr Gachet*, which he had had on consignment from Kessler for two years and had finally bought himself in February for around 14,000 francs (£700). Georg Swarzenski, director of the Städel Museum in Frankfurt, opened negotiations to buy it when it was on view in London. The sale finally went through at 20,000 francs early in 1911.

Swarzenski's enthusiasm contrasts bleakly with the behaviour of another museum director, Sir Charles Holmes of the London National Gallery. Holmes had initially agreed to serve on the honorary committee of the exhibition, but once he saw what was on the walls he asked for his name to be removed from

37. Van Gogh, *Portrait of Dr Gachet*, 1890

the catalogue. Sir Claude Phillips, writing in the *Daily Telegraph*, was more measured: ' ... out of those things that have been done in absolute sincerity – mistaken sincerity it may be – out of the very few which are truly attributable to the desire to express "the emotional significance that lies in things" may yet emerge the painting of the future.' Arnold Bennett was ashamed of London's guffaws: 'For the movement has not only got past the guffawing stage; it has got past the arguing stage. Its authenticity is admitted by all those who have kept themselves fully awake. And in twenty years London will be signing an apology for its guffaw.' Fry himself also predicted that it would take two decades for the 'custard islanders' to be converted. He was left to rue the opportunity that Britain had lost when the van Gogh *Dr Gachet* was bought by Frankfurt, where, in Fry's words, 'it will take its place beside the masterpieces of Dutch and Italian art. We in England shall probably wait twenty years and then complain that there are no more van Goghs to be had except at the price of a Rembrandt.' Fry, of course, knew all about the price of a Rembrandt in 1910. With his other gentleman-dealer's hat on, he had just sold one to Frick for £60,000 (see p. 356).

In London, mockery of the new French art was an easier game to play. A splendid show was mounted at the Chelsea Arts Club in December 1910 as a satire on the Fry exhibition. It was entitled 'Septule and the Racinistes', and provided a fascinating insight into how London viewed avant-garde Paris. The catalogue described the Racinistes as 'that brave band of fighters who gathered round Quintin Septule after his flight from Paris and formed the little artists' colony at Chateaudun'. These revolutionaries were on the very cutting edge of modern art; Septule himself was a Cubist painter, and the work exhibited by him showed an unexpectedly assured command of the new visual vocabulary. The point was, of course, that Septule never existed, and the painting was a spoof by the cartoonist H. M. Bateman, a member of the Chelsea Arts Club. A surprisingly good spoof, in fact, unwitting confirmation that good caricaturists (as we shall see with Juan Gris and Louis Marcoussis) make good Cubists. Great fun was had inventing other artists for the exhibition: Charles Turletin, for example, 'whose uncompromising independence had closed to him the gates of all public exhibitions'. Another work was actually signed 'Henri Matisse', the name alone being enough to raise a laugh. Other brilliant geniuses were called Schufflin, Rotton, Gaga and Aspic. It was noted that all these men had variously shot themselves, gone mad, become drug addicts, or died in convulsions from the poisonous exhalations of certain pigments of their own invention.

The excitement and controversy generated by Roger Fry's exhibition extended into the new year of 1911. Continental modern art was ridiculous of course, but its power to shock was really rather fun. Fashionable London decided that the most effective defence against alarming artistic innovation was to drown it in frivolity. An event called the Post-Impressionist Ball was held in February, for which the guests – shrieking with laughter – turned up in Gauguinesque costumes. Two months later another colourful cultural import from continental Europe arrived, the Russian Ballet. Considerable excitement was aroused in artistic circles, and performances were sold out. But audience enthusiasm was not universal. The entry in Arnold Bennett's diary for 21 April, when *Swan Lake* was playing, reads as follows:

> London Palace Theatre. Pavlova dancing the dying swan. Feather falls off her dress. Two silent Englishmen. One says, 'Moulting.' That is all they say.[22]

In May 1912 Roger Fry pushed his luck by mounting an exhibition of modern British art in Paris, at the Galerie Barbazanges. He included work by Vanessa Bell, Duncan Grant, Charles Ginner, Wyndham Lewis and Fry himself. It sank without trace. Fry was reduced to sending an invoice to Wyndham Lewis for £1 0s 6d to cover return shipping costs of the works he had lent. It didn't improve relations between them. Back in London Fry tried again, with a second post-Impressionist exhibition that opened at the Grafton Gallery in October. Although the focus was still chiefly on French art, he leavened the show with a few home-grown examples. Despite their domestic upheavals, the Stein family were again generous lenders, so the British public were admitted to an even closer familiarity with the latest work of the Parisian avant-garde. Reactions were as outraged as ever. Lytton Strachey observed: 'I must say I should be pleased with myself, if I were Matisse or Picasso – to be able, a humble Frenchman, to perform by means of a canvas and a little paint, the extraordinary feat of making some dozen country gentlemen in England, every day for two months, grow purple in the face.'

But among writers and intellectuals there was increasing acceptance and understanding of what Fry was pioneering. Rupert Brooke spoke of the new 'Expressionism' in painting. 'It recognises what is, roughly, the main reason of this modern art – a very sensible one – namely that the <u>chief</u> object of a good picture is to convey the expression of an emotion of the artist and <u>not</u> as most people have been supposing his impression of something he sees.' Arnold Bennett went to the exhibition on 8 October and was struck by the beauty of the Matisse drawings, while noting the unevenness of the quality of the show. Bennett recorded:

> I met Frank Harris. He was prepared on principle to admire everything, though there was a large proportion of absolutely uninteresting work. When I said I had seen much better Picassos than there were there he hardened at once. 'I find it all interesting,' he said grimly.[23]

Throughout it all Roger Fry continued to proselytise for the new French art, and particularly Matisse. Eddie Marsh reports an example of the Fry technique:

> Fry was taking Lady Violet Bonham-Carter round the Post-Impressionist Exhibition ... and finally led her up to *La Ronde*, which was hanging in the place of honour on the end wall of the Grafton Gallery. 'What do you think of *that*?' Lady Violet, whose soul was already a little fatigued by its adventures among so many novel masterpieces, gazed upon it in stupefaction, and at last brought out apologetically, 'I don't think I quite like the shape of their legs.' 'Ah!' said Roger in a tone of triumph, 'but don't you like the shape of the spaces *between* their legs?'[24]

At the beginning of October 1912 Sir George Birdwood – quite possibly one of Lytton Strachey's purple-faced British country gentlemen – wrote a letter to *The Times*. In it he argued that, if a fire broke out, it would be better to allow a live baby to burn than the Dresden *Sistine Madonna* by Raphael. 'I would try to save both,' he explained, 'but if the direful choice were forced upon me, I should certainly save the Dresden Madonna first.

One can get another baby any day.' On 9 October the *Sketch* illustrated four examples of extreme modernism from the just opened second post-Impressionist exhibition, including a van Dongen, a Picasso and a Wyndham Lewis, and invited its readers to choose between saving any of these or a live baby. There was little doubt that, if the *Sketch* and its readers had anything to do with it, there would be no increase in the infant mortality rate.

What this meant was that if you wanted to see works by Picasso, Kokoschka or Franz Marc in London in the years 1912–14, the best way to do it was to get yourself invited to the private quarters of the German embassy. Here Mechtilde, Princess von Lichnowsky, wife of the German ambassador, hung her personal collection of modern art; she was a writer and poet, and she bought from the young German dealer, Alfred Flechtheim. Presumably the emperor was kept unaware of the collection's existence. Its guilty secrets were hastily packed up and returned to Germany in August 1914.

Back in Paris, what may have been the most significant contribution by a British artist to the advance of European modernism before the First World War took place in early 1914. It is recounted by Duncan Grant in a letter to Clive Bell of 26 February:

> [Gertrude Stein] took me to see Picasso, which I very much enjoyed. I promised to take him a roll of old wallpapers which I have found in a cupboard of my hotel and which excited him very much as he makes use of them frequently and finds [them] very difficult to get. He sometimes tears small pieces off the wall, he said.[25]

These wallpapers were the materials Picasso was using for the collages with which he was pushing synthetic Cubism to its limits. You couldn't get more cutting edge than that. It is a cause of quiet national pride that they were at least supplied by an Englishman.

Chapter Thirteen

Paris and Russia

Whereas Paris was not much interested in the German avant-garde and barely registered London's feeble attempts to establish its own version of modernism, it was more intrigued by what came out of Moscow and St Petersburg. A telling incident involved the young British painter Christopher Wynne Nevinson, when he came to study in Paris as a young man in the years before the First World War. He found people were suddenly much more interested in his work when his name was accidentally transcribed as 'Nevinsky'. A Russian painter was considerably more exciting to Paris than a British one.

The fascination could be traced back to a big exhibition of Russian art shown as part of the Salon d'Automne in 1906. It comprised works by a number of young contemporary artists including Natalya Gontcharova and Mikhail Larionov and was orchestrated by that master entrepreneur of the visual arts, Sergei Diaghilev. In the wake of the political upheavals of the previous year in Russia, Diaghilev articulated a sense of the more general revolution that he perceived to be unfolding: 'We are living in the awesome time of a turning point. We have been doomed to die so that a new culture may be born, a culture that will sweep away what remains of our tired wisdom.' If Paris was intrigued by the distinctive and unfamiliar art of the east, the impact of Paris on those Russian artists who travelled with the show was even greater. Larionov, in France for the first time, was 'stupefied' by the 'Paris innovations in art'. It was his first encounter with Fauvism. Wassily Kandinsky also exhibited at the Salon d'Automne. He was already familiar with western

Europe, having studied for some years in Munich, and settled in Sèvres just outside Paris in June that year. At this point he was struggling with the accommodation of what he called 'the inner necessity' in his art. He knew its expression had a lot to do with colour: for now it was the colour conjured out of the simplified shapes of illustrations to Russian fairy tales. That winter of 1906/7 he also sent work to the Die Brücke exhibition in Dresden. A tracery of international modernist connections was being established across Europe. But at its centre was Paris.

Back in Russia the collector and critic Nikolai Ryabushinsky was stirring things up. 'I love beauty,' he announced, 'and I love many women.' In pursuit of each, he ran through five wives and quite a lot of his family's huge wealth, which had been amassed in industry and banking. But it was art that gripped him, and new art particularly. He had recently founded a magazine called *Zolotoye Runo* (*Golden Fleece*). Ryabushinsky, like Diaghilev, was in no doubt as to the momentousness of the early twentieth century. In the first issue he wrote: 'It is at a formidable time that we embark upon our path. Around us, like a raging whirlpool, seethes the rebirth of life ...' In 1908 Ryabushinsky organised a major exhibition in Moscow under the sponsorship of the *Golden Fleece*. It contained work by van Gogh, Cézanne, Gauguin, Matisse, Derain and the Impressionists, and included works by the leading Russian avant-garde artists: Ryabushinsky had gathered in loans from the Paris art trade and sympathetic collectors. As Kean points out, it is remarkable that far-distant Moscow managed to mount such an advanced show fully two years before Roger Fry put something of equivalent modernity on in London. Among the paintings that Vollard now sent to Ryabushinsky were four of Derain's London series. What better illustration could there be of the ubiquity and innovation of modern art dealers? Vollard was marketing in Moscow views of London by a French artist who he himself had sent to paint in England two years earlier. The exhibition in Moscow was well attended, attracting 6,000 visitors. Among the van Goghs lent was *The Night Café* which Ivan Morozov had just bought in

Paris for 7,500 francs. The two great Russian collectors of French modernism, Shchukin and Morozov, were now important channels through which the latest Parisian art reached Moscow.

The cross-fertilisation between Russia and France was remarkable in these years. 'French more sensual, Russians more spiritual' said the *Golden Fleece* in March 1908. In 1908, the artist positioned most centrally to this cross-fertilisation remained Matisse. Apart from the increasingly high regard that Shchukin had for him, there was his newly established role as teacher and theoretician. When Matisse published his thoughts on art in Paris in December, under the title 'Notes of a Painter', the first language into which it was translated was Russian. The flow of artists making their own way from Russia to study in Paris increased. On top of that came the impact of the Ballet Russe, whose sensational first season in the French capital in 1909 kept Russian art and culture in the foreground of the Parisian imagination.

In Moscow, new modernist groupings and exhibitions now began to assemble, dissolve and reconfigure with an enthusiastic and acrimonious regularity. The *Golden Fleece* group published the final edition of their journal and dispersed. But by December a new avant-garde group had been established by Gontcharova and Larionov, the Jack of Diamonds. The young Malevich was one of the exhibitors in its first show, and explained: 'the name Jack stood for youth, and diamonds for – beautiful youth. The exhibition shook severely the aesthetic foundations and consequently the foundation of art in society and criticism.' This was precisely the aim of all these imitation 'salons d'automne' that emerged across Europe, founded in homage to Paris.

Like other nations, what the Russians learned from Paris was first Fauvism and then Cubism. When Vladimir Burliuk painted a portrait of the writer and critic Benedict Livshits in 1911, he did so in modishly faceted Cubism fresh from Paris. But in Moscow a reaction was setting in: Gontcharova and Larionov had left the Jack of Diamonds association in the summer, objecting to what they saw as its excessive submission to the influence of western

38. V. Burliuk, *Portrait of Livshits*, 1911

art. They were mounting their own mini Russian version of the Vinnen protest. A growing determination not to be pushed around by the French (or the Italian Futurists) was articulated by Gontcharova in 1913: 'Contemporary Russian art has reached such heights that, at the present time, it plays a major role in world art. Contemporary Western ideas can be of no further use to us.' It was certainly true that Moscow and St Petersburg now rivalled Paris, Berlin and Munich as centres of avant-garde experimentation. Malevich's art was evolving: he was painting in blocky, primitive forms and would soon move on to works of a more intricate Cubist geometry. Malevich was exceptional in that he had never been to Paris, but he was certainly well aware of what was going on there.

Russia and Diaghilev – in the form of the Ballet Russe – caused their greatest sensation in Paris with the production of

39. Vladimir Tatlin,
Constructivist Guitar, 1914–15

40. V. Makowsky, *The Last Steps*, 1914

Stravinsky's *Rite of Spring* in May 1913. It provoked riots and had a huge impact on avant-garde art in its abstract alliance of music and movement. Stravinsky explained himself in a statement in the new arts magazine *Montjoie!* on 29 May (note the early use of the exclamation mark as a signifier of modernity). He made a declaration of faith in abstraction, and a wish to express the disruptive dynamism of the force of life. His theme was the cyclical energy of all life as a continual process of regeneration – fashionably Bergsonian – and in the first scene the opposing rhythms of groups of dancers is intended to express the clash of universal forces. The balletic emphasis on rondes and spirals echoes Futurist lines of force.

Not long before the war the Russian artist Vladimir Tatlin visited Picasso in Paris, and in 1914 showed his first reliefs or 'synthetic-static compositions' in Moscow. Inspired by the Cubist experiments with collage, *papier collé*, and other materials that he had seen, Tatlin went further, creating sculptural constructions using 'wood, metal, glass, plaster, cardboard, gesso, tar, etc.,' while 'the surfaces of these materials were treated with putty, gloss paints, steam, sprinkled with dust, and other means'. By any standards this was revolutionary: and later Tatlin traced back 'what happened from the social aspect in 1917' to these Paris-inspired developments in his art of 1914. It would have been a source of gratification to Picasso, had he made the retrospective connection, that his role as a progenitor of Constructivism thus endowed him with indirect responsibility for the Russian Revolution.

While Tatlin was stringing up his Constructivist guitar, the conventional Russian genre painter Vladimir Makowsky painted a picture in 1914 entitled *The Last Steps*. It shows an ancient Russian general arrayed in a splendid uniform being helped down the staircase of some palatial interior by a deferential footman. The general and his setting are an image of the apparently unchanging might of traditional Russia. But the old warrior is on his last legs. He is a poignant metaphor for the imminent collapse of the tsarist regime. He will shortly trip over Tatlin's guitar and be gone forever.

41. Jan Sluyters, *Parisian Dance Hall*, 1907

CHAPTER FOURTEEN

Paris and the Rest of Europe

Like a stone dropped in the centre of a pond, the influence of the latest modern art movements rippled out from Paris across Europe, creating waves that reached its furthest flung boundaries. More and more painters in distant parts were emboldened by the example of Matissean Fauvism to experiment with violent non-naturalistic colours applied in flat planes. The intrepid band from Sweden and Norway who enrolled at Matisse's newly opened academy, and indeed soon comprised more than half the student numbers, prompted the formation back in Sweden of a movement called De Unga (the Young Ones), an avant-garde group led by Birger Simonsson. In 1909 they held their first exhibition in Stockholm. 'The public crossed itself as if confronted by an epidemic of French disease', reported Simonsson with some satisfaction.

There had been similar dismay in Amsterdam in 1907 when Jan Sluyters exhibited at the Rijksakademie the work he had produced since being awarded the Prix de Rome in 1906. As a modern young man with his wits about him, Sluyters had of course chosen to go to Paris rather than Rome to further his studies at the academy's expense. The authorities were horrified to find that Sluyters' painting was now infected with the influence of the Fauves and the unspeakable van Dongen – one Dutchman being led astray by another. In the furore, they decided to withdraw Sluyters' bursary.

In Prague Emil Filla's antennae were as sharply tuned as anyone's to the new tendencies in Paris. In the summer of 1908 he had moved on from his mood of Munch-induced despair

42. Derain, *Bathing*, 1908–9

and was now painting Fauvist landscapes along the Dubrovnik coastline. But by 1910 there had been a further change in the messages being received from France. In February there was an exhibition of the 'Paris Independents' in the Czech capital, organised by Bohumil Kubista and the Manes Group. The star exhibit of the show was Derain's *Bathing* (1908–9), a composition in which the Primitivistic female nudes seem to have escaped wholesale from Cézanne's *Grandes Baigneuses* and are looking about, uncertain what to do with their new-found freedom. Emil Filla was so moved that he led a campaign to buy it for the Czech nation; subscriptions towards its purchase price were gathered throughout the artists' cafés of Prague. In the end the sum of 800 crowns was raised and the picture stayed in the Czech capital. In tribute Filla promptly painted his own landscape with multiple bathers (*Autumn*), but by the end of 1910 Bohumil Kubista had been to Paris and discovered even more up-to-the-minute manifestations of Cubism; already the Derain was looking if not old-fashioned then somewhat less relevant. A few months could make a lot of difference in these times of constant awareness of new developments in the Parisian avant-garde.

Meanwhile, back in Amsterdam a new artists' association was established called the Moderne Kunst Kring. Jan Toorop, unofficial president emeritus of Symbolism in Holland, was its chairman, with the young Piet Mondrian and Jan Sluyters on the committee. This was set up specifically as Amsterdam's own Salon d'Automne, with distinguished guest contributors from the Paris avant-garde. By 1911 the waves rippling out from Paris were Cubist rather than Fauve, and the first Moderne Kunst Kring show, which was held in the Stedelijk Museum that year, reflected the new mood. It included twenty-eight Cézannes from the collection of Cornelis Hoogendijk, a pioneering Dutch admirer of post-Impressionism who died that year. There were also works by Braque and Picasso from 1908 and 1909, the first examples of early Cubism to be shown in Holland. They made a deep impression on Mondrian, convincing him that he must move to Paris. He was there by the end of the year, by which time he was painting still lives in a distinctly Cubist language.

The country whose modern art was least in thrall to Paris in 1905–14 was Austria. In Vienna, Munch, van Gogh and Hodler were more influential than Gauguin, Cézanne, Matisse or Picasso. The Parisian avant-garde was not much interested in Austria, either: Paris had gone beyond art nouveau and on that account dismissed Klimt and early Schiele; Paris also had little sympathy for the brutality of Germanic Expressionism and was thus disinclined to embrace Kokoschka and Schiele's later work. When Klimt travelled outside Austria, he was most at home in Berlin, while his biggest commission abroad came from Brussels, where his decoration of the Villa Stoclet occupied him for five years from 1906. It is one of the glories of the Vienna Werkstadt, in combination with Klimt at his Jugendstil peak. But it is difficult to imagine it being undertaken in Paris.

In February 1913, the art magazine *Montjoie!* first appeared in Paris, under the editorship of Ricciotto Canudo, lover of the redoubtable Valentine de St Point. *Montjoie!* was unashamedly a mouthpiece of 'French cultural imperialism' and took its name from the war cry of the Capetian knights who, as a symbol of their readiness to fight France's enemies, seized the standard of St Louis from the basilica of St Denis. In a nationalistic statement the magazine came out against the anti-tradition of the Italian Futurists and on the side of French Cubism, which, as Gleizes argued, traced its roots back to the realism of le Nain and the pure painting of Cézanne. The dominance of Paris over the artistic avant-garde needed restating. Italian Futurism and indeed the Russian version were perceived as threats to France's hegemony.

The longer term threat, as it turned out, was from the other side of the Atlantic. Early in 1913, arguably the most important event for the future development of the European art world took place in New York. The Armory Show, billed as a survey of avant-garde art in Europe, ran from 17 February to 15 March. It generated considerable press interest, and a predictable degree of outrage and mockery. It was driven by a group of forward-thinking American artists, who had spent a few weeks in Paris at the end of 1912 visiting studios and making selections. Exhibitors included Matisse, Picasso, Braque, Picabia, Gleizes, Leger, Brancusi and the three Duchamp brothers: the painter Jacques Villon, the sculptor Raymond Duchamp-Villon and Marcel Duchamp. There were also works by Cézanne, van Gogh and Gauguin, plus a representation of American contemporary art.

It was a lot for bemused Americans to assimilate. Brancusi's sculpture of Mlle Pogany, in which the sitter was reduced into two basic three-dimensional shapes, was mocked in the local press as 'a hard-boiled egg balanced on a cube of sugar'. But it was the work of Matisse that produced the angriest reactions. The *New York Times* critic called his pictures 'ugly', 'coarse' and 'revolting in their inhumanity'. Another critic in *The Nation* dismissed them as 'an art essentially epileptic'. In the course of the exhibition a journalist called Clara MacChesney was even despatched by the *New York Times* to Paris to interview the beast in his lair, and was amazed to find that Matisse was 'a fresh, healthy, robust, blonde gentleman ... whose simple and un-affected cordiality put me directly at my ease'.

One of the odder and more immediate effects of the Armory Show was to launch Marcel Duchamp into a kind of local super-stardom, based on the American public's fascinated incomprehension of his *Nude Descending a Staircase* (see p. 282). In Paris it had been rejected by the Salon des Indépendants in 1912 as too Futurist. Now, in New York, it was the image of the show, its most talked-about painting. People came to the exhibition in numbers, many of them specifically to see the Duchamp and react in amazement and amusement to it. Was the figure a man or a woman? How could you tell the figure was going downstairs rather than upstairs? Were these Europeans crazy? Nonetheless, a San Francisco dealer, Frederick C. Torrey, wired from Albuquerque on 1 March that he would pay the full asking price for the picture, $324, sight unseen. This was what happened when European modernism met American entrepreneurialism. As far as the exhibiting European dealers were concerned, the object of the exercise had been achieved: the opening-up of the American market had begun. Indeed sales were made to people who would later become major collectors of European modern art, such as John Quinn, Lilian Bliss and Albert Barnes. The highest price achieved was for a Cézanne landscape, *The Poorhouse on the Hill*, which was bought by the Metropolitan Museum for $6,700 and became the first work by the artist to enter an American public collection. The Armory Show was the first act in the ceding of Paris's position as art capital of the world to New York, a drama completed later in the century.

Part III

LOSING CONTROL

Chapter Fifteen

Trouble with Women

Following your instinct was all very well, but it also had its perilous consequences for artists. When members of the Chelsea Arts Club put on their satirical show of spoofs of modern French art in London in December 1910, they identified a number of them. The brilliant young geniuses they invented had variously shot themselves, gone mad, become drug addicts, or died in convulsions from the poisonous exhalations of certain pigments of their own invention. As a list of the pitfalls of the new freedom in art, it was surprisingly accurate. It even made dark references to artistic 'seraglios', which was as close as any Englishman was going to get to mentioning sex.

In European avant-garde circles the complicated connection between sex and artistic creativity was a continuing subject of debate and practical experimentation. In the process new questions arose about the place of women in the art world. Under the traditional scheme of things women functioned most productively as models and muses. Even that limited role brought dangers for susceptible male artists, like the misery and distraction from your work that entanglement with the wrong woman could cause, or the complication of an unexpected pregnancy. The new dispensation that modern artists allowed themselves, at all costs to follow their instincts, only intensified these perils. On top of that, as women became increasingly empowered in the new century, they developed an alarming tendency to answer back, to start asserting themselves and their rights. A new sort of woman was emerging in the modernist artist's studio, resolute, independent and determined to do battle with

43. Modigliani, *Beatrice Hastings*, 1914

lazy assumptions of male superiority.

Take Beatrice Hastings, for instance. In the summer of 1914, she became Modigliani's girlfriend. She was English, of South African origins, and she was a fully fledged modern woman: strong-minded, of no fixed attachments, drawn to Paris as the centre point of advanced European culture, where she wrote poetry, lived passionately and sent dispatches back to London in occasional articles for the journal *New Age*. And as a new woman she was in Paris to make conquests of men: she was alleged to keep a tally in notches on her bedhead. Her relationship with Modigliani was a sequence of violent skirmishes, strategic retreats, passionate engagements, occasional ceasefires and all-out war. In her own words, he could be a pig or he could be a pearl. Over the next two years their relationship produced a series of fourteen portraits of her; works which were important catalysts in Modigliani's resumption of painting after a period of focusing his energies on sculpture. But they were not produced without considerable ordeal.

If Modigliani was kept at full stretch by women like Beatrice Hastings, the process went both ways. It needed a particularly strong woman to cope with the moods, obsessions, cruelties and charm of a character like Picasso. Fernande Olivier lived with him off and on from 1904 to 1911, which entitled her to some sort of endurance medal. She was no fool. Unlike most artists' models, she understood the wisdom of the maxim, 'Keep a diary and one day it will keep you'. Her journal records the ups and downs of their relationship and is now regarded as the most important eyewitness account of what Picasso was actually up to in those early years. Picasso was immediately smitten by her. She had the capacity to get under his skin. He didn't like her sitting for other artists, but she did, sometimes nude, to Kees van Dongen in the studio next door. Unable to bear children herself, she persuaded Picasso that they should adopt a thirteen-year-old girl from a local orphanage. Given the unconventional nature of the set up at the Bateau-Lavoir, it was an arrangement unlikely to win the approval of today's social services. It was probably for the best that Fernande decided to give her back at the end of the summer. In most things, Fernande generally got her way.

She got her way until the final fracture with Picasso, which was set in motion when Picasso met Eva Gouel, the mistress of the Polish painter Louis Marcousis, and began an affair with her. It was initially clandestine: in October and November 1911 Picasso painted a Cubist work that included letters forming the words 'Ma Jolie' in its composition, a camouflaged love letter to the new woman in his life. In another, 'j'aime eva' is inscribed microscopically in the margins. The Cubist painting becomes briefly a patchwork not just of signs and symbols but also of amorous encrypted text messages. Eva had a frail and delicate beauty in piquant contrast to Fernande's buxom physicality. But her appearance was deceptive: she proved an unscrupulous manipulator, precipitating Fernande's demise from Picasso's favour. Fernande confided in Eva, whom she trusted as her friend, about a one-night stand she had enjoyed with an Italian Futurist. Eva lost no time in revealing the infidelity to Picasso. So Fernande was unloaded. The break was final this time, and Eva and Picasso disappeared into the sunset.

George Bernard Shaw's play *Man and Superman*, which had its first performance in London in 1907, documented the changing balance between the sexes. Its title may have paid fashionable tribute to Nietzsche, but its theme was the power that the new thinking gave women over men. The superman could only be created if the woman willed it. It was the woman who embodied the 'life force'. Confronted with the feminist threat, some male modern artists panicked in their efforts to assert their virility. As part of his preparations for their Gauguinesque trip to the south seas in 1914, Max Pechstein – determined to take back control – insisted that his wife (and model) Lottie should have herself sterilised. The prescription of 'contempt for women' that Marinetti proposed as part of the Futurist manifesto in 1909 should similarly be seen in the light of the insecurity that men felt in the face of women battling for their rights. Somewhere

44. Munch, *The Death of Marat*, 1908

in the depths of the male modernist soul lurked the awful suspicion that the new freedom to indulge your instincts applied to
women too.

Munch's relationships with women were fraught at the best
of times. Ominously, the painting that he showed at the Salon
des Indépendants in the spring of 1908, *The Death of Marat*,
revisited his toxic relationship with his model and muse Tulla
Larsen, the sexual entanglement that had ended in 1902 with
him shooting himself in the fingers. Munch depicts himself now
as Marat, lying naked and bloodied on the bed, and Tulla as his
murderer, Charlotte Corday. 'Tulla' Corday is also naked and
she stares out at the spectator with a disturbingly detached look

45. Kokoschka, *Murderer Hope of Women*, 1909

on her face. This re-engagement with the subject of the woman as destructive predator was not a good start for Munch. The year went further downhill in an alcoholic haze, punctuated with occasional fights, brawls and brainstorms. His persecution complex – being done down by women, by his critics, by his fellow countrymen – gave him no peace. He got on to a train. He drank a bottle of wine. He didn't know where he was going. He got off the train. He looked up and saw that the name of the station was Copenhagen. Soon after that he lost consciousness. When he woke up he was in a clinic run by the eminent Danish psychiatrist Daniel Jacobsen.

Although examples of his work were loaned to the 1909 Vienna Kunstschau, Munch himself did not travel to Austria for the exhibition. He was still under the supervision of Dr Jacobsen. It was probably for the best that he stayed away, thus missing the young Oskar Kokoschka's controversial experimental play, *Murderer Hope of Women*, whose premier coincided with the exhibition. Indeed the plot of the play might have been deliberately constructed to inflame Munch's worst instincts, pre-Jacobsen: put simply, a woman holds a man captive in a cage; the man breaks free; the man kills her. It is the work of an artist prone, as Kokoschka was in his early days, to unhappy love affairs with deeply unsuitable women. The poster that Kokoschka designed for his play depicts the sort of tormented and menacing female familiar to Munch in his most lurid nightmares.

It wasn't just the young avant-garde who struggled with their instincts. Rodin – an ageing Don Juan – was also afflicted with problematic sexual entanglements, particularly with models and muses possessed of delusions above their station. First, there had been the whole Camille Claudel saga. Claudel had been the very gifted pupil of 'the master', and posterity now acknowledges her as possibly the greatest female sculptor of the nineteenth century. She became Rodin's lover; she became his muse; she became his collaborator. She became miserable. Did he even steal ideas from her? In 1905 she was stricken with mental illness and faded from his life, though she remained a lingering embarrassment. The next year, when Rodin sculpted his *Monument to Whistler*, he turned to the British painter Gwen John as his model. But history repeated itself: John was not happy to be cast solely in such a passive role. She saw herself as collaborator in the creation of the work rather than mere sitter, and wanted acknowledgement. The fact that she was also having an affair with Rodin complicated the issue. Sadly for Gwen John, in 1906 there was no recourse to intellectual property lawyers.

Used to lionisation and an inveterate philanderer, Rodin was in later years ensnared in an increasingly suffocating love affair.

46. Münter, *A Boat Trip with Kandinsky*, 1909

The Duchesse de Choiseul, a bossy and domineering widow of ample means, appropriated him in 1908 and assumed a role in his life that was part nurse, part femme fatale, and part business manager. Rodin allowed his eye to continue to roam, but found himself stifled by the duchesse's attentions. Also, his powers were waning. He had operated most of his life on the principle that *not* to make a pass at a woman was caddish behaviour, insulting to the lady's femininity. Now, approaching old age, he found himself occasionally having to apologise: 'Madame, I regret, but my doctor has forbidden me to ...' So for the next few years he sunk under the control of the duchesse.

Even the serious-minded Matisse had his problems with the opposite sex. Olga Meerson, a young Russian painter of considerable talent, was one of the new breed of ambitious, independent and single-minded young women. Having first studied in Munich, where she had arrived with Maria Werefkin and become a friend of Gabriele Münter, Meerson enrolled in Matisse's school and latched on to the master with a kind of romantic and professional tenacity which was difficult to resist even for a man of Matisse's artistic focus. In the *Nymph and Satyr* that Shchukin bought in 1909, the Satyr's pose, arrested in mid-pounce as he approaches the young woman lying before him, speaks of a lifetime of sexual indecision on the artist's part, and reflects the strangled passion that Matisse felt for her. Meerson repeatedly caused trouble for Matisse over the years 1910–12, but it was not until 1912 that he felt strong enough finally to grapple with the continuing problem that she had become to him. She was packed off to a sanatorium in Switzerland for treatment of (a) drug addiction, (b) neurasthenia and (c) attachment to an unreliable male artist who was already married to someone else and would always prioritise his painting over his mistress and even his wife.

There is not much joy in Meerson's story from a feminist point of view, but a small breakthrough was the admission that women, too, could suffer from neurasthenia. In the nineteenth century it had been the medical term for a nervous breakdown only among male artists, the equivalent female condition being generally dismissed as hysteria. But it still wasn't easy to be a woman artist at the beginning of the twentieth century, particularly not one of modernist inclinations. Pioneers such as Münter, Werefkin, Meerson, Gwen John, Claudel, Modersohn-Becker, Kollwitz, Sonia Delaunay, Marie Laurencin and Valentine de St Point were battling against huge male entitlement. They had to be strong just to survive, let alone thrive.

Although on one level Gabriele Münter's *A Boat Trip with Kandinsky* is a splendid Expressionist image of summer on the lake at Murnau in 1909, painted in vibrant Fauvist colours, on

47. Klimt, *Nude study*, 1906

another it is emblematic of the subsidiary role that women artists were expected to adopt in the vicinity of their male *Chef de l'École*. Kandinsky stands at the end of the vessel in a pose of visionary leadership, surrounded by a coterie of adoring females, one of whom gamely rows the boat so that the master should not be distracted from his artistic or theosophical ruminations. The message is clear: as a woman, too strong an assertion of your independence as an artist in your own right would not only rock the boat but probably precipitate everyone into the lake.

Marie Laurencin was another woman trying to function as an artist in a difficult environment. Introduced by Picasso to

Apollinaire in 1907, she became his mistress, which put her at the very epicentre of modernism. Their relationship was complicated: the physical side of it exercised Apollinaire, who had a visceral and no doubt deeply Freudian aversion to the use of his bed for lovemaking. Hence their knowledge of each other was only ever acquired on an armchair, which in view of the poet's girth must have presented logistical problems. Under these restrictive circumstances it is testament to their mutual regard that their relationship lasted as long as it did. In 1909, the same year that Münter depicted Kandinsky in command of his craft on Lake Murnau, Douanier Rousseau painted Apollinaire and Laurencin in a double portrait. He entitled it *The Muse Inspiring the Poet*. But Marie Laurencin, who in this early phase of her career was a bold and adventurous experimental artist, might legitimately have queried why the picture could not just as well have been called 'The Painter inspired by her Muse'. Contemporary gender stereotypes, however, were still too strong.

In 1906 Gustav Klimt, free of the official painting commitments that he had jettisoned the previous year, was now at liberty to pursue his own projects: one was a series of erotic drawings to illustrate Lucian's *Dialogues of the Courtesans*, a book being produced by the Vienna Werkstadt. This was a lot of fun, with naked models swarming about his studio. And meanwhile his day-to-day financial needs were met by the lucrative commissions he was able to pull in painting portraits, generally of women with modernistic inclinations and rich husbands. But there was a downside to all this joyous cavorting among the models and society ladies. Quite how many illegitimate children he had fathered is not definitely established, as he was a man of considerable appetites. His most prolific year had been 1899, when he had produced at least two, one born to Maria Ucicka in July and another to Marie Zimmerman in September. For the avoidance of doubt as to paternity, in each case the child had been christened Gustav. But around 1906, the Klimt scholar Alfred Weidinger believes, Klimt became aware that he was suffering from syphilis. As a result Weidinger suggests that his active sexual engagements diminished, and the erotic drawings were the function of his new status as a voyeur rather than a participant. Still, after a year or two of taking it easy he was back in productivity. In 1912 Klimt moved into a new Vienna studio, Feldmuhlgasse 11, and celebrated by fathering another illegitimate child, this time with Emma Huber. It was another son, and as ever he was called Gustav.

Unplanned pregnancies were an increasing hazard in the lives of advanced artists and their muses in the years 1905–14. Picasso was responsible for one such accident with the gamine Madeleine, Fernande Olivier's predecessor, for whom an abortion was arranged in the summer of 1904. Picasso, who was in many respects not a very nice piece of work, exorcised the experience and his own part in it by making several drawings of Madeleine as a madonna with child. Across the modernist studios of Europe, female victims of the assertion of male instinct accumulated. In May 1910 Schiele discovered that he had impregnated a young woman whom he managed to consign to the care of Viennese gynaecologist Dr Erwin von Graff. Graff was apparently an early admirer of Schiele's art, and it may well be that his fee for 'arranging things' was paid in Schiele drawings.

In 1911 Schiele met one of his most sympathetic (and long-suffering) models, Walburga 'Wally' Neuzil. Together they decided to move out of Vienna to the small town of Krumau, where Schiele painted a series of powerful works, landscapes and studies of Wally. Unfortunately the Krumau bourgeoisie were less tolerant than the Viennese, and local disapproval of the fact that Schiele and Wally were not married, and that nude painting sessions were observed in the couple's garden, forced them to leave Krumau in the summer. Schiele now had a taste for the country, however, and looked round for somewhere else to live. They decided on Neulengbach, a small rural community picturesquely set amid the Vienna woods. It promised to be idyllic; or as idyllic as an artistic practice could be, whose rendering of the female nude was pushing very close to the boundaries of pornography.

48. Schiele, *Nude study*, 1912

There was still a terrible shortage of money. Schiele wrote despairingly to his patron Arthur Roessler: 'Can it go on like this? Won't anyone help me? ... I have no money to buy canvas. I want to paint, but I have no colours.' Production of fairly lurid nude drawings continued, often featuring Wally as model. To raise cash, Wally was despatched to Vienna (an hour away by train) to offer these drawings to likely punters in the more worldly capital. Some of these punters were collectors, genuine admirers of Schiele as a draughtsman. Others were more susceptible to the frisson of excitement occasioned by the fact that the saleswoman was herself the subject depicted in these highly sexualised drawings. It was a selling point to which Schiele himself had no objection; Wally, on the other hand, needed all her credentials as a tough new woman to endure the discomfort of the situation. But the bills had to be paid somehow.

In 1912, however, events in Neulengbach turned nasty for Schiele. Tatjana Mossig, the teenage daughter of a local dignitary, ran away from home. The police investigating her disappearance questioned Schiele. He had certainly met the girl, but there was no evidence to suggest that he and Wally had abducted her. Then another more serious accusation, of the sexual assault of a minor, was brought against him and he was imprisoned in the town jail for three weeks. Fortunately, when the sexual assault case came up at the district course in St Polten, it was dismissed for lack of evidence. But Schiele's troubles weren't over: the police searched his studio and came across a number of 'indecent' drawings which they confiscated. Executing obscene drawings was not in itself an offence, but Schiele had allowed local children to enter his house where one such obscene drawing had apparently been pinned up in his bedroom. Of the offence of displaying pornography to minors Schiele was found guilty and sentenced to twenty-four days' imprisonment. The experience left a deep scar of outrage and resentment. He was particularly traumatised by the court's decision to destroy the offending drawing that had hung in his bedroom, which the judge did by burning it in the courtroom. 'Anyone who has not suffered as I,' Schiele wrote in his diary on the day of his release from prison, 'will have to feel ashamed before me from now on.'

There is no doubt that Schiele – not unlike the Die Brücke artists frolicking with Franzi in the Moritzburg lakes – had an uncomfortable interest in underage girls as sexual objects, as his drawings up till 1912 attest. It is also clear that he felt that the following of his instincts was a more urgent imperative than obeying the legal regulations, dictated by what he regarded as an outmoded sexual morality. From 1912 onwards, however, while his drawings are no less sexually explicit, Schiele's female models tend to be older. He had learned a painful lesson.

Kokoschka, meanwhile, had taken up with Alma Mahler: he was obsessively and destructively intoxicated by her. Their affair produced at least one masterpiece. In 1913, Kokoschka painted his elegaic *Bride of the Wind*. The artist and his lover float over a blue night landscape, their El Greco-ish bodies entwined. 'He painted me,' said Alma, 'lying pressed trustingly against him in a storm amid high winds – entirely dependent on him, a tyrannical expression on his face, radiating energy as he calms the waves.' Kokoschka described it to his dealer Herwarth Walden as 'my strongest and greatest work, the masterpiece of all my expressionistic efforts'. Oh, and by the way he needed 10,000 crowns for it.

If ever two people were predisposed by their natures to cause maximum disruption to each other's lives it was the promiscuous Alma, recently widowed wife of the composer, and the passionately over-sensitive Kokoschka. Almost inevitably Alma became pregnant. Kokoschka wanted to keep the child, but Alma, already tiring of her lover's stifling attentions, was less keen. As we have already seen, one of the most important amenities for a young artist in Vienna or Paris in these years was access to an art-loving gynaecologist to deal with situations like this. Kokoschka, albeit unwillingly, found one in the young Doctor Ludwig Adler, who agreed to terminate Alma's pregnancy. He also painted the physician's portrait the same year, though it is unclear whether this was in payment for the procedure or simply an act of self-flagellation. The ongoing psychological anguish that Alma caused Kokoschka can be measured by an event five years later. In 1915, just at the moment when Kokoschka, having enlisted in the Austrian army, came back from the front wounded, Alma left him for Walter Gropius. In July 1918 Kokoschka, still looking for ways to exorcise her, commissioned the Munich doll-maker Hermine Moos to make him a life-size doll to look exactly like Alma. It was an enormously painstaking project, with Kokoschka on hand to ensure every detail was perfect. Once delivered to his studio, Kokoschka entered into a somewhat ambiguous liaison with the doll; certainly one aspect of it was professional, because he frequently used it as a model for paintings, drawings and watercolours. As to any other aspects, all one can say is that Freud was not consulted; but Kokoschka's doll stands as a potent symbol of the troubled relationship that male modernist artists found themselves drawn into with the opposite sex.

Chapter Sixteen

Descent into Madness: The Case of Edvard Munch

Given what he had put his body through over the previous twenty-five years, it was a tribute to the extraordinary physical toughness of Edvard Munch that he was still alive in October 1908, when friends checked him into the Copenhagen clinic of the renowned psychiatrist Dr Daniel Jacobsen. Jacobsen was a smooth and confident operator who recognised that many of his richer patients were simply in need of a rest, which he gave them in comfortable surroundings. He also cultivated a reputation for curing artists, having successfully treated the famous Danish author Amelie Skram, who had entered the clinic suffering from hallucinations and suicidal tendencies.

'I am having shock treatment and massage and I feel very well in the peaceful atmosphere here, surrounded by very kind nuns and a very capable doctor,' Munch wrote to his friend Jaap Nilssen on 27 December 1908. 'My mind is like a glass of cloudy water. I am now letting it stand to become clear again. I wonder what will happen when the dregs have settled on the bottom?' In the first months of 1909 he began to find out.

Earlier in his life he had explicitly rejected medical help to alleviate his sufferings. He had declared, 'they are part of me and my art, they are indistinguishable from me, and it would destroy my art. I want to keep those sufferings.' In fact, he went further: 'For as long as I can remember I have suffered from a deep feeling of anxiety which I have tried to express in my art. Without this anxiety and illness I would have been like a ship without a rudder.' So putting himself into Dr Jacobsen's clinic at this time was an admission of defeat, a realisation that he must find some other way of steering his ship through the tumultuous seas of his life, that art alone was not the answer. And the treatment worked, up to a point. There were a lot of baths, mild electrolysis, sensible nutrition and doses of chloral to ensure long sleeps. Another aspect of the Jacobsen technique was to employ attractive nurses, which worked a treat with Munch in his new incarnation as a neutered tabby cat. He described them as angels.

After seven months in Copenhagen under the doctor's care, Munch had taken himself in hand and found some peace. Half jocularly, he claimed in a letter to his niece Sigurd that from now on he would confine himself to 'nicotine-free cigars, alcohol-free drinks, and non-poisonous women (either married or unmarried)'. But there was a nagging feeling that the treatment had also taken something from him: 'I have lost something remarkable, something inexplicable, something that combines both joy and pain, of that I am sure,' he reported to Nilssen. Perhaps as a result, there was a residual resentment towards Jacobsen. The doctor had wrought a cure, but at what cost? When he was well enough to leave his bed Munch undertook a full-length portrait of the doctor, of which he said, 'When I was painting it I was master. I felt that the man in whose hands I had been was now in mine.' The idea persisted in Munch's mind that Dr Jacobsen, in treating him, had somehow got the better of him. The resulting portrait shows, in Munch's words, a man looking 'just as conceited and pleased with himself as he really is'. Painting it was therapy, of course. And it was revenge of a sort. Confronted with the finished work, Dr Jacobsen was inclined to see it as evidence of residual madness, confirmation that there was an element of the incurable in his patient. But the reaction of the painter Ludwig Karsten, who was shown the portrait on a visit to Munch in the clinic, unnerved the nerve specialist. Karsten went down on his knees and described it as 'pure genius'.

Another instance of an artist painting his doctor, van Gogh's *Portrait of Dr Gachet* (see p. 117), makes an interesting comparison

49. Munch, *Dr Jacobsen*, 1909

with Munch's interpretation of Dr Jacobsen. Whereas Munch resented his doctor for relieving his condition, van Gogh felt a huge sympathy with the melancholy Gachet for his inability to find a cure for either van Gogh's or indeed his own mental frailty: he wrote to his brother that Gachet 'certainly seems to me as ill and distraught as you or me'. Behind these two portraits lie two different attitudes to artistic madness. 'If I could have worked without this cursed disease – what things I might have done,' van Gogh speculated ruefully. Munch felt the opposite: what things he might have done could he have gone on working *with* his cursed disease.

Munch was changed by his sojourn in the clinic. His angst became more manageable in the years that followed, and his style less innovative and more repetitive. His subject matter inclined to the pastoral and the lyrical. Yes, there remained the underlying duality in his nature, occasionally surfacing in images such as the two plough horses which strained to pull in different directions; but now the horses are better controlled, yoked together by the farmer. The earlier, angst-ridden works of the 1890s do indeed stand in contrast to the artist's more innocuous and decorative later works, so much so that one twenty-first-century American collector persuaded himself that they were the work of two different painters. He didn't like the earlier more fraught works of the artist called Munch. But he collected the later, more gently coloured paintings by an artist he knew as Munch (to rhyme with 'lunch').

What would the world have lost if Munch had not got up from the Copenhagen gutter in which he found himself lying in October 1908? From an artistic point of view, not a lot. It is a sad truth that with certain artists it might have been better had they painted less in their later years. But Munch's exceptional physical constitution ensured his longevity. He even survived a dose of the Spanish flu in 1919, the lethal strain that ravaged Europe, seeing off weaker specimens like Egon Schiele. There is, however, a natural span of high achievement to the careers of innovative geniuses, spans that they may outlive. Munch is a cautionary example, a warning to van Gogh of how the Dutchman might have run out of inspiration and intensity had he continued working after 1890. While he was in the clinic, Munch was made a Knight of the Order of St Olav in his native country. It was a further symbol of the way the once angst-ridden genius was now being fettered by the comfortable shackles of respectability. And something else changed, too. Jens Thiis, newly appointed director of the Oslo National Gallery, bought Munch's early painting *Spring* for 10,000 kroner. Now Munch's pictures started selling for large sums of money. A successful exhibition of his work followed in the summer of 1909, held at Blomquist in Oslo. It raised 60,000 kroner. For the rest of his life he was financially secure, not always the best condition to stimulate an artist's creativity. From being confined to an institution, he had become one.

Artists were prone to pushing themselves too far. In December 1910 Matisse travelled to Spain where, exhausted by the effort he had put into painting *Dance* and *Music* and the stress of their reception, he collapsed with a physical and emotional breakdown. Fortunately, he fell into the hands of a capable doctor, who – a bit like Jacobsen with Munch two years before – prescribed a regime of rest, tranquillisers, and warm baths three times a week. What Matisse wrote to his wife Amélie at the time could have been written by Munch two years earlier, in explanation of his precarious state of mind: 'All artists have this particular make-up, that's what makes them artists, but with me it's a bit excessive. Perhaps that's what gives their quality to my pictures.' That genius was close to madness was not a new insight. But the unstable mood of the years leading up to the First World War made it a particularly relevant one. Artists who painted by instinct balanced unsteadily on the cusp between the two.

CHAPTER SEVENTEEN

Altered States: Drugs and Alcohol

Did you paint better under the influence of mind-altering substances? Could alcohol or drugs be deployed to bring you closer to your instincts? Or did indulgence merely offer a refuge from the ordeal of creating a work of art? Could it even be that, far from liberating, drugs actually damaged you as an artist? In the mid nineteenth century, Baudelaire and Rimbaud had already struggled with these questions. Rimbaud wrote in 1871: 'The poet must make himself a seer by an immense, long, deliberate disordering of all the senses. He seeks in himself all forms of love, of suffering, of madness. He exhausts from them all their poison, to keep only their essence.' How to disorder the senses? Alcohol, or even better opium, seemed to offer an attractive short cut.

The idea that genius could be liberated by opium had its roots even further back, in the Romantic movement. It was re-energised in the first years of the twentieth century by the prevailing wisdom among young modern artists that anything which cleared the way to a direct expression of instinct was to be encouraged. Paul Alexandre, the doctor who was Modigliani's first and most important patron, became an advocate of the use of drugs as an aid to creativity. Modigliani's wilder drug-fuelled journeys into the unknown were thus made with the imprimatur of medical science – not that he needed any persuasion. The looming, sphinx-like Egyptian heads that he carved out of limestone in 1911 and 1912 form a curious link with the early nineteenth-century English romantic poets, who were driven to an opium-induced ecstasy by the unveiling in the British Museum

50. Modigliani, *Egyptian Head*, 1911

in 1818 of a newly discovered work of Egyptian art, the granite bust of Rameses II, the 'Young Memnon'. Its mood of sightless trance was admired by De Quincey as the personification of opium reverie. The blind eyes that Modigliani gave his Egyptian heads are tinged with the same feeling. Modigliani set candles on the tops of these heads as illumination in his studio during evenings of drink and drugs, and worse. Augustus John, a visitor to Paris, attended several of these soirées and was so moved by Modigliani's heads that he bought one; a century later, when it came on to the art market and fetched $70 million, a residue of the coloured wax from the candles remained visible, ingrained

51. Picasso, *Boy with Pipe*, 1905

into the stone. And perhaps, wafted on the air conditioning of the auction house gallery, a whiff of opium was still detectable too.

There was, however, a limit to what artificial stimulants could achieve. Perhaps genius could indeed be liberated by opium, in the same way that genius could be liberated by following your instincts. But neither drugs, nor living in close rapport with your instincts, could create genius if it wasn't there in the first place. Picasso certainly took a lot of opium in his early days, but as a relaxant and because it was pleasurable rather than in order to unlock his artistic intuition. Fernande was his accomplice, noting in her journal 'I love to smoke opium, I love Pablo. He is tender, kind, amorous; he pleases me. How can I have been blind for so long ... I love him; I'm going to love him so much.' Through the later part of the summer of 1905 Fernande had grown closer to Picasso, culminating in her moving in with him on 3 September. In the blur, money was short but what the hell? 'We're managing to survive on 50 francs a month,' she added, 'and sometimes we have enough left over to pay the bill at the paint shop.' Fernande also recorded the change that came over Picasso's art in 1905. 'The paintings he's doing are quite different from those I saw when I first came to the studio last summer,' she wrote, 'and he's painting over many of those canvases. The blue figures, reminiscent of El Greco, that I loved so much have been covered with delicate, sensitive paintings of acrobats ...' What was probably his masterpiece of 1905, *The Boy with the Pipe*, is suffused with a euphoria summed up by the wreath of roses that Picasso placed in the boy's hair as a finishing touch. The pipe in the young man's hand may well have contained something more than tobacco. Richardson suggests that opium 'flavours the theme and mood of many late Blue and early Rose period works'. But while it may flavour their theme and mood, it doesn't generate them as works of art. Picasso's use of drugs remained recreational rather than creative.

The sad fact also had to be faced that not everyone's experience of mind-altering substances was beneficial. In many cases such experimentation was destructive rather than inspirational. The young German artist Karl-Heinz Wiegels, schizophrenic, eccentric, homosexual, in flight from the Teutonic restriction of his native Dusseldorf, was a fellow tenant of Picasso's in the Bateau-Lavoir. Fernande recounts how one evening in 1908 Wiegels 'took ether, hashish, and opium in quick succession. He never regained his senses, and several days later, despite our efforts to care for him, he hanged himself.' It was a sobering lesson for everyone in the building.

CHAPTER EIGHTEEN

Alienation from the Public

'Artists and public have never been so isolated from each other as they are today,' wrote Georg Swarzenski in 1911. The director of the Frankfurt Städel with his modernist sympathies was well positioned to measure the chasm of misunderstanding that had widened between the two. He was right that in the years 1905–14 the avant-garde advanced further beyond bourgeois taste than ever before. They made the advance rejoicing. If the public didn't get it, then that was their loss. Artists were there to remain true to themselves, not to please their public. It was all very well, however, to adopt Schoenberg's position of bowing only to the musicians in the orchestra at the end of their performance of an atonal piece, not to the audience. But there was a financial consequence. A ticket-paying audience was a prerequisite to survival as a musician. If no one bought your pictures, how were you going to eat? The Munich dealer Hans Goltz bravely staged his first exhibition of the work of Egon Schiele in 1913, and afterwards wrote to the artist: 'Herr Schiele, while I am always delighted by your drawings, and while I am happy to go along with your weirdest moods, who is supposed to sell the paintings? I can see very little opportunity for that.'

One of the unforeseen consequences of the modernist revolution in the early years of the twentieth century was the extent of material suffering inflicted on the young avant-garde, unable to find buyers for their paintings because they were too advanced. Was there more poverty among the avant-garde in 1905–14 than in previous generations? A small group of young Impressionists had certainly suffered deprivation in the 1870s and 1880s, but

now there were numerically more artists of a rebellious disposition so the problem was more widespread. Some of the new
generation resorted to commercial work, drawing illustrations
for the comic papers in order to survive. After his arrival in Paris
in 1906, Juan Gris, for instance, worked for a time as a cartoonist
for popular magazines such as *l'Assiette du Beurre*, *Le Charivari*,
and *Le Rire*, earning a reasonable living from this graphic work.
So did other avant-garde artists earlier in their careers, including
van Dongen, Frantisek Kupka, Louis Marcoussis, Jacques Villon
and Marcel Duchamp. There is a certain irony in the double life
they lived: rebels by conviction, but pandering to a bourgeois
sense of humour by necessity.

Poverty was hard enough to navigate if you were young
and single, but even more of a problem if you had dependents.
Emil Nolde, half a generation older than the young men of Die
Brücke to whose train he temporarily linked his wagon in 1906,
had a wife to support. Ada Nolde – whose background was the-
atrical – nobly tried to reinvigorate their finances by returning
to the stage in a music hall act accompanied by a trained goose.
Never work with children or animals: the performance was a
failure and Ada suffered a physical and mental breakdown. The
subsequent career of the goose is not recorded. Fortunately new
patrons gradually emerged for Nolde, such as Karl Osthaus in
Hagen, and the lawyers Hans Fehr and Gustav Schiefler. In their
instinctive understanding of the new art, these collectors were
nonetheless the exceptions rather than the rule.

It was the same thing in Austria. The Viennese bourgeoisie,
in the words of Otto Friedlander, continued to 'vegetate in its
own happy mediocrity', roused to anger, it seemed, only by
the more extreme manifestations of advanced art. In this the
Viennese took their cue from the heir to the throne, the Archduke Franz Ferdinand, whose verdict on Kokoschka was that he
would like to break every bone in the young man's body. Such
violent hostility to modernism, while it might initially stimulate
rebellion in artists, could ultimately wear them down. Matisse,
protected by the carapace of what Gertrude Stein called his

'brutal egotism', appeared to be coping with the string of critical rebuffs that blighted his career from 1905 to 1910. He rode out the derision and abuse poured on him as the perceived leader of Fauvism, culminating in the debacle of his first big exhibition in Germany, at Cassirer in Berlin in 1909. But he finally cracked, and had a breakdown in December 1910. Picasso, on the other hand, took a more aggressive line. When Kahnweiler informed him of a collector's adverse reaction to an early Cubist painting, his response was 'Good, let's get everyone against us'. It was as if Picasso welcomed ignorant opposition as validation of his new work's quality.

Even an artist as eminent as the elderly Rodin suffered the hostility of the public, although he was by now financially secure. A flashpoint was the large version of *The Thinker*, which in 1906 the city of Paris agreed to put up in front of the grand staircase of the Panthéon. It was envisaged as a tribute to the man widely accepted as the greatest French sculptor of his generation, and perhaps an oblique acknowledgement of the power of French thought. But not everyone was in favour and opposition to the idea – deeply wounding to Rodin – was voiced by the writer Joséphin Péladan, on the grounds that its pose 'suggests a scatological idea'. The physician Max Nordau, who made his name as a specialist in degeneracy, declared that its 'bestial countenance with its bloated, contracted forehead, gazes as threateningly as midnight'. The plaster mock-up initially put in place was even attacked by a man with a hatchet. Despite all this, the piece was finally installed on 21 April.

Nietzsche was in no doubt about the self-protective power vested in the armoury of the artist. 'The artist is related to the lovers of his art as a heavy cannon is to a flock of sparrows,' he wrote. If such volleys of artillery fire were to impact even an artist's admirers, how much greater would be the shock on an unsuspecting general public? And in the case of a more advanced artist, in touch with his instincts and with all guns blazing, perhaps the general public could be forgiven for taking immediate evasive action.

CHAPTER NINETEEN

Suicide, Death, Morbidity

Life lived on the cusp between genius and madness, and perilously pared down to the instincts, produced among avant-garde artists a dangerous obsession with death and morbidity. At moments of crisis and extremity, the idea of suicide was regularly invoked, as a threat, a release, or an inevitability. Confronted with Picasso's extraordinary *Les Demoiselles d'Avignon* in the artist's studio in 1907, Derain had only one reaction. 'This can only end in suicide', he told Kahnweiler. 'One day Picasso will be found hanging behind his *Demoiselles*.' In 1912 Boccioni went into crisis: 'I worked for six hours today on my sculptures and I don't understand the results', he wrote to Severini. 'Planes upon planes, muscles and faces sectioned, and then what? What about the total effect? Do my creatures have a life of their own? What is going to happen? ... I can always find a pistol.' The pistol was a constant option. 'The only right an artist has in a materialistic age,' wrote Kokoschka, 'is that when he has no more illusions left – that is, when he is exhausted – he has the freedom to take his own life.'

It was in Vienna that artists lived most precariously on their nerves. In 1912 Schiele painted an extraordinary and disturbing portrait of himself and Klimt, which he called 'Hermits'. Schiele explains that these are 'the bodies of men weary of living – suicides – but men of feeling'. The implication was that men of feeling were more quickly worn down to become weary of living. The relevant case history here is the twenty-four-year-old Richard Gerstl. Fresh from his arrogant refusal to exhibit with the Klimt Gruppe, Gerstl again went to stay in the country with

52. Schiele, *Hermits*, 1912

the Schoenbergs in the summer of 1908. It was a momentous and tragic two months for all concerned. In July Gerstl painted two group portraits of his hosts and fellow guests, which in their technique establish Gerstl's claim to be the earliest Austrian Expressionist. Thick loops of paint are splurged on to the canvas in what seems more a display of painterly pyrotechnics than an expression of inner emotion, but then Gerstl only pulled out all the emotional stops when he was painting himself. Simultaneously, Schoenberg was making his final leap into atonality, achieved at the end of the month in the fourth movement of his *Second String Quartet*. Then on 26 August everything fell apart. Gerstl and Schoenberg's wife Mathilde, their mutual passion

53. Gerstl, *Self Portrait*, 1908

rekindled, were discovered by Schoenberg in flagrante. In the turmoil that followed, Gerstl and the composer's wife ran off to Vienna together.

On 18 October Gerstl set up in a new studio on the top floor of 20 Liechtensteinstrasse. Significantly, it overlooked Freud's consulting rooms. Here he painted an extraordinarily powerful naked self-portrait; the nude study of Mathilde that he also managed is much less animated by comparison. But the explanation may be that Mathilde, having half returned to her husband, was by now only able to give Gerstl brief, clandestine sittings. It was in Liechtensteinstrasse that Gerstl took his own life on 4 November, stabbing himself in the heart as he simultaneously hanged himself from a noose set up from a rafter. It was all done in front of the large studio mirror: he was not to be denied this dying glimpse of himself, one final, horrifying self-portrait for his eyes only.

The Viennese preoccupation with illness and death continued. On 17 February 1910 the writer and art critic Ludwig Hevesi committed suicide. Ludwig Wittgenstein, arriving in Cambridge from Vienna in 1912 to study philosophy with Bertrand Russell, shocked his tutor by claiming to have contemplated suicide every day of his adult life. The writer Karl Kraus described the Austrian capital at this time as 'an experimental station for the collapse of mankind'. In Vienna in 1910 Klimt held a show of erotic drawings at the Galerie Miethke. The press described them as 'obscene' and 'morbid'. Once again, Nietzsche had seen it all coming. In *Will to Power* (1885) he identified 'exceptional states that condition the artist – all of them profoundly related to and interlaced with morbid phenomena – so it seems impossible to be an artist and not to be sick'. Thus it was not entirely unexpected that Kokoschka and Schiele, the two *enfants terribles* of Austrian modernism, should also this year be drawn independently to subjects involving malady and mortality.

In January 1910 the chief savage (*Oberwildling*) of Viennese art, as Hevesi had earlier christened Oskar Kokoschka, set out to a sanatorium in the Alps. He had been commissioned by the Viennese architect Adolf Loos to paint a portrait of Loos's girlfriend, the English dancer Bessie Bruce, who was under treatment there. When he arrived, Kokoschka didn't just paint Bessie Bruce. He found several further subjects for portraits in the rich and degenerate cast of patients holed up on the mountain, who, if they weren't about to be carried off by tuberculosis, were in danger of succumbing to death by boredom. Loos, already an admirer and collector of Kokoschka's work, paid for the artist to stay on and paint them. What emerged was a succession of masterpieces, psychologically penetrating portraits of the sick and decadent executed in an appropriately vivid, manic, swirling technique: there was an urgency to his method, involving

54. Kokoschka, *Portrait of Sanatorium Patient*, 1910

the use of the end of the brush, the hand, the fingernails, and small bits of cloth to wipe away paint. As Kokoschka said later, 'Look, the route from the brain via the arm and then through the brush is much too long. If it were possible I would paint with my nose.'

Of the patients he painted in the sanatorium, he wrote: 'They were like shrivelled plants, for whom even the Alpine sunshine could not do much.' The violent Expressionist technique that he unleashed on them produced portraits of such merciless psychological penetration that their subjects recoiled. It was fortunate that Loos was on hand to buy them from Kokoschka, because the sitters certainly weren't going to. Kokoschka's slightly later portrait of the psychiatrist, myrmecologist and philosopher Auguste Forel, a similarly ruthless piece of intuitive

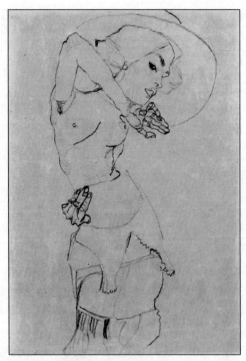

55. Schiele, *Study of Gerti*, 1910

Expressionism, provoked the sitter to exclaim that he looked as though he had had a stroke. When, two years later, he did have one, Kokoschka rather callously took this as confirmation of his own gifts as a clairvoyant of humanity. 'It's my task as a painter to see,' he claimed, 'to see what's really going on in the world. I'm a seer.'

In 1910 Schiele was still employing as a model his pretty younger sister Gerti, who had no objection to posing in the nude for him. Theirs was a complicated relationship, with overtones simultaneously morbid and erotic, entirely in keeping with the mood of the time in Vienna. Four years earlier, in 1906, Schiele had marked the occasion of the death of his father (a railway employee) by using his late father's rail pass to take the then twelve-year-old Gerti to Trieste, retracing the itinerary of their parents' honeymoon and spending one night in a hotel with her. It was clearly not a conventional family life. Now, pursuing his interest in death and disease, Schiele turned to his friend at the gynaecological hospital, the obliging Dr von Graaf. A trifle rashly von Graaf allowed Schiele access to some of his female patients for artistic purposes. Schiele produced a series of deeply disturbing studies of dead or dying often pregnant women, sometimes disconcertingly sexual. Are the eyes fluttering at the approach of ecstasy or of death?

Artistic morbidity extended to a fascination with homicide, too. In London on 11 September 1907 a prostitute called Emily Dimmock had her throat slit by a client on a bed in a seedy rented room in Camden Town. This crime had unexpected repercussions for modern British art. Walter Sickert, who had already made rather a speciality of painting defeated-looking nudes on iron bedsteads in dank north London boarding houses, became obsessed with the story. He adapted existing works and produced new ones as pieces of topical painterly reportage on the theme of the murdered woman. Sickert's naturally dimmed palette deepened the bleakness of the subject; although familiar with France, having lived there for periods of his career, there was no suggestion of Fauvism in his colouring. Rather, he seized on the Dimmock murder as a document of the sort of seaminess that in its realism would shock the complacent traditionalists of the Royal Academy, and in Britain at least would constitute modernism. Poor Sickert. Little did he know that his choice of subject matter would be dredged up a century later and used to fabricate a sensationalist theory that he had in fact been the notorious East End serial killer, Jack the Ripper. So the sex murder entered the repertoire of the advanced artist in the years 1907 to 1909: Sickert (*Camden Town Murder*) – man kills woman; Munch (*Death of Marat*) – woman kills man; Kokoschka (*Murderer, the Hope of Women*) – woman imprisons man, man escapes, man kills woman.

Squalid mortality invaded not just the work of British artists but, in the case of John Currie, his life as well. Currie was one of the most promising young artists of his generation in London.

56. John Currie, *Dolly Henry*, 1913

He had enrolled at the Slade School in 1910 where he befriended Nevinson and Gertler, and began to paint in that peculiarly British 'advanced' style of the time in which the human form is treated with a kind of lumpen monumentality; Will Rothenstein characterises this as 'a tendency ... to give more power to forms than they can comfortably carry – as though one pumped more air into a tyre than it needed'. Gaudier-Brzeska called Currie 'a great painter, and a magnificent fellow'. But he was a magnificent fellow with a tempestuous temper, and a lack of moral sense caused, according to Nevinson, by 'an over-reading of Nietzsche'. In late 1913 he left his wife and infant son to live with a young model, Dolly Henry, with whom he was obsessed. Their relationship was not a calm one. Currie was catastrophically jealous, and in September 1914, enraged by rumours that

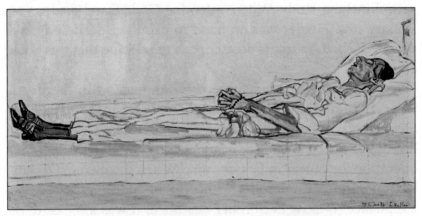

57. Hodler, *Valentine Gode on her Deathbed*, 1915

Dolly had posed nude for a photographer, he shot her dead in the Chelsea flat that they shared. Then he turned the gun on himself. London's answer to Richard Gerstl died a few days later.

You could lose control, of yourself, of your fate, of your instincts, and the consequences were often dire. But there was a compensation: those consequences could be turned into art. The morbidity intensified. In 1913 Hodler's mistress Valentine Gode-Darel, like so many artists' models, 'fell pregnant'. In October she went into hospital in Geneva and gave birth to their daughter, Pauline. But Valentine was not well: she was discovered to be suffering from an illness that was first thought to be tuberculosis, but in January 1914 was diagnosed as cancer. As an artist, you have to work with what you are given. So Hodler began painting her as an invalid, producing a series of works that painstakingly documented her decline. It was a merciless record of the progressive loss of all trace of her former beauty, given an extra chill when one remembers that Hodler was simultaneously engaged in a new relationship with another woman. So these were works of observation, as much scientific as emotional, as much about the living artist as the dying woman. Perhaps they achieved the final rapprochement with death for Hodler, an expiation and catharsis through the art of unflinching study. When Valentine Gode-Darel died on 26 January 1915, Hodler was on hand to paint her dead body laid out on the bed – a tragic postscript to the decade that this book covers.

Such a subject, involving artistic immersion in the death throes of a loved one, would not normally have attracted Picasso. His mistress Eva Gouel, whose condition, like Gode-Darel's, had initially been diagnosed as tuberculosis, underwent her first operation for cancer in January 1914. When she died in December 1915, Picasso – despite his horror of mortality – was inn attendance to draw her on her deathbed. It was a measure of the power of his feelings for her. But, like Hodler, it didn't deter him, as the illness of his lover worsened in the first months of the war, from holding several surreptitious auditions for the role of her successor.

CHAPTER TWENTY

Studio Gruffness and the Rewriting of History

As an avant-garde artist, pushing boundaries on the front line could be a lonely business. You were isolated because you were so far in advance of conventional art. Thus you gravitated gratefully to any other rare spirit whose work was in sympathy with yours. Groups coalesced and movements were founded. Die Brücke, the Blaue Reiter, the Futurists, the Jack of Diamonds, the Golden Section and the Vorticists were all assemblies of artists of like sympathies that came into existence not just to collaborate on innovation but also to offer mutual support. And then gradually, artists being only human, dissension arose. Rivalries intensifed and movements disbanded. And later, as artists brooded on the past and histories of modernism started to be written, disagreements rankled, jealousies surfaced and the temptation to adjust the record and exaggerate your role in the story became almost irresistible.

The artists of Die Brücke put a particular emphasis on the camaraderie of shared studios and models. As they strove to break free from the artificiality of Jugendstil and to replace it with something more spontaneous and instinctive, Fritz Bleyl, one of the founders of the movement, described how

> we met regularly, once a week, at Kirchner's. Our wish to draw the live model became reality and was immediately carried out, not in a conventional academic way but in 'fifteen minute poses'. Thus the artist and the model would not tire, but rather through fast-changing poses, the spontaneity of expression was strengthened.[26]

But working communally also had its disadvantages. Comparisons of work were inevitable. Mutual criticism occasionally turned rancorous and hostilities arose. There was a regrettable tendency to what Pechstein's biographer refers to as '*unverfalschter Atelierruppigkeit*', a distinctively Germanic concept which translates literally as 'unadulterated studio gruffness'.

The Germans, having invented the name for it, found themselves rather good at it. The Brücke group yoked together a number of abrasive personalities. Kirchner could be difficult, pumped up with his own self-importance. Pechstein had an uncanny ability to rub people up the wrong way, and was rather better at promoting himself than his colleagues, so that his prices were infuriatingly higher than those of other members. Things got worse when artists from both Die Brücke and the Blaue Reiter decided to show together in the Neue Secession in Berlin in 1911. Relations between the two groups were already precarious. The exhibits were chosen by a selection committee, in which Pechstein – never the most diplomatic of characters – was felt to have too prominent a voice. Studio gruffness turned into loud and bitter disagreement, with the result that Pechstein withdrew from the Neue Secession in a huff, taking the other Die Brücke artists with him. An infuriated Franz Marc described Pechstein as 'the little Napoleon of the Berlin art scene'.

The artists of Die Brücke continued their assault on Berlin in 1912. But having made enemies in the Secession and the Neue Secession, Kirchner and his associates had to look elsewhere for a place to exhibit. In April they found a temporary home in the Galerie Fritz Gurlitt in Berlin for their annual exhibition. Relations within the group, however, were deteriorating. Kirchner, Heckel and Schmidt-Rottluff were accused by Pechstein of 'blatant egotism'. Then Pechstein was invited to become a member of the Berlin Secession, where Cassirer was about to assume the presidency. Pechstein's acceptance was seen as disloyalty by the other Die Brücke members.

In May 1913 the Die Brücke group dissolved. The level of studio gruffness between its members had finally become intolerable. Its demise was hastened by Kirchner writing a self-promoting 'history of the movement' which upset just about everyone. The last exhibitions took place in Basel and Munich, but by now the original stylistic innovations of the group were being lost in the encroaching seas of Cubism, Futurism and Orphism. That summer, Kirchner retreated to Fehmarn on the North Sea coast where he painted landscapes, but the great achievements of his year were in Berlin, where he worked on a powerful series of paintings of city life. Schmidt-Rottluff withdrew to Nidden, and Heckel to Osterholz on the Baltic Sea. As a symbol that the fight had gone out of them, when the Berlin Secession invited all the former Die Brücke artists to exhibit, they all accepted. But this precipitated another row, this time within the Berlin Secession. The more conservative members objected to all this dangerous new blood, and the consequence was the departure of Liebermann, Slevogt and Cassirer. These were volatile times.

Pechstein left the Secession too – he wrote that the only time he enjoyed being a member was when he signed his resignation. He was also pleased to be rid of Die Brücke, explaining why in mid May: 'because these people are totally finished in terms of their humaneness, and their works at the current Secession Exhibition prove to me once more their addiction to appearing modern at all costs'. Before too long cracks also appeared in the façade of unity erected by the artists of the Blaue Reiter. Jawlensky and Werefkin had already signalled their divergence from Kandinsky's programme, finding themselves unable to follow his advance on all-out abstraction. Then August Macke made a drawing entitled 'Satire on Blue Rider', which mocked Kandinsky. Macke wrote of him: 'There is more mysticism in a tabletop than in all his pictures put together. They no longer have any resonance for me.'

Were you a Futurist or a Cubist, a Simultanist or a Rayonist or a Vorticist? These allegiances were upheld with an almost religious sectarianism, and disputes could lead to violence – even in London. On 12 June 1914 a bunch of maddened Vorticists, led by Wyndham Lewis, marched on an exhibition of Futurism at the Doré Gallery to attack their former colleague Christopher Nevinson, who had thrown in his lot with the Futurists. These things really mattered.

Over time, studio gruffness hardened into deeper jealousies and resentments. In the years after the First World War some sort of historical perspective became possible on what was now understood to have been the critical decade of modernism, 1905–14. Artists started brooding about their personal place in history. The precise dating of works within that crucial period became more and more important as they jostled each other retrospectively to establish their own priority in the judgement of posterity. Such had been the speed of the development of new movements that even a year's difference in a work's execution could make a lot of difference to its perceived significance. It became clear, for instance, that a Fauve work painted in 1905 or 1906 was usually more important than one painted in 1907 or 1908, and certainly more significant than one painted in 1910 or 1911. Similarly with Cubist or Futurist works: ideally they needed to sit in that exciting cusp of 1910–14. Anything from 1915 onwards was reckoned a bit late. And even within those sacred five years, you didn't want to be caught out as still painting like an Analytical Cubist in 1914, when you should have moved on to something more Synthetic. Malevich was not the only artist guilty of a little bit of later adjustment in the dating of works from his Cubist phase.

One of the worst culprits in this respect was Kirchner. Like most of his fellow masters of modernism, he was under-appreciated prior to the First World War and a lot of what he painted remained unsold in his studio until some years later. The longer it hung around, the more tempting it became to fiddle with it, to redate it, to make out that it had been painted earlier than it actually had and thus reinforce his own significance in the history of modern art. The impact of Matissean Fauvism went deep with Kirchner, perhaps deeper than he would care to admit. He first saw Matisse's work properly in

58. Kirchner, *Girl Under Umbrella*, 1909 (dated 1906)

the Cassirer exhibition of January 1909, and later in the year he painted a violently Fauvist *Girl Under Umbrella*. At some later point he added to it the false date of 1906. Another Kirchner of 1909 is his *Self-Portrait with Model*. This he rather more modestly later redated to 1907. These are not the only examples of works executed by Kirchner in the years 1909–11 but redated to 1905–7. Kirchner, of course, wanted to give the impression that he had come to Fauvist colouring independent of any influence from

Matisse, so well before he had seen his Berlin exhibition. Hence his rewriting of history. The modern historian learns to treat the dates on Kirchner's paintings with suspicion. They occupy a moral no-man's land, an almost surreal territory. They are not fakes, in that they are indeed painted in the artist's hand and are intrinsic to the work; but they impart false information.

Another artist later eager to exaggerate his own importance to Fauvism was Michael Larionov. On his first visit to Paris in 1905 he confessed to being 'stupefied' by the new art. So stupefied was he by the experience that it fogged his memory. In the Musée Pompidou today hangs a Fauvist landscape by Larionov that he dated 1905. It was actually painted in 1912, by which time attention was shifting in Paris and Moscow to Futurism.

With Futurism, too, dates of execution became retrospectively of increasing importance. The Futurists made their trip to Paris in the autumn of 1911 in order to spy out the latest Cubist developments before they made their own sensational debut in Paris in February 1912. The movement was driven by a new and exciting dynamism. However, Balla's *Street Light* (now in the Museum of Modern Art, New York), painted in 1910, was removed from the Paris exhibition at the last moment. It was apparently censored by Boccioni. Why? 'They did not want me in Paris and they were quite right,' explained Balla after the event. 'They are much more advanced than I am but I'll work on it and I'll also improve.' Presumably *Street Light* was deemed still too divisionist, and not dynamically Futurist enough. Rather than repainting it, Balla took it away and opted for the less demanding course of redating it to 1909, thus neatly repositioning it as a forward-looking early work in the development of Futurism. In any other era, these minutiae of chronology would be of minor interest. But just at this point they become crucial. The failure of advanced artists to sell their work as soon as they painted it put temptation in their way: had they been able to shift it immediately, it would not have hung around their studios offering later opportunities to reimagine dates and adjust history in their favour. There is boring, rational truth and imaginative, instinctive truth. Some artists succumbed to the latter.

There were more radical ways of rewriting or even suppressing history. Rather than redating their works, modernist artists sometimes committed more drastic acts of self-censorship by destroying them. There was a mysterious fire in Derain's studio in early 1908. Most of the paintings that he hadn't already sold to Vollard were lost. It may well be that, torn between Fauvism and the directions in which Cézanne and Picasso were pulling him, he could see no way forward and so set light to them himself. Posterity is therefore denied a fuller understanding of his struggles with the human figure in 1906–7. The ambitiously titled *Prouesse*, shown at the Salon des Indépendants in 1906, is missing; so, too, is *La Source*, which seems to have been painted as a companion piece to Matisse's *Le Bonheur de Vivre* in the same exhibition. *La Source*, like the Matisse, was slated for being mere decoration, based on poorly understood Far Eastern prototypes and described by one critic as 'the woolly result of lofty prattle and poorly digested reading'. Victims of disheartening critical hostility, these works may well have been among those that went up in smoke in an act of oeuvre-editing by Derain. Matisse would not have supported such destruction. 'I do not repudiate any of my paintings,' he wrote in 1908, looking back on his career to date, 'but I would not paint one of them in the same way had I to do it again. My destination is always the same but I work out a different route to get there.'

Not everyone, however, was as well balanced as the sanctimonious Matisse. The pace of change was frenetic in these years of feverish invention, and Léger also succumbed to a bout of Derain syndrome. Having achieved the radical advance represented by *Nus dans un paysage* (begun in 1909 and exhibited in 1911 – see p. 253), he decided to wipe from the record all his previous efforts at painting. Today collectors search pretty much in vain for works by Léger executed in 1908 or before. Wherever he could lay hands on something he had done early in his career he destroyed it. An equally drastic act of self-censorship was performed by Juan Gris. Looking back in the 1920s on the work he had done in the early years of Cubism, he reached the conclusion that it had indeed been excessively geometric, too informed by measurement. He therefore gave instructions to his widow and his dealer to destroy several hundred working drawings of the period, which they duly did when he died relatively young in 1927. Artists can make bad critics and worse autobiographers.

Sometimes early works by the artists of modernism didn't survive for other reasons. In April 1909 Max Pechstein exhibited *Women with Yellow Robe* at the Berlin Secession. Large and very Gauguinesque, it attracted the shocked attentions of the press. One critic talked about 'Gauguin-mad colour orgies' displaying 'all the repulsiveness of bad digestion'. Here is another lost painting from the crucial years leading up to the Great War. We only know it from an old photograph.

But it is unlikely that the artist himself destroyed it, as was the case with Derain and Léger. Pechstein was little given to self-doubt, and had a high regard for his own oeuvre. The problem was that these early works of modernism initially sold, if they sold at all, for relatively small amounts of money. As curiosities of meagre value, their first owners sometimes tired of them and relegated them to attics, whence it was not unknown for them to pass on to unappreciative heirs who disposed of them before their importance became acknowledged decades later. In Germany, the artistic suppressions of the Nazi regime from 1933 onwards were also a significant factor. German Expressionism was top of the Third Reich's proscribed list. Ownership of an example made you politically suspect. It's sad but not surprising that several – possibly including *The Yellow Robe* – ended up on the rubbish tip.

PART IV

BEYOND INSTINCT

Chapter Twenty-one

Breaking Boundaries

From 1910 to 1914 there was a climactic acceleration of innovation and invention in European modernism. Such was the manic pace of change that it would have taken a superhumanly perceptive commentator at the time to step back from the maelstrom and assess the confused new directions of contemporary art. But from the vantage point of more than a century later, it is clear that visual art was being deployed in pursuit of unprecedented new objectives, objectives unimaginable even five years earlier: with Kandinsky and Marc, an investigation into synaesthesia; with the Futurists, the depiction of pure dynamism; with de Chirico, a pictorial evocation of the philosophy of Nietzsche; with the Cubists a journey of exploration into the fourth dimension. Braced by its renewal at the font of Instinct, visual art was now straying deep into the territories of music, dance and poetry, even into those of mathematics, geometry and philosophy. Had it gone too far?

An awful lot of dense and high-flown theory was written and spoken by artists themselves, trying to explain or justify what they were doing, to give intellectual heft – or alternatively mystical drama – to the particular -ism that they had just invented and were striving to promote. Never had there been such jostling for position in a pantheon of modernism that was being reimagined from new angles on an almost daily basis. Just occasionally something illuminating emerges from the verbiage; but generally Picasso got it about right by either refusing to elaborate verbally on his artistic practice or by putting forward explanations that were deliberately absurd. Early on in his career he stole from a Paris tram a sign that read 'Do not Talk to the Driver', which he displayed in his studio to discourage questions about his work. He preferred to let it speak for itself. The last months before the war saw a staggering range of new -isms blossom: besides the offshoots of Cubism – Futurism, Orphism, Simultanism, Rayonism and Vorticism – there were less well-known variations such as Synchronism and Synchromism, Cerebrism (the invention of Canudo and Valentine de St Point, themselves an exotic combination of the cerebral and the sensual), and Henry Valensi's Effusionism or Musicalism (whose most famous example was a visual rendering of the Funeral March of Chopin in 1912). Most came and went, minor growths in an exotic hothouse of competing ideas. Many had strident manifestos attached. Some were remarkably silly.

But by 1914 so much had happened in such a short time that it was impossible not to be excited about what had been achieved, and even more excited about the future. Marc wrote in January:

> Today art is moving in a direction of which our fathers would never even have dreamed. We stand before the new pictures as in a dream and we hear the apocalyptic horsemen in the air. There is an artistic tension all over Europe. Everywhere new artists are greeting each other ... everywhere new forces are sprouting like a beautiful unexpected seed.[27]

He went on to claim 'a secret connection between all new artistic production', comprising subtle links with 'Gothic and primitive art, with Africa and the vast Orient, with the highly expressive, spontaneous folk and children's art, and especially with the most recent musical movements in Europe and the new ideas for the theatre of our time.' Apollinaire took the avant-garde temperature in 1914 and came up with a similarly optimistic reading: 'These experiments show that a universal art is being created, an art in which painting, sculpture, poetry, music and even science in all its manifold aspects will be combined to transform our vision of the world and to arrive, at last, at an understanding of the universe.' It was as if a new Golden Age was dawning.

The chapters that follow examine in more detail the five intense years leading up to the outbreak of war. They investigate how artists now travelled beyond where instinct had led them, and arrived, if not at an understanding of the universe, then at least in places where they had never been before.

Chapter Twenty-two

Supermen

On 25 July 1909 the world changed: the French pioneer airman Louis Blériot made the first cross-channel flight from Calais to Dover in thirty-seven minutes. The conquest of the air captured the imagination of everyone, particularly artists. In September many forward-thinking artists thronged to the exhibition that opened in the Grand Palais celebrating aerial locomotion. Technological advance was intoxicating. True modernism had found its natural expression in the flying machine. 'Just as work by Cimabue was paraded through the streets,' explained Apollinaire, 'our century has seen Blériot's aeroplane, bearing the weight of humanity, of thousands of years of endeavour and of necessary art, triumphantly paraded through Paris to the Arts-et-Métiers Museum.' Marcel Duchamp accompanied Brancusi and Léger to the exhibition that autumn. 'Painting is finished,' he told his companions. 'Who could do better than that propeller? Can you do that?' Giacomo Balla needed no convincing: having christened his first daughters Luce and Elettricita in tribute to the marvels of twentieth-century technology, he now called his third one Elica (propellor). The cult of the aviator was born, and intensified in Paris in the following years. Apollinaire, for instance, felt moved to write a poem called 'Zone' depicting Christ as a high-flying record-breaking airman.

André Salmon paid a visit to Picasso's studio on 21 September 1911. 'Welcoming and mocking,' he reported, 'Picasso is dressed like an aviator.' This was the ultimate praise: by now the aviator was the epitome of heroic modernity. Aviators bridged the Nietzschean gap that so fascinated de Chirico between God and the acrobat; they were the new supermen. Harry Kessler tried to commission Maillol to sculpt a memorial to Nietzsche the same year, and suggested it might take the form of a giant nude statue of the superman. The idea didn't work out. A more appropriate guise for the twentieth century would have been to clothe the superman in the overalls of a pilot, the new master of the universe.

For the avant-garde, the staggering technological advances of the early twentieth century were proof that the old art was not adequate for the age of the motor car and the aeroplane; that new artistic breakthroughs were needed to match and reflect these scientific ones. And came they did with all the -isms of the next five years, radical movements that in their different ways were all responses to the heroism of twentieth-century life. Who were the new heroes? They emerged in a procession of men of action: not just the aviator, but also the racing-car driver, the cyclist, the boxer, the footballer and the dancer.

Particularly the dancer. Dance, indeed, was now everywhere in the visual arts. It was the theme of Sergei Shchukin's greatest commission from Matisse, the painting that became one of the most celebrated and influential of the twentieth century. There was also the Ballet Russe, whose choreography broke new boundaries of expressiveness and athleticism, while the costumes and the set designs were thrillingly daring and exotic. Van Dongen was one of the many to be enchanted by the visual and musical treat that it offered: on 2 June 1909 he saw Anna Pavlova perform in *Cléopâtre*, and in tribute he painted his *Souvenir de la Saison de l'Opéra Russe*, a swirl of gorgeous colour. In 1913, in the wake of the Ballet Russe's sensational performance of *The Rite of Spring*, the journal *Montjoie!* saw a clear link between the new ballet and other advanced branches of the visual arts, commenting admiringly that Stravinsky 'participates in the aesthetic of our time, in Cubism, Synchronism and Simultanism on the one hand, and all the nervous banality of arrhythmia on the other'. And if you wanted an extra helping of nervous arrhythmia in 1913, there was also Valentine de St Point's Futurist *Métachory*

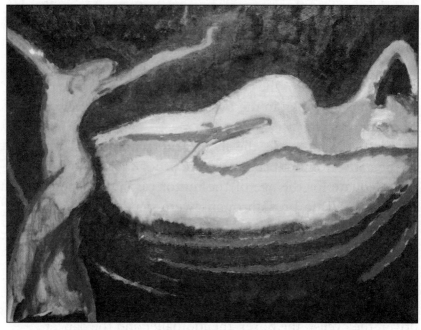

59. Van Dongen, *Souvenir de la Saison de l'Opéra Russe*, 1909

or 'Beyond Dance', her stage performance of body movement which set out to celebrate 'lust' and 'the art of the flesh' in an up-to-the minute assault on rhythm, tonality, morality and logic.

The body's capacity to communicate abstract ideas was of continuing fascination to artists, and links with dance and music were enthusiastically investigated. In 1892 the American modern dancer Loie Fuller had brought to Paris her 'free dance', which featured swirlingly expressive costumes lit with dramatic coloured lighting. Ferdinand Hodler, who depended directly on the human figure as the means of giving his art its expressive power, was a friend of the Geneva-based composer Émile Jacques-Dalcroze, who pioneered rhythmic gymnastics and the experience of music through movement. Hodler developed the idea of rhythm in the visual arts as an echo of the rhythmic laws that permeate nature. Nothing delighted him more than the lines of girls draped in sheets cavorting through the Alpine landscape that the freer spirits in dance, music and painting were busy orchestrating. In the coming years the eurhythmics of Mary Wigman, a German pupil of Jacques-Dalcroze, would plumb even deeper the psyche's travails and states of being as expressed by the human body, and have considerable influence on later Expressionist painting.

In his search for what he called 'pure plastic rhythm', Boccioni sculpted his famous *Unique Forms of Continuity in Space*. He was aiming for 'not the construction of bodies, but *the construction of the action of bodies'*. The obvious place to find bodies in action was the sports arena, and in the years leading up to the Great War sport was increasingly depicted by modern artists. Football was a particularly popular subject, although there was sometimes a confusion in artists' minds as to whether the version they were watching was rugby or soccer. It had all started in 1908, when Douanier Rousseau had painted his *Footballers*, the progress of their game inconveniently constricted by an arbitrary avenue of trees running across the middle of the field of play. Duncan Grant's large composition *Football* followed in 1911: it features players of improbably balletic stature, prancing about in such a way as to suggest only a hazy familiarity with the offside rule.

Things got serious in 1913, when Gleizes painted his *Joueurs de Football*, Boccioni produced a powerful *Dynamism of a Footballer*, and a third great football picture was dreamed up by Delaunay. Little did the Cardiff rugby team suspect the vital contribution they were making that year to the history of art. But Delaunay seized upon a rugby game as reported and photographed in a Paris sports magazine in January, and elaborated it into a dynamic composition of leaping players, advertising hoardings and the obligatory view of the Eiffel Tower, further energised by impressions of a ferris wheel and a biplane. Then, somewhat mystifyingly, because the game depicted was between two French clubs, he gave it the title *l'Équipe de Cardiff*. But artists aren't necessarily the most

60. Delaunay, *L'Équipe de Cardiff*, 1913

factually accurate reporters. Baffled scholars have suggested
that Delaunay was acknowledging the then perceived inferiority
of French rugby to British rugby; yet what counts here is not
competitive nationalism but dynamism and colour, creating
a memorable image of modern life. When the picture was
exhibited at the Indépendants in March, Apollinaire described it
as 'the most modern work in the Salon'.

The cyclist offered further opportunities to the Cubist and
the Futurist to investigate the body in motion. Cycling had been
the rage for some time, and had caught on in advanced circles.

61. Metzinger, *Cyclist*, 1912

Félix Fénéon was so devoted to it that in his days as art critic on *La Revue Blanche* he doubled as the journal's cycling correspondent. Braque similarly thought nothing of bicycling from Paris to the south of France for a summer's painting. In 1902 Jarry had decided to take on Nietzsche and go one better than the Superman when he wrote his novel *Le Surmale*. Marcueil, the 'super-male' hero of the story, surpasses all human physical limits as both bicyclist and lover. He dies only when an electric 'love-inspiring machine', overwhelmed by his superior powers, falls in love with him, shorts out and kills him in a climactic spasm. You can imagine Picasso's delight in such a fantasy. When the sculptor Zadkine designed a monument to Jarry, he showed him simultaneously riding a bicycle, pointing a gun, writing in a notebook on the handlebars, and looking into the sky, the whole thing lit from within.

The velodrome – and the boxing ring – attracted many modernist artists, including Metzinger, Archipenko, and the Vorticist William Roberts. Besides being dynamic subject matter, boxing was also a metaphor for the professional antipathies that were felt ever more strongly in advanced circles of the Paris art world by 1914. Arthur Cravan, the poet-cum-boxer who prided himself on pulling no punches as an art critic, was an ace troublemaker. Swiss by birth, his formal education was terminated when he was expelled from an English military academy, allegedly for 'spanking a teacher'. In 1914, he founded his own literary magazine called *Maintenant!* (the exclamation echoes the better known *Montjoie!*) which he distributed round Paris in a wheelbarrow. Art was 'situated more in the guts than in the brain', he decided, an appropriate declaration for a critic of his violent disposition. He conceived a virulent hatred for Delaunay, whom he likened to a piece of soft cheese. Rather ungallantly, Cravan also took issue with Delaunay's wife Sonia for being Russian. 'I'd rather sleep with a member of the Collège de France – Henri Bergson, for instance – than with most Russian women,' he asserted pugnaciously. 'But I won't pretend that I wouldn't do it with her just once, because like most men I am a collector.' Cravan was found guilty of defamation in court and sentenced to eight days in jail, a punishment revoked on appeal at the request of the Delaunays, which was generous of them. In the same review, Cravan criticised so brutally a self-portrait by Marie Laurencin that her lover Apollinaire felt obliged to challenge him to a duel. It doesn't seem to have got as far as the Parc des Princes. But when war broke out in August, it was Cravan who fled the country and Apollinaire who joined up.

One place where boxing did not feature was the Olympic games held in Stockholm in the summer of 1912. In keeping with the honourable traditions of Swedish pacificism, boxing was banned by the organisers, but an unexpected inclusion as a competitive sport was Art. In the painting category the gold medal was won by an Italian artist, Giovanni Pellegrini (1866–1937), for three friezes representing winter sports. Walter

62. Kirchner, *Berlin street scene*, 1914

Winans, an American marksman and sculptor, won the silver medal for shooting and gold in the sculpture category for a bronze statuette *An American Trotter*. Had Norway done the obvious thing and selected Edvard Munch to represent them he might have won gold for painting, but it is unlikely that he would have brought home any medals for marksmanship.

There is one additional hero (or heroine) to be added to the pantheon created by modernist artists in the years leading up to the First World War. The street scenes that Kirchner painted in Berlin in 1913–14 are arguably his greatest achievements. His is not Meidner's apocalyptic view of the city, nor does he recast urban life in the dynamic lines of force of the Italian Futurists. But there is still a palpable energy: he charts the human traffic of the teeming metropolis, surging along its pavements, dodging motor cars and illuminated by the strange new glare of electric light. The displaced angles and violent colours of his figures perfectly express the interplay between the men and women who eye each other as they pass in a mixture of lust and financial calculation. The prostitute, said Kirchner, is the heroine of modern times. As so often with the advanced artists of 1905–14, Baudelaire had anticipated him. In *The Painter of Modern Life* he had already identified the whore as an emblem of heroic Primitivism, 'a perfect image of savagery in the midst of civilisation'. 'Sometimes they effortlessly adopt poses, both provocative and dignified, that would be the joy of the most fastidious sculptor … Nobility should be seized even in the mire'. Wyndham Lewis went further and characterised the artist himself as a 'sacred prostitute', 'defiled by the world but at odds with it'. It was a description of his profession that might have taken the elderly Sir Edward Poynter, the then President of the Royal Academy, a little by surprise.

CHAPTER TWENTY-THREE

Abstraction

'What does the artist create?' Paul Klee asked in his diary in 1905. 'Forms and spaces! How does he create them? In certain chosen proportions.' Although Klee himself never quite made the final jump out of representationalism, he was articulating one of the underlying modernist trends of the ten years before the First World War: the advance on abstraction. It was an advance given momentum by Fauvists and Expressionists in their flat planes of garish, non-naturalistic colour, and by Cubists and Futurists in their drastic distortions and deconstructions of natural form. In the final breaching of the citadel in 1913, all references to the natural world were drained from painting and sculpture, leaving a pure plastic residue for a few daring pioneers to work with and infuse with new meaning.

Artists noted the progress of this process as it happened. Henri Le Fauconnier, an enquiring young painter trying to get the measure of the new post-Fauve, Cézanne-driven direction of travel, put it like this in 1908: 'Our pictorial research is leading us to an aesthetics that is less changeable, more stable, and more theoretical … in the last resort painters are withdrawing more and more towards pure plastic art, doing away with all literature.' 'We are moving towards serenity by simplification of ideas and means,' Matisse explained in 1909. 'Our only object is wholeness. We must learn, perhaps relearn, to express ourselves by means of line. Plastic art will inspire the most direct emotion possible by the simplest means.' At this point the avant-garde had reached extreme simplification of forms, but not yet the eradication from them of all resemblance to nature. That advance was not far ahead. By 1913, when Franz Marc analysed the exhibition of international avant-garde art that he had helped Walden put together at Der Sturm, his excited overall impression of the show was that the new art displayed 'a significant preponderance of abstract forms'. Non-figurative, pure painting was now much discussed. 'Why should we not conceive of pure painting?' wrote Henri Valensi (inevitably in *Montjoie!*) that summer. 'In the same way that the musician uses notes, why shouldn't we suppose that colour, by its intrinsic force, has the power to express the thought of the painter?'

Several different artists pushed such ideas so far in 1913 that at various different points they crossed the final boundary to abstraction. As they did so they became aware of the ultimate dilemma of totally abstract art. How do you give an abstract composition meaningful content? How do you prevent it sliding into mere decoration? Both Matisse and Picasso drew back from the problem: pure abstraction was never part of their agenda. But Kandinsky, Léger, Delaunay, Malevich, Larionov and Mondrian, who each made the final step in different ways in 1913, all came up with different answers.

Orphism, as Delaunay later put it, was 'a visual art whose forms, rhythms and development derived from painting itself, just as music does not deduce its sonority from nature, but from musical relationships. Painting becomes painting.' At the heart of Delaunay's Orphism were its simultaneous contrasts, which evolved out of his *Fenêtres* series. These were created by different areas of colour acting on each other reciprocally to produce pictorial form and space. Looking back on her life, Sonia Delaunay identified the years 1912–14 as the high point: 'What intense, explosive years for Robert and me!' she rhapsodised. 'We had found in the sky the emotive principle of all artwork: light, movement, and colour.' Delaunay's 'formes circulaires', emerging in 1913, intensified these effects, but with a hint of the didacticism of a scientific colour chart.

In his extraordinary series of 'contrastes de forms', Léger reached abstraction by a different route. Multi-coloured geo-

63. Delaunay, *Fenêtres*, 1912

metric shapes rendered in a brisk, painterly brushstroke spill across the composition with a tense dynamism. In the words of Christopher Green, they achieve an effect 'both of surface conflict and of tangible, weighty form'. Léger, too, subscribes to the ideal of pure painting, pursuing a realism that he characterised as true to the picture rather than to nature. In a lecture delivered to the students of the Académie Wassilief in Paris on 5 May 1913, he explained: 'pictorial realism is the simultaneous ordering of the three great plastic quantities: lines, forms, and colours.' But it was perhaps a fear of losing meaningful content that caused Léger, too, to draw back from totally subjectless painting. By the end of 1913 and into 1914, vague representational elements were creeping into his work once again. He was still painting powerful 'contrasts of form', but they now had titles: *Nature morte, Le Village dans la forêt, L'escalier.* They were no more than hints

64. Léger, *Contraste de Formes*, 1913

of a subject, but they returned a structure to his compositions without sacrificing their power and their dynamism. Léger was at the high point of his career, and the years 1913–14 represent his supreme achievement.

And 1913 was also Kandinsky's greatest year. His was the most spectacular final crossing of the boundary into complete abstraction, underpinned as it was by an elaborate synaesthetic theory and experienced by the artist as profound spiritual revelation. The major compositions of 1913 – and there were an extraordinary number of them – unfolded on a large scale and involved many preparatory studies on paper. From now on Kandinsky divided what he produced between Impressions (the product of the observation of nature), Improvisations (the spontaneous product of the unconscious), and Compositions

65. Kandinsky, *Bild mit weissen Linien*, 1913

(the result, as prescribed in his 1911 essay *On the Spiritual in Art*, of 'a slowly formed inner feeling, which comes to utterance only after long maturing'). The musical parallels are obvious and intentional. The distinction between an Improvisation and a Composition is particularly important here: Improvisations are more direct transcriptions of motions of the soul, but works such as *Bild mit weissen Linien* (painted in October) and *Composition VII* (painted in November) – both masterpieces – evolve gradually over days. Yes, they contain elements that can be read as having reference to forms in nature, but these are subjective, evanescent interpretations.

What Kandinsky achieved in 1913 was a genuine breakthrough, the sort of moment of definition not seen often in the history of art. Kandinsky described it in his *Reminiscences*, published by Herwarth Walden in 1913: 'Thus the realm of art drew farther and farther apart from the realm of nature for me, until I could thoroughly experience both as independent realms. This only happened in its full magnitude this year.' Painting, to Kandinsky, is now

> a thundering collision of different worlds, intended to create a new world in, and from, the struggle with one another, a new world which is the work of art. Each work originates just as does the cosmos – through catastrophes which out of the chaotic din of instruments ultimately create a symphony, the music of the spheres. The creation of works of art is the creation of the world.[28]

Taking the raw material of chaos and recasting it into a symphony is not a modest artistic ambition. But in 1913 Kandinsky felt himself ready to attempt the challenge.

Malevich's progress into abstraction was not fully complete until 1915, but he made major advances in 1913 along the road to what would become Suprematism, an absolutely pure, geometrical abstract art. It was a distinctively Russian phenomenon, the product of Malevich's association with poets, playwrights and philosophers in Moscow and St Petersburg. Indeed his innovation was all the more remarkable for the fact that he himself never went to western Europe. The Cubo-Futurist vocabulary which he incorporated into his paintings in 1912–13 was learned at second hand. He wrote on the back of one such work, *Cow and Violin*, that 'the alogical juxtaposition of the two forms' was 'an aspect of the struggle against logic, natural order, and bourgeois meaning and prejudice'. Later he falsely dated the *Cow and Violin* to 1911, which was perhaps another act in the same struggle.

The crucial moment in his breakthrough to abstraction took place in St Petersburg in December 1913, where Malevich was involved in the staging of an avant-garde opera, *Victory Over the Sun*. He masterminded the lighting, which contributed to the creation of a new sort of Cubist abstraction. The critic Benedikt Livshits, who was in the audience, reported:

66. Malevich, *Black Square*, 1913–15

Within the limits of the stage box, a painterly solid geometry was born for the first time, a strict system of volumes
reducing to a minimum the elements of chance which have
been thrust on it from without by the movements of the
human figures. The figures themselves were sliced by the
blades of the beams; alternately hands, feet and heads were
eliminated, since for Malevich they were only geometrical
bodies.[29]

Malevich was also responsible for the set and costume designs,
which gave birth to the original version of his most famous
abstract composition, the black square on a white background.
Later Malevich himself recalled:

In the year 1913 in my desperate attempt to free art from the ballast of objectivity, I took refuge in the square form and exhibited a picture which consisted of nothing more than a black square on a white field ... The black square on a white field was the first form in which non-objective feeling came to be expressed. The square = feeling, the white field = the void beyond this feeling.[30]

It is questionable whether he actually exhibited such a picture in 1913, but the image had its first visual realisation that year in the context of *Victory Over the Sun*.

Elsewhere in Russia, 1913 saw the birth of Rayonism, which at first sight seemed like a Russian version of Futurism. It was the brainchild of Larionov, with the help of Gontcharova. Together they issued their Rayonist manifesto at the Donkey's Tail exhibition in July: 'We proclaim the whole brilliant style of modern times – our trousers, jackets, shoes, trolleys, cars, airplanes, railways, grandiose steamships – is fascinating, is a great epoch ... that has known no equal in the entire history of the world.' So far so Futurist, and indeed Rayonism's ray-lines and interacting planes parallel Futurism's lines of force and dynamism. But Larionov went on: 'Painting is self-sufficient; it has its own forms, colour and timbre. Rayonism is concerned with spatial forms that can arise from the intersection of the reflected rays of different objects, forms chosen by the artist's will.' The Rayonists were thus marking out a new kind of abstraction, one that was simultaneously scientific and mystical, mediated by something that Larionov calls 'the artist's will'. 'The artist must be a clairvoyant,' the Russian philosopher P. D. Ouspensky had written in 1911. 'He must see that which others do not see; he must be a magician: must possess the power to make others see that which they themselves do not see but which he does see.'

It was time for art to invade life, decided Larionov, so he also started face-painting. 'We paint ourselves because we want to herald the unknown, to rearrange life, and to bear man's multiple soul to the upper reaches of reality,' he explained. 'The

67. Larionov, *Rayonist Composition*, 1913

painting of our faces is the beginning of the invasion. That is why our hearts are beating so.' But other avant-garde Russians were less kind about Rayonism: in late 1913, Malevich dismissed 'these sticks of Larionov' as facile by comparison with a pure Cubist work. Nor did it stand up well against Futurism, according to Livshits: 'Rayonism,' he said, 'with which Larionov tried to outstrip the Italians, fitted into Boccioni's waistcoat pocket.'

Piet Mondrian, who had arrived in Paris the year before, also took large strides to pure abstraction in 1913. Apollinaire correctly identified him as a painter who 'seems above all to have been influenced by Picasso', although his 'highly abstract Cubism', while arising out of a close study of the method of Picasso and Braque's analytical period, was now driving him in a new direction. Gradually references to the figure, indeed to

68. Mondrian, *Composition*, 1913

all representationalism, were eliminated from Mondrian's compositions. What was left was a network of short vertical and horizontal lines across the surface of the picture, a precursor of his later grid system, but as yet without its regularity. Mondrian, regrettably unconstrained by the inherent sexism of his thinking, characterised the vertical as male and the horizontal as female. The vertical and horizontal are all that remain after the reduction of the diversity of nature to its essence, to the 'primordial and the absolute' relation. By now titles have been abandoned and Mondrian calls his works simply *Tableau no. 1* or *Tableau no. 2*. But in late 1913, he approached a crisis: within the limited parameters that he allowed himself, how was he to avoid obtaining the same pictorial result every time he picked up a paint brush? Thus in 1914 Mondrian would return now and then to the 'particularity of the motif', for instance by the addition of random configurations of letters to his otherwise abstract composition. But the cat was out of the bag: back in Holland his example had persuaded the young Dutch artist Jakoba van

Heemskerck to follow him in dispensing with titles to her paintings. The practice, she felt, was 'just disgustingly romantic'. She was not alone: through the rest of the century there followed a monotonous procession of works of modern art called variously 'Sans Titre', 'Untitled', 'Senza Titolo', or 'Ohne Titel'.

Larionov headed to Paris again in summer 1914, accompanied by Gontcharova. The 'Exposition de Natalie Gontcharova et Michel Larionov' opened at Paul Guillaume's gallery on 17 June. Here was the chance for Paris to acquaint itself with Rayonism, and the show was visited by the luminaries of the avant-garde: Picasso, Duchamp, Delaunay, Léger, Modigliani and of course Apollinaire. In the April edition of *Montjoie!* Larionov had prepared the way with an article explaining his new movement. Larionov the scientist based his Rayonist theory on the tenets of reflectivity, luminosity and recent discoveries of radioactive and ultraviolet rays. But Larionov the artist was still aware of the danger of merely 'transcribing phenomena', of limiting his art to the scientific representation of the infravisible. That was not enough. He needed to take the whole thing further, to amplify its spiritual and emotional dimension. Larionov was not modest in his claims: 'Ultimately,' he elaborated, 'a Rayist computation allows for the possible physical definition and measurement of love, ecstasy, talent, spiritual qualities, and the epic state. In a word, everything that pertains to the sphere of feelings in the human and animal world.'

These constituted an ambitious agenda. Apollinaire was prepared to acknowledge Rayonism as 'a genuine aesthetic discovery', but how far the movement actually achieved 'the physical definition and measurement of love, ecstasy, talent, spiritual qualities, and the epic state' is open to debate. Rayonism shares with many movements of the frenzied five years before war broke out – Orphism, Futurism, Cubism – a supporting structure of ambitious scientific theorising. In earlier centuries, expeditions exploring unknown lands and peoples would be accompanied by an official artist whose task it was to make a visual record of their findings. The avant-garde artist of the

69. Hilma af Klint, *Sjustjärnen*, 1909

early twentieth century fulfils an equivalent role, except that the expeditions he accompanies and visually documents are probing into obscure regions of a different nature: into the human brain and psyche, into aspects of the visual process, into new frontiers in philosophy. Art, therefore, becomes a record of phenomena ranging from the scientific to the metaphysical, operating like some sort of magic X-ray or infrared machine. The danger in this process is that the artistry, its aesthetic content, is limited to the chance beauty of an X-ray or a many times magnified photograph. Lines of force, light-rays, forms in space, emanations of the cosmic spirit, synaesthetic colour equivalents of music, visual expressions of Bergsonian duration are all wonderful, no doubt. But are they art? Wyndham Lewis struggles manfully to explain Vorticism: 'A mental-emotive impulse (by this is meant subjective intellection, like magic or religion) is let loose upon a lot of blocks and lines of various dimensions and is encouraged to push them around and arrange them as it will.' Brave words, but they still sound more like a laboratory experiment than a work of art.

The race to Abstraction in 1913 was all very exciting, but did a female painter called Hilma af Klint, working away in eccentric obscurity in Sweden, get there first? Her 'Temple' series of large-scale abstract compositions, begun in 1907, eluded the attention of scholars until recently. They were painted in isolation in Stockholm as part of a crazy Theosophist-inspired mission to reform the world by giving abstract visual expression to the motions of the soul. Are they among the earliest works of Abstract art? Yes. Are these contrived and overly geometric compositions therefore greater works of art than the Kandinskys, Légers and Maleviches of the next decade? No. Af Klint minutely records mystical phenomena with pseudo-scientific meticulousness. She stands in the same relation to Kandinsky as a botanical artist painting a sunflower stands to van Gogh.

CHAPTER TWENTY-FOUR

The Blaue Reiter

In 1908 a young art historian in Munich, Wilhelm Worringer, published a book called *Abstraction and Empathy*. His thesis, that the crucial element in our appreciation of art is our capacity to empathise with it, was not new. But he took a more radical line in arguing that art's beauty and power does not necessarily depend on its accurate reproduction of external reality. There is a different kind of art, one which embodies the urge to abstraction, and is exemplified by the Egyptian, the Byzantine, the Gothic or the Primitive. This sort of art answers a different need in humanity, one which expresses man's insecurity and alienation, and addresses his spiritual anguish. At self-confident historical periods – classical antiquity, or the Renaissance – the rendering of the external world meets man's spiritual needs and generates what Worringer calls an 'objectified delight in the self'. But at other, more anguished times, the artist seeks to abstract from objects something more than their outward appearance. Here was an exciting justification for the distortions of modernism in general and Expressionism in particular, and an acknowledgement that modern times, being the product of spiritually hostile elements such as industrialisation, demanded a special heroism if they were to be navigated by the new generation of artists. These were ideas that would have appealed to Paul Klee, ploughing his own lonely furrow and as yet barely known in the art world. 'How shall I most freely cast a bridge between inside and outside?' he asked himself in his diary in 1908. It was still a question absorbing most of the European avant-garde.

Four artists who would have found Worringer's book profoundly interesting took a house together in Murnau, outside Munich, that summer of 1908: they were two couples, Kandinsky and Gabriel Münter, and Jawlensky and Marianne Werefkin. By day they roamed the Alpine landscape in search of *plein-air* subjects, which included the brightly painted houses of the village. In the evenings they discussed the spiritual power of art, the expressive potential of colour, and the relationship of the visual arts to music. Münter and Werefkin – painters of considerable ability themselves – were support acts to the men. Werefkin believed profoundly in Jawlensky and, having money of her own, was prepared to fund him. Münter, too, was ready always to put Kandinsky's interests before her own. Kandinsky and Jawlensky had a lot in common. Both were Russian, and both had spent recent time in Paris. Jawlensky actually visited Matisse in his studio in 1907. But Kandinsky's natural instinct was to be the boss. He took on occasional pupils whom he would corral into the Alps to paint the landscape, summoning them to particular viewpoints with a sharp blast on the whistle he carried for the purpose. You didn't argue with the master.

For Münter 1908 was a summer of revelation. She described it as being a time when 'I took a great leap forward, from copying nature – in a more or less Impressionist style – to abstraction, feeling the content, the essence of things ... I particularly enjoyed showing my work to Jawlensky, who praised it lavishly and also explained a number of things to me: he gave me the benefit of his wide experience and talked about "synthesis".' What was synthesis? At this early stage in the evolution of the Blaue Reiter group it meant an expression of inner feelings through a simplification of the painting of nature, a paring down to the essential by means of flattening planes and exaggerating colour. There was also a willingness – more evident in the work of Münter and Kandinsky – to learn lessons from the primitivism of Bavarian folk art, and from children's drawings. But Kandinsky's sights were already set higher, trained on a more spiritual realm than that achievable by simple 'synthesis' as understood by the others. His Murnau landscapes from now on progress along a road that led ultimately to total abstraction; the others did not follow him so far.

Kandinsky's return to Bavaria in 1908 made clear to him how sorely Munich was in need of a wake-up call. He spoke of the slumber into which art had sunk in the city where he had begun his studies a decade earlier. 'When I returned to Munich,' he wrote, 'I found everything in the same old place. And I thought, this really is that fairy kingdom in which pictures sleep on the walls, the custodians in their corners, the public with their catalogues in their hands, the Munich artists with their same broad Munich brushstrokes, the critics with their pens between their teeth.' But Kandinsky also sensed that the place was ready for change: 'They're waiting for something', he said. 'Something's got to happen. Everyone who knows about such things realises it can't go on like this.'

In order to make something happen, Kandinsky, Jawlensky, Werefkin and Münter got together in Munich in January 1909 to form the Neue Kunstler Vereinigung (the NKV). Other artists they recruited included Alexander Kanoldt, the reclusive Alfred Kubin and Karl Hofer. The premise of this new group was restated as 'the belief that the artist, apart from those impressions that he receives from the world of external experiences, continually accumulates experiences within his own inner world'; and what united them was 'the search for artistic forms by which to lend expression to all these interacting and mutually permeating experiences ... in short, the quest for artistic synthesis'. The year before, Klee had been asking himself how best to throw a bridge between the inside and the outside. Here was the answer.

That summer Kandinsky painted a number of landscapes which go beyond anything he had achieved before. *Landscape with a Green House* is clearly discernible as being set in the main street in Murnau, but there is an electric charge running through it that is immensely exciting to the eye and does indeed conjure a synthesis between the 'outer' and the 'inner' Kandinsky;

70. Kandinsky, *Landscape with a Green House*, 1909

between what he sees and what he feels. After months of preparation, the first exhibition of the NKV was held at the Galerie Thannhauser in December. It was panned by the local press as 'an orgy of colour', meant disparagingly. Only the newly arrived Hugo von Tschudi, now director of the Munich Museum, had a good word to say for it.

Franz Marc was a young painter separately looking for something more mystical and instinctive, what he was to call 'a pantheistic empathy into the shaking and flowing of the blood in nature, in trees, in animals, in the air'. In 1909 he met the young August Macke, who was based in Bonn but had spent time in Paris in 1907 and 1908 where he had been deeply impressed by the work of Matisse. Macke had also taken the wise precaution for an avant-garde artist of marrying the niece of a very rich and modernistically inclined collector, Bernhard Koehler. The meeting with Macke, besides opening Marc up to French art, also introduced him to Koehler, who became as enthusiastic in his patronage of Marc as he already was of his nephew by marriage. Throughout 1910 Marc was at work on the challenge he had set himself to reinvent the animal picture. He was leaving naturalism behind and striving to find a means of expression to capture the essence of animality. The process was increasingly informed by a highly individual colour theory that Marc was developing. He explained it to Macke as follows: '*Blue* is the *male* principle, austere and spiritual. *Yellow* is the female principle, gentle, bright and sensual. *Red* is *matter*, brutal and heavy, the colour which the other two have to fight against and overcome.'

In the summer of 1910 Kandinsky's Murnau landscapes, already distanced from naturalism by their thrillingly lurid colouring, were fragmented into images that came closer to abstraction. Bits of Murnau – the church tower, the hills, odd roofs of houses – are thrown together as if in a washing machine and are glimpsed in a mêlée of unexpected shapes and angles. The second exhibition of the NKV took place on 1–14 September 1910 at the Galerie Thannhauser, and was considerably more ambitious than the first. Apart from contributions from Kandinsky and his friends, it included an impressive consignment from Paris with international artists represented, including Picasso, Braque, Derain and van Dongen. The hand of Kahnweiler may be detected here, establishing market connections in his native land. While he discouraged his artists from exhibiting in Paris, Germany was a different matter. There was always the chance that a new buyer might be found in Germany. And adverse press reviews were less damaging for his artists in far away Munich than in the cauldron of Paris. Adverse they certainly were: on 10 September the *Munchner Neueste Nachrichten* devoted some column inches to what it called, noting the foreign origins of Kandinsky, Jawlensky and Werefkin, 'this Munich assembly of East Europeans'. It went on, 'Taken as a whole, their exhibition is sheer nonsense, but one also finds in it a synthesis of the shortcomings and futile mannerisms of the art of every known people and region, from primitive cannibals to Parisian neo-decadents.'

71. Kandinsky, *Autumn Landscape*, 1911

Now Franz Marc joined the fray. He saw the NKV exhibition in September, and wrote admiringly of the group's attempt pictorially to articulate 'spiritualised and dematerialised inwardness of feeling'. The synaesthesia of colour and music and the visual expression of inner emotion were threads that united the efforts of Kandinsky and Marc through 1910 and 1911, culminating in their establishment of the Blaue Reiter group in later 1911. Kandinsky's first meeting with Franz Marc took place on New Year's Day 1911 at a party in Munich thrown by Maria Werefkin. There was an instant rapport. Marc described Kandinsky and Münter as 'wonderful people' and went on: 'Kandinsky is the most charming of them all, even more so than Jawlensky. I was completely captivated by his refinement and distinction: altogether a splendid fellow. I can well understand why Münter, whom I like *very* much, is madly in love with him.' The next day they went to a Schoenberg concert, which led to a sympathetic correspondence between Kandinsky and the composer. It culminated in Schoenberg's declaration quoted earlier that, 'Art belongs to the *unconscious*! One must express oneself! Express oneself *directly*! Not one's taste or one's upbringing, or one's intelligence, knowledge or skill. Not all these *acquired* characteristics, but that which is *unborn, instinctive.*'

Kandinsky's highly charged colours advance, via a kind of apocalyptic folklorism, towards an almost abstract art in 1911. In December that year he published his treatise *On the Spiritual in Art*, which articulated an increasingly synaesthetic view of the function and power of colour. Each colour corresponded with a particular emotion, parallels which Marc, too, was defining. But what was even more important to Kandinsky were the musical equivalents that he established: different shades of green, for instance, echoed the sound of stringed instruments. Mid green evoked the quiet, mid-ranged tones of a violin, while yellow-green corresponded to the higher notes of the violin and blue-green to the muted alto violin. Red, on the other hand, is a colour that can 'cause pain … through association with running blood' but also 'gives a feeling of strength, vigour, determination and triumph. In music it is a sound of trumpets, strong, harsh, and ringing.' Kandinsky takes the musical analogy further: 'Colour is the keyboard, the eyes are the hammers, the soul is the piano with many strings. The artist is the hand that plays, touching one key or another purposively, to cause vibrations in the soul.'

There is also ordeal, violence and subversion of convention in the momentous modern art that Kandinsky envisages: 'The strife of colours, the sense of balance we have lost, tottering principles, unexpected assaults, great questions, apparently useless striving, storm and tempest, broken chains, antitheses and contradictions, these make up our harmony.' The pursuit of a harmony born out of anarchy was now an international phenomenon of the avant-garde, expressing itself across the arts: in arrhythmia in dance, dissonance and atonality in music, and distortion in painting.

Harmony through dissonance may have been achievable artistically, but harmony between increasingly fractious modern artists was more elusive. At the end of the year 1911, disagreements came to a head among the Munich avant-garde. The Vereinigung exhibition was scheduled for December, but in its preparation the jury voted to exclude Kandinsky's nearly abstract *Composition V*. Jawlensky and Werefkin viewed these developments uneasily: they were not keen on the totally non-representational direction of Kandinsky's art, nor on the 'cosmological', mystical aspect of his theory that was emerging from *On the Spiritual in Art*. For the time being they stayed with the Vereinigung. But Kandinsky and Marc broke away, followed by others, including Münter and Kubin. The defectors quickly organised their own exhibition at the Galerie Thannhauser, under the name of the Blaue Reiter, the title of the almanac devoted to European contemporary art that they were about to publish. The exhibitors at the first Blaue Reiter show, which opened on 18 December, included the Burliuk brothers from Moscow, Macke, Münter and Heinrich Campendonck, a young artist close to Marc. And then there were works by three others, each representative of an aspect of advanced contemporary art important to Kandinsky and his friends. There was a painting by Arnold Schoenberg. In the brave new world of the Blaue Reiter, where music and visual art were all but interchangeable, what could be more natural than a painting by a composer? Privately Macke did not think much of it, but Kandinsky was fierce in its admiration. There was a self-portrait by Douanier Rousseau which everyone could agree was an important demonstration of twentieth-century Primitivism. And there was work by Robert Delaunay, a particular favourite of Franz Marc. Delaunay's fragmentation of form into interpenetrating planes of light and colour from now on provided a visual language which Marc and Macke increasingly adopted to express themselves.

The Blaue Reiter Almanac itself is one of the great early documents of modernism. Its editors were Kandinsky and Marc, and it was in the planning through most of 1911. Who could they get to fund it? The potential benefactors that the group discussed constitute a roll call of the most enlightened modern patrons in Germany at the time: Karl Osthaus, the young dealer Alfred Flechtheim, Hugo von Tschudi (who sadly died in the course of the year), and Macke's uncle by marriage, Bernhard Koehler. No doubt Herwarth Walden would have been on the list had he not already been publishing his own art magazine *Der Sturm*. In the end, it was Koehler who stumped up. The contributors worked on it with gathering enthusiasm throughout the autumn of 1911, and what was finally published in May 1912 constituted an extraordinarily wide-ranging and well-informed *tour d'horison* of the artistic avant-garde in Europe. It included illustrations of Picasso's *Woman with Mandolin*, Delaunay's *Eiffel Tower*, Matisse's *Music* and *Dance* from the Shchukin collection, Rousseau's self-portrait, Kokoschka's *Portrait of Else Kupfer*, as well as works by Marc, Macke and Kandinsky. Also featured were Asian art, folk prints and children's drawing. 'Without exception,' wrote Kandinsky, 'in each child's drawing the inner sound of the subject is revealed automatically.' For Kandinsky the 'inner sounds' of things were what linked art, literature and music, and provided the basis for a viable synaesthesia.

Kandinsky distinguishes between 'inner necessity', whose expression is the essence of the true work of art; and 'outer necessity', art motivated only by ambition and greed. 'In daily life we would rarely find a man who will get off the train at Regensburg when he wants to go to Berlin. In spiritual life, getting off at Regensburg is a rather common occurrence.' It is a metaphor for the difference between life lived constricted by reason and convention, and the glorious freedom from logic of living by your instincts. Still, if you had arranged to meet Kandinsky's train at Berlin railway station, you shouldn't have been surprised if he wasn't on it.

The Blaue Reiter movement cast their net widely across Europe for their second exhibition, held at the Goltz Gallery in Munich in February 1912. Apart from the regulars, such as Kandinsky, Marc and Macke, Paul Klee contributed seventeen drawings. The Die Brücke artists were invited to show, too, and Heckel, Kirchner, Mueller, Nolde and Pechstein all sent work; from Paris, Braque, Picasso and Vlaminck contributed; and from Russia, where of course Kandinsky had strong links, Gontcharova, Larionov and Malevich exhibited. Malevich was going through a neo-Primitive phase, portraying strong, blocky figures with titles like *Mower*, *Woodcutter*, and *Taking in Rye*. Modernist connections were indeed being made all over Europe. For instance, Klee visited Paris in April 1912. Unlike his trip there in 1905, when he had very little idea where to find the avant-garde and ended up seeing a Whistler exhibition, this time he went straight to Delaunay's studio and the next day visited von Uhde, Picasso and Braque.

There was a surge of the spiritual and the synaesthetic among the artists of the Blaue Reiter in 1912. Later in the year, Kandinsky published his book *Klange* (*Sounds*), comprising thirty-eight prose poems and fifty-six woodcuts which aimed to combine words and images, the aural and the visual, the concrete and the imaginary. By now he was talking of the 'sound', the 'feel', and even the 'taste' of a painting.

Franz Marc, on the other hand, his style energised by seeing the Italian Futurist exhibition in Berlin in the summer of 1912, was continuing his attempts at pictorial empathy into the animal's view of nature. In a painting such as *Deer in the Monastery Garden*, Marc was now not so much putting the deer into the landscape as the landscape into the deer. His work makes a telling contrast with that of Wilhelm Kuhnert, a conventional animal painter of great popularity in Germany, who was producing big set pieces like *Grollende Löwen* in 1912. Kuhnert knows his public and what they want from the wild animals he depicts: realism, of course, and a touch of anthropomorphic nobility; but to Kuhnert they are ultimately trophies. He paints them only as a prelude to shooting them.

'Is there a more mysterious idea for an artist than to imagine how nature is reflected in the eyes of an animal?' Marc wrote. 'How does a horse see the world, how does an eagle, a doe, or a dog? It is a poverty-stricken convention to place animals into landscapes as seen by men; instead we should contemplate the

72. Marc, *Deer in the Monastery Garden*, 1912

73. Wilhelm Kuhnert, *Grollende Löwen*, 1912

soul of the animal to divine its way of sight.' His words echo the philosopher Theodor Lipps, for whom empathy, 'projecting oneself on to the object of perception', was all-important in aesthetics. Under Lipps' influence the poet Rilke was working on the same idea, practising *'einsehen'*, or 'inseeing' on animals with a view to penetrating their souls. Nijinsky explored the same common ground between the animal and the human in his interpretation of the faun in the scandalous Stravinsky ballet *L'Après-Midi d'une Faune*, that premiered in Paris in 1912. His movements on stage, according to an eyewitness, were 'virile and powerful and the manner in which he caressed and carried the nymph's veil were so animal that one expected to see him run up the side of the hill with it in his mouth'. But Ludwig Wittgenstein brought a merciless philosophical logic to the question. If lions could talk, he said, we wouldn't understand them.

There were widening divisions of opinion within the Blaue Reiter about how far to follow Kandinsky's route to mystical abstraction. Marc was the one who remained most loyal to Kandinsky through the extraordinary year 1913, in which the Russian made such dramatic steps forward. On 30 January 1914 Kandinsky gave an address at the opening of the last significant exhibition of his work before the war, Galerie Ernst Arnold's 'Die Neue Malerei' show in Dresden, in which he re-emphasised his conviction that 'the birth of a work of art is of cosmic character. The originator of the work of art is thus the spirit.' On 25 February he finished *Painting With Red Spot*, his last pre-war masterpiece, which features the conflicting relations of colours in what seems like a battlefield of diverse formless elements. By this point Kandinsky's inclination is towards transcendentalism, seeking truth in the realm beyond the material world, while Franz Marc seeks the truth in the material environment. Marc nonetheless pretty much attains total abstraction himself in works such as *Fighting Forms (Abstract Forms I)* of 1914.

His route there, however, had been different from Kandinsky's, and owed more to Delaunay. Both Marc and Macke had been deeply impressed by Orphism, and their approach

74. Macke, *Figures in the Park*, 1914

continued to show it. By 1914 Macke too was constructing his paintings in compartments of colour that no longer depended on perspective, volume or modelling by light and shadow. In February he wrote to his artist friend Hans Thuar: 'Finding these space-defining energies of colour instead of being content with dead chiaroscuro – that is our finest goal.'

There was still the second edition of the *Blaue Reiter Almanac* to work on. In its preface Marc expressed the loneliness of life as a mountaineer – or perhaps in his case, given his animal sympathies, the loneliness of life as a mountain goat – in the difficult upper reaches of modernism: 'The common herd is unable to follow us,' he wrote. 'The path is too steep and as yet untrodden.' As 1914 unfolded Kandinsky also became discouraged, increasingly troubled by what the future held in store and less able to work. The outbreak of war at the beginning of August meant that as a foreign national he had to leave Germany, and he reached Russia again – via Switzerland – in December, something of an exile in his own country.

75. Klee, *Tunisian Landscape*, 1914

A last idyllic hurrah for happy painting had been sounded in April 1914, when Klee and Macke travelled together on an expedition to Tunisia. It was a brief trip, but it made a deep impression on both painters. On 8 April Klee spoke in his diary of the 'intoxication' of painting in the Arab quarter. On 10 April Macke wrote to his wife from Tunis: 'You can turn around here and find a thousand motifs ... I am going flat out and enjoying a work-lust that's entirely new to me. The African country-side is far more beautiful than the Provence. I'd never have imagined it.' On 16 April it was Klee's turn to rhapsodise again: 'Colour possesses me. I don't have to pursue it. It will possess me always, I know it ... Colour and I are one. I am a painter.'

Klee's words are a fitting summing up of the excitement and positive energy generated by the movement. Four months later war had broken out, and Kandinsky was on his way back to Russia. Two years later both Macke and Marc were dead, killed in action. The era of the Blaue Reiter was over.

CHAPTER TWENTY-FIVE

Matisse: Beyond Fauvism

When Matisse exhibited *Le Bonheur de Vivre* at the Salon des Indépendants in spring 1906, it was a signal that he had already moved beyond the first explosive phase of Fauvism and was looking to do more than detonate primary colours like 'sticks of dynamite'. In the years to come he never lost the fundamental belief in the expressive power of line and colour. Journeys into the fourth dimension, synaesthesia or pure dynamism were not for him, although journeys to north Africa and borrowings from Islamic art were. And he believed that you worked best when you worked instinctively. But now he found he needed to re-engage with the human figure in order to advance. He was on his own, no longer a member of a group. He was mocked and reviled by the general public. He didn't get any easier to live with.

Not everyone, however, derided *Le Bonheur de Vivre*. The Russian merchant, Sergei Shchukin, had professional, textile-related reasons to travel regularly to Paris, where he was devoting more and more time to looking at new art. He saw *Le Bonheur de Vivre* and was fascinated by it. Although he was not yet ready to commit to buying such modernity, the dancing circle in the back of the composition must have made a subliminal impact on his visual memory. Three years later it would be repeated as the motif of *The Dance*, his most famous commission from Matisse. Shchukin's role as Matisse's most important patron in these years is examined in more detail, in the context of collectors of modern art, later in this book.

Matisse continued to exhibit widely across Europe in 1906. In May he sent paintings to the 'Libre Esthétique', the exhibition of a grouping of advanced artists in Brussels, and four works to Munich in a travelling international show. It was hard to escape explosive metaphors: Kandinsky, now based in France, heard reports that the reaction in Munich to Matisse was like a bomb going off. It was probably in early summer 1906 that Matisse first actually met Picasso, at the apartment of Gertrude and Leo Stein. Matisse unsettled Picasso. Later that year, Picasso drew a peevish distinction between himself and Matisse: 'Matisse talks and talks. I can't talk so I just say oui oui oui, but it's damned nonsense all the same.' He makes an important point: Matisse was a theoriser, constantly wanting to say the unsayable, to put into words the functioning of his visual imagination. Picasso, by contrast, according to Leo Stein, had 'nothing to say except the occasional firework, his work developing intuitively with no plan'.

In the summer of 1906 Matisse headed south, to Collioure again. But the experiences of the previous year were not to be repeated. He had gone beyond the landscapes of the Mediterranean rendered in shadowless, extravagant colour. This time Matisse moved on to Algiers, in search of something else. It had much more to do with the human figure. He looked at belly dancers, and he looked at African and Egyptian sculpture; and he was intrigued by the boldness and spontaneity that he observed in his own children's art. His own modelling in clay intensified, focused on the naked female form. When he returned to Collioure and started painting from the nude model, he was well on the way to a radical reinvention of the human body. Not so many miles away, at Gosol in the Pyrenees, Picasso was engaged in the same challenge.

What emerged from Matisse's trip to North Africa was a painting that he exhibited at the Salon des Indépendants in March 1907, his *Blue Nude, Memories of Biskra*. Picasso was intrigued but baffled by it: 'If he wants to make a woman, let him make a woman. If he wants to make a design, let him make a design. This is between the two.' Matisse's new engagement with the human form results in something of a parody of the

76. Matisse, *Blue Nude, Memories of Biskra*, 1907

reclining female nude, a figure whose awkwardness contributes to its extraordinary power. Once again, the people who appreciated it first, and therefore bought it, were Gertrude and Leo Stein. But of all the Steins, Matisse grew closest to Sarah, Leo's sister-in-law, in the course of this year. She understood him as a painter to an extent unmatched by anyone else.

The rivalry between Picasso and Matisse was by now a potent and pervasive feature of the weather in the thin air of advanced modernism. So the exchange of paintings that took place between the two of them in the summer of 1907 could have assumed the momentousness of an exchange of nuclear weapons between two superpowers. As it turned out, what Matisse handed over was more a grenade than an atom bomb: Picasso chose Matisse's portrait of his daughter *Marguerite*, a flat, two-dimensional Fauvist work, sweet rather than challenging. Matisse, on the other hand, came away with Picasso's still life, *Pitcher, Bowl and Lemon*, which was considerably more advanced, playing with space in a way that both alarmed and fascinated in its prefiguration of Cubism. I am sorry to have to say that while Matisse sat at home and agonised over what Picasso was up to in the painting that he had chosen, Picasso showed less respect for the portrait of Marguerite. Visitors to his studio, where it hung, were encouraged to throw darts at it. Admittedly they were rubber-capped darts, but still. Although they cloaked their excesses in a certain Jarry-esque self-irony, Picasso and his gang could sometimes behave like louts.

In early summer, while Picasso was confined to his studio grappling with his monumental *Demoiselles d'Avignon,* Matisse was off again heading south, first to the Midi and then on to Italy, where he was impressed less by the great masters of the Renaissance – whom he could not look at without being revolted by their materialism – than by Giotto, Duccio and the Sienese primitives. In the Renaissance masters Matisse detected the stench of corruption, wrought by the wealth of both church and state at whose disposal these artists put themselves. Here was work, complained Matisse, 'manufactured for the rich. The artist sinks to the same base level as his patron.' This was a bit ironic, considering that Matisse was travelling in some luxury to Italy on the strength of a cheque for 18,000 francs that he had just banked from the Galerie Bernheim for various paintings bought from him by Félix Fénéon, the former anarchist newly in charge of stocking the gallery with modern art. It also puts into perspective the 2,500 francs that Vollard had paid the same February to Picasso for a quantity of his pictures. Yes, Matisse continued to agonise; but he now did so in relative comfort.

After Italy Matisse returned to Collioure. Like many advanced artists in that summer of 1907, Matisse's focus turned again to the subject of the naked human figure on the beach. He came up with *Le Luxe,* a large, upright, two-metre-high canvas dominated by three female nudes, their awkward, hefty masses simplified, flattened and stylised to rhyme with the undulating coastline and sky beyond. His recent experience of Giotto and Duccio had only increased the effect of sparseness. Its title shows that Matisse was still dreaming a dream of sensual Arcadian idyll; but if this was luxury, it was a rather more austere version than before. He showed the picture at the Salon d'Automne, where it baffled and outraged; critics had problems with its lack of finish. Fortunately Sarah Stein and her husband Michael stepped forward to buy it.

Matisse saw the year out cultivating his image as a '*cher maître*'. The desire within him to attempt artistic self-explanation, or to spout 'damned nonsense' as Picasso called it, led to the opening of a school under his name. It was attended by a circle of largely German, Scandinavian and American acolytes: the Steins, Hans Purmann, Oskar and Greta Moll were among the pupils. As Hilary Spurling points out, the lessons he gave were as much a process of illustrated autobiography as instruction. Matisse, who was always more of a painter than a teacher, expressed himself most lucidly when examining the solutions he himself had reached in confronting the various challenges of his career. In the end what Matisse had couldn't be taught, so what he said, although it was lapped up adoringly by his pupils, didn't actually get them very far as painters. They were exhorted to put their faith in their instincts, to try to attain harmony, to aim for the essence of the subject rather than its detail. A year later Matisse published his *Notes of a Painter*, which said the same things over again in greater detail. You can understand why Picasso never opened his own school.

Through 1908 the patronage of Shchukin became an increasingly important factor in Matisse's life, and Shchukin commissioned from him *Harmonie en Rouge*, a feast of orgiastic colour. In January 1909 the big show intended to launch Matisse in Germany was held in Berlin at the gallery of Paul Cassirer. Matisse returned from the opening disheartened by the negative local response. But there was one compensation: Shchukin was becoming an increasingly enthusiastic admirer, and back in Paris Matisse sat down with him to plan the future. A major new decorative project for Shchukin's Moscow palace was broached between them. By spring, the idea had germinated further in Matisse's mind: 'I am to decorate a huge staircase with three

77. Matisse, *The Dance*, 1910

flights of stair', he told a French magazine. 'The first panel will be of a dance, a *ronde* on the top of a hill. By the time [the visitor] reaches the second panel, he is already in a more silent area of the house, so I see there a music stage with an attentive audience.' In the same interview Matisse explained the thinking that now underlay his art: photography had eliminated the task of copying nature. He repeated his conviction that what the painter now needed to do was 'present emotion as directly as possible by the simplest means'.

The challenge was on for Matisse. He was going to be working on an unprecedented scale – the panels for *Dance* and *Music* were each 2.6 by 4 metres, so he needed a bigger studio. He built one in the garden of the house on the edge of Paris at Issy-les-Moulineaux where he moved his family. The two paintings commissioned by Shchukin were scheduled for unveiling at the Salon d'Automne in October 1910. Up until then they occupied most of Matisse's creative energy. In February 1910 there was a distraction when Félix Fénéon mounted a large

Matisse exhibition at Bernheim comprising sixty-five works, of which twenty-five were borrowed from the Steins. For Matisse, it was something of a retrospective, perhaps an opportunity to take stock (at forty), to show the public once and for all that there was what he saw as a logical progression to his career. But if he was looking for Paris to redress the balance after the critical mauling he had got in Germany a year earlier at the Cassirer exhibition, he was to be disappointed. The Bernheim exhibition provoked another storm of brutal and uncomprehending malice. Octave Mirbeau questioned Matisse's sanity, and went on to speak with contempt of the 'Russians and Germans, male and female, drooling in front of each picture, drooling with joy and admiration, naturally'. This was tough on Matisse: far from drooling, most Germans had actually disdained his work a year earlier. But it suited the political mood in Paris – and in London in December, where Matisse made his British debut at Roger Fry's show – to characterise Matisse's 'ridiculous' modern art as the sort of thing that gave pleasure to gullible Germans.

Matisse's sympathisers realised that he was dredging in deep waters. Matthew Prichard, an eccentric scholar with a love of Eastern art based in Paris, was that rare phenomenon: a perceptive English admirer of Matisse. 'Much of what Matisse gives us is to be found in our unconscious life', he explained. 'To find what it is we must plunge there in a state of trance or ecstasy, we must swim along the bottom of our stream of existence.' Prichard is identifying Bergson's 'instinctual stream of consciousness that surges beneath mere knowledge' as Matisse's true territory. It took Bergsonian intuition to get there, both for artist and spectator.

So on 1 October 1910 at the Salon d'Automne, *Dance* and *Music* were unveiled. Would the critical response be any more positive than in Berlin in 1909 or at Bernheim in February? The answer was no. The problem was that the two panels were so large you could not miss them. The extravagance of their size compounded the insult conveyed by the distorted simplification of their composition and execution. The critics were unwilling or unable to plunge into the requisite Bergsonian state of trance or ecstasy to understand them. The reviews in the Paris press were so bad that Amélie felt obliged to hide them from her husband. Wisely Matisse left after a week to meet up with his new friend Matthew Prichard in Munich, to see the exhibition 'Masterpieces of Islamic Art'. It was a show that would have considerable influence on the direction of Matisse's painting over the next three years. After some heart-stopping indecision on Shchukin's part, the Russian finally took delivery of *Dance* and *Music* in Moscow at the end of 1910. Matisse, who was travelling in Spain at the end of the year, sighed with relief then collapsed in a physical and emotional breakdown.

The following year, 1911, was more positive. While the rest of advanced Paris was increasingly caught up in the cobwebs of Cubism, Matisse stayed immune. Colour was too important to him. In the course of these twelve months he produced a series of exceptional paintings, all on a large scale. Size did not frighten the avant-garde in the twentieth century: the bigger the picture the more important the statement. Extra square footage gave more scope for self-expression, for the broad brush of instinct as opposed to the small-scale detail of calculation. Two of Matisse's large canvases were bought by Shchukin: *The Pink Studio* and *The Painter's Family*. Another, *Interior with Aubergines*, was bought by Michael and Sarah Stein. Shchukin himself came to Paris for a brief visit at the end of July to see his new acquisitions, and arranged for Matisse to visit him in Moscow at the end of the year to discuss, among other things, the hanging of the two works. Before that, in August, Matisse went once more to Collioure. The problem was that he was accompanied by his strong-willed pupil, the young Russian painter Olga Meerson, and Matisse omitted to tell Amélie about it. But they muddled through. And in October Matisse, minus Meerson, was on the train to Moscow.

When Matisse arrived in Moscow that month he found that he wasn't just a hero in the eyes of his patron, but something of a celebrity in the city's art circles. Shchukin's more intelligent friends were also beginning to appreciate *Dance* and *Music*. Seen in the context of the eighteenth-century elegance of the Shchukin palace, the two paintings were oddly stimulating. 'Matisse is such a contrast he has the effect of strong pepper,' said one, echoing the culinary imagery that Leo Stein used to explain the appeal of Matisse six years earlier. Dinner parties were held for him in the houses of the cultural elite, and young radical artists in Moscow queued up to meet him. He stayed three weeks instead of two, and was asked to be the first member of the Jack of Diamonds association. His two latest works – *The Pink Studio* and *The Painter's Family* – arrived during the final week of his stay and brought to twenty-seven the number of Matisses in Shchukin's collection.

There seems to have been a genuine rapport between Shchukin and Matisse, who was the only artist in his collection with whom the Russian formed a personal relationship. 'For me Matisse is above all the rest,' wrote Shchukin, 'better than them all, closest to my heart.' Surveying the full range of his most radical work, as represented here in sympathetic company, was the kind of retrospective that Matisse had wished for but hadn't got at Cassirer in Berlin or at Bernheim in Paris the year before. He arrived back in Paris in December from Russia in much better shape than at the end of the previous year when he had tottered home from Spain.

For those avant-garde artists whose driving force was colour, there was a geographical progression southwards in the years 1905–14. First, there were summer pilgrimages to the French Mediterranean coast; then, sometimes via Spain, artists reached North Africa, where light and colour were even stronger; where the people were simpler and more primitive; and where the element of Islamic art added new decorative stimulus. Van Dongen was there in 1910; Klee and Macke followed in 1914. Matisse, of course, had been to Biskra in 1906. But in 1912 he went to Morocco and settled down for several months' productive engagement with 'orientalism'. At the end of September, he was joined in Morocco by Charles Camoin and Amélie. Camoin, who was between girlfriends, visited the local brothels. Sometimes Matisse accompanied him, but made it clear that he was there only in a professional capacity, in search of models for art, not sex. 'Like a doctor', he told Camoin. Perhaps this was the origin of the clinical white overall which he dutifully put on later in his career whenever he painted naked female flesh.

Orchestrated by Félix Fénéon, an exhibition of his most recent work was held at Bernheim in Paris from 14–19 April 1913. A corner had been turned, and he now had more admirers in France; regret was expressed that virtually all the paintings in the show had already been bought by Shchukin, or Morozov, who had also become an admirer. There was increasing demand for his work from Germany, too. While there were not yet any collectors of his work in Britain – nor indeed America – his controversial brand had been established. It may have been synonymous with all that was outlandish in modern art, but most people in cultured circles in London at least knew the name of Henri Matisse.

The summer and autumn of 1913 were spent by Matisse in painting his wife. It was a challenge reminiscent of Picasso's struggle to paint Gertrude Stein in 1905–6. There were at least eighty sittings. The face, with its faint smile and half-closed eyes, is a mask. It reveals little of the woman behind it. As an artist you cannot submit your model to eighty sittings if your primary object is the depiction of her humanity. There comes a point at which the loss of spontaneity undermines the emotional and psychological insight. But if you are treating her as some sort of species of still life, a compositional problem to be resolved solely in formal terms, then the process can indeed be extended ad infinitum.

Perhaps that was the reason why the sitter wept when she finally saw it. Matisse had painted her (with barely more than a single sitting) in 1905 and the resulting highly controversial portrait, with which this book begins, had yielded a much needed 500 francs thanks to Amélie's determination not to accept a lower

78. Matisse, *Window*, 1914

offer. Now Matisse's prices started at ten times that amount, and the family finances were secure. But was her husband, the brutal egoist of Gertrude Stein's unkind description, actually any happier? Matisse was in one of his phases of turmoil, in a paring-down mood. He did a variety of further fairly bleak portraits of women in 1914. Perhaps his most memorable picture of the year was one he painted in Collioure that summer. Nine years earlier, the glories of Fauvism had been announced by a vibrant image of the sea and fishing boats seen through the open window of his hotel bedroom (see p. 33). Now he painted a work on a similar theme, an interior with a window whose shutters are open; but this time the view is gone. There is no longer a sparkling sea beyond. All that confronts the eye is a dark empty space. What did that empty space mean? Swimming along the bottom of his stream of existence only took him so far. In fact, it is arguable that the period of his greatest innovation as an artist was now behind him; that – as the next forty years of his career bore witness – there was nowhere left to go beyond ravishing repetition for this supreme decorator and colourist.

CHAPTER TWENTY-SIX

Picasso and Cubism

If Picasso had been run over by a bus in 1905, how would he now be remembered? As a young artist of huge talent and imagination, certainly, a kind of souped-up Puvis de Chavannes. He had first come to Paris from Barcelona when he was barely out of his teens and had begun painting pictures which married a Spanish energy and vigour to a subject matter and style that initially owed much to Toulouse-Lautrec. The art dealer Ambroise Vollard, that ace *dénicheur*, or talent spotter, had already given a show to him in his ramshackle gallery as early as 1901, when Picasso was barely twenty. Thereafter, his art entered a phase that drew on human suffering for its subject matter: beggars, blind men and frugal meals, increasingly bathed in a glacial blue light. His figures were distinctive: gaunt, attenuated by hunger, their long skeletal limbs drawn with a mannerist exaggeration. Like many of his contemporaries he was moved by El Greco and by the French Symbolist painters. It was clear that he was extraordinarily gifted, and extraordinarily confident in himself as an artist. But he had not yet achieved anything that set him apart as a revolutionary modernist.

Fortunately Picasso avoided errant buses in 1905. Newly ensconced in a studio at the legendarily squalid Bateau-Lavoir, he entered his pink period, which ushered in a gentler, more sensual, more lyrical approach to figure subjects. Then, at the end of the year, he began to engage with Primitivism. His growing interest in tribal art showed itself in the simplified forms of his nudes through 1906, a direction given momentum by his experiments that summer at Gosol. He was also embarking on an era of deliberate seclusion, no longer showing at Paris exhibitions. It was as if he sensed that he was now following a path which only he understood.

With the benefit of hindsight and the authoritative prompting of Alfred Barr, the all-powerful director of the Museum of Modern Art in New York in the 1930s and 1940s, art historians generally take the view that the most important event of 1907 was the painting by Picasso of the *Demoiselles d'Avignon*. It now stands in the same relation to Cubism as the assassination of the Archduke Franz Ferdinand at Sarajevo in 1914 does to the First World War. And yet only a handful of people were aware of its existence that year, or indeed in the years after. It certainly wasn't revealed to the public, nor indeed did the artist necessarily consider it finished. It wasn't until 1916 that it was actually exhibited, when it was shown at the Salon d'Antin in Paris. It is easy to overestimate its contemporary impact from our vantage point more than a century later. Our perception of it is influenced by its later history, entering as it did the Museum of Modern Art in New York in 1937, and rapidly being established, both literally and figuratively, as the centrepiece of Alfred Barr's prescriptive interpretation of the evolution of modernism. Had it ended up in some different museum at a different time would it have assumed such significance?

The only people who actually saw it in 1907 (at different stages in its development) were the very few visitors to Picasso's studio in the Bateau-Lavoir who were allowed a viewing, and even though they were by definition sympathetic to the avant-garde, their reactions ranged from the uncomprehending to the downright derisive. It was a very large, violent, challenging picture unlike anything anyone had seen before. It had its origins in Picasso's experimentations with the human figure at the end of 1906. Picasso now took as his theme the interior of a brothel, with the naked *filles de joie* displaying themselves across the canvas in various attitudes of availability and menace. The figures exist in the airless, perspectiveless, hallucinatory jumble that the artist had begun to fashion in Gosol the previous

79. Picasso, *Les Demoiselles d'Avignon*, 1907

summer. They are angular, vertiginous constructs of female body parts; their faces, particularly the two on the right, would have been inconceivable without Picasso's recent entrancement with the masks of primitive art, both African and Iberian. It has prompted many different interpretations. Possibly it is indeed, as some have claimed, the ultimate in artistic misogyny; and even – the favourite resort of imaginative art historians when all other speculation has been exhausted – evidence of a possible bout of venereal disease suffered by the artist at the time.

Most disheartening to Picasso must have been the fact that even his most supportive patrons, the Steins, didn't get it. They came to the Bateau-Lavoir in mid May, and, as Picasso described it later, Leo 'brayed' with laughter, 'holding his sides, doubled up'. Around the same time the young German *march-and amateur* Wilhelm von Uhde was shown it. Ever loyal, he was polite, but clearly did not understand it. Matisse saw it, too. His reaction was uneasy, outraged laughter. He may have suspected that it was a practical joke; worse, he may have suspected that it wasn't. When Picasso's future fellow Cubist pioneer Georges Braque was shown it, he recognised its incendiary potential; it was, he said, 'as if [Picasso] had swallowed petrol', the implication being that he was now performing as a fire-eater. In August Kahnweiler was granted a viewing. His first reaction was negative, on the grounds that it was unfinished and seemed not to have fulfilled its purpose. Derain, as we have seen, recoiled from the picture as evidence of Picasso's imminent suicide.

Was there anyone in Paris who would have understood it in 1907, apart from the artist? The reaction of the subversive writer Alfred Jarry might have been more sympathetic. He was in poor health, and died on 1 December, aged thirty-four; but had he seen it, he would probably have appreciated its iconoclasm and its whiff of anarchy and absurdism. Like Jarry, Picasso set out deliberately to shock, and succeeded. But there is a difference between a work of art that is delivered as a subversive shock and one that is intended as a deliberate confidence trick. It's the difference between the emperor parading naked as an act of anti-conventional performance art and the emperor parading naked because he is under the deluded impression that he's wearing elegant and fashionable clothes. Despite Matisse's misgivings, Picasso's subversions were serious, and whatever else *Les Demoiselles* may have been, it was no hoax.

During the summer – which for once Picasso did not spend in the south – he was heavily under the influence of tribal art, and in August he produced a magnificent *Nu à la Draperie*, a reworking of one of the *Demoiselles d'Avignon* in the language of faceted angles and tribal scarification. Richardson suggests that it was triggered by the Strauss–Wilde opera *Salome*, first performed in Paris in May 1907: its original title was *La Danse aux voiles*. But it is not a sexy picture. It is powerful, menacing, primitive, airless, perspectiveless. It was completed in August, and the Steins (Leo having got over his initial reaction to *Les Demoiselles*) bought it direct from the artist's studio when they returned from Italy in September.

An unexpected windfall of 1,000 francs came Picasso's way in early autumn when the collector André Level bought the *Saltimbanques* (see p. 77) for his recently established art fund. Money in his pocket always made Picasso look at life rather more positively, and in December he patched up a particularly violent row he had had with Fernande and she moved back in with him in the Bateau-Lavoir. She was in time to resume duties as a model. Yet another reinterpretation of her form was to follow, this time as a piece of monumental sculpture. It's no longer sex but power: gigantic limbs are petrified in an airless space. For her part, Fernande noted that Picasso was undergoing a gradual change in his habits. He was becoming more serious, in her words 'increasingly preoccupied' with his work and with his health. 'For several years,' recounts Fernande, 'I never saw him drink anything except mineral water or milk, or eat anything but vegetables, fish, rice pudding and grapes. Perhaps it was this diet that made him miserable and bad-tempered so much of the time.' That's not to say that Picasso did not still relish the absurd, enjoy mocking people, and find occasional solace in the opium pipe. But he was nothing if not instinctive: it may be that he sensed something momentous was approaching in his artistic career and the time for single-mindedness had come.

The bemusement as to what Picasso was up to now was shared by older modernists, too. Pierre Bonnard was at one of Vollard's dinners in February when the latest Picassos were brought out from Vollard's storeroom, and the dealer explained that 'the young artists are returning to Negro Art'. 'This will remain as a document of our artistic corruption', commented Bonnard. 'That a man who has all the skill, all the range of colours, should feel the need to come back to this ... They have all the means of expression and nothing to express.' Picasso was dismissive of Bonnard: he called his work 'a pot-pourri of indecision'. The decorative intimism of Bonnard's Nabi phase in the 1890s, which was delicate, disciplined and subtle, had now given way to something freer and more colourful and classical. He turned inwards again, but this time into the bathroom, where he depicted women shedding their clothes, washing themselves and performing various other functions of their toilet. What Picasso was trying to do – to invent an art that was real in relationship to itself rather than realistic in relation to nature, that had volume and weight rather than colour and prettiness – was totally at odds with Bonnard's apparent objectives. Picasso was never one to underestimate himself in relation to other artists. 'If I hadn't been a genius,' he once said, 'I would have painted like Jacques Émile Blanche.'

Georges Braque now enters the story in a big way. His transition from Fauve landscapist in 1906 to Cézanne-besotted proto-Cubist later in 1907 roped him closer into the embrace of Picasso. He had spent the summer of 1907 painting at Le Ciotat and L'Estaque in the south of France, when his approach was still essentially Fauve; but in October he returned to L'Estaque and, after the revelation of Cézanne at the Salon d'Automne, nothing was quite the same. The exaltation of Fauvism had left him: what he brought back was a series of landscapes cast in Cézanne-esque blocks. One of the first places he went upon his return to Paris in November was to the Bateau-Lavoir, where he found Picasso's focus had turned to figure painting. Over this winter of 1907–8 Braque, too, began to grapple with the figure.

The Salon des Indépendants, which opened its doors on 20 March 1908, contained the first evidence of the new directions that the most advanced young artists were following. In the same room hung two compositions, each depicting a trio of gigantesque women, one by Derain (*La Toilette*) and one by Braque (*La Femme*). Each artist, having jettisoned Fauvism, was struggling to come to terms with what they had recently seen in Picasso's studio. Gellet Burgess, an American journalist visiting Paris on a mission to get to the bottom of modern art for his readers back home, was at the Indépendants and described it as 'a universe of ugliness'. He pursued Braque for an explanation as to why he had painted what looked like the same model from three different angles. 'To portray every physical aspect of such a subject requires three figures, much as the representation of a house requires a plan, an elevation, and a section,' Braque apparently told him in an interview. Both the Braque and the Derain are works that could not have been produced without Picasso's influence, even though as usual Picasso did not exhibit publicly himself. Oddly neither painting has survived: the Braque is only known from a pen and ink sketch of its composition, and the Derain from an old photograph, which shows that it was an awkward, stilted picture. Perhaps it, too, found its way into one of its creator's despairing bonfires.

In the absence of anything written down by Braque or Picasso about what they were doing in these early years of Cubism, we are forced to rely on the accounts of an odd variety of witnesses: a group of over-imaginative poets; the memories of Picasso's mistress; the later testimony of his dealer. And this year there was Gellet Burgess, who recorded interviews with Picasso as well as with Braque in 1908. It's not quite clear whether Burgess (a) thought the whole thing was a huge joke; (b) was being sent up by Braque and Picasso; or (c) managed to catch some important insights. Probably it was a bit of all three. Picasso, as ever in such situations, was evasive in his answers to Burgess's questions. But Braque at least tried to be more helpful. One major figure painting that has survived from 1908 is his *Large Nude*, a response to what he had seen in Picasso's studio and not without some lingering influence from Matisse. He explained further to the American, in words that are particularly apposite to *Large Nude*:

I couldn't portray a woman in her natural loveliness ...
I haven't the skill. No one has. I must therefore create a
new sort of thing, the beauty that appears to me in terms
of volume, of line, of weight, and through that beauty

80. Braque, *Large Nude*, 1908

interpret my subjective impression ... Nature is a mere pretext for subjective composition, plus sentiment. It suggests emotion, and translates that emotion into art. I want to express the Absolute, and not merely the factitious woman.[31]

Here is the Absolute again, the word that Derain was using in 1906 when he was thrashing around trying to find something more solid than the mere colour of Fauvism. It was the search for the Absolute that led Derain to a conflagration in his studio; but for Braque it led on to Cubism.

Picasso spent June and July in Paris, working on in his studio in the summer heat. He was still struggling with the challenge

81. Léon Comerre, *Leda and the Swan*, 1908

82. Picasso, *Dryad*, 1908

of the female figure, constructing follow-ons from the *Demoi-selles d'Avignon:* women with mask-like faces and massive limbs who meld ambiguously in and out of their backgrounds so as to compress space and heighten menace.

The *Dryad* dates from this time. It is a reminder of quite how outlandish Picasso's work would have seemed in the context of the conventional art being produced in Paris this year. A useful point of comparison is *Leda and the Swan* by the elderly acad-emician Léon Comerre, also painted in 1908. Both works are set in the Arcadian woods of classical myth, but they come up with very different results. Comerre depicts a nude woman, in this case the mythological Leda, lying full length in some sylvan grove, pleasantly absorbed by the amorous attentions of a swan (the disguise which Zeus assumed to seduce her). The atmos-phere is idyllic, unthreatening and a trifle saucy. Picasso's *Dryad*, thundering through the forest, is made of different stuff. Any halfway intelligent swan would think twice before attempting relations with this proto-Cubist Amazon who clenches her left fist in menacing mimicry of the wringing of a neck. There are no misty recessions in Picasso's airless woodland; but the *Dryad* – in classical myth a nymph who sprang out of a tree – is a good subject for Picasso in this mood. In 1908 trees and human beings were being reconstituted as a kind of homogeneous pictorial matter by Picasso; soon space, too, would be drawn into this dynamic Cubist porridge.

One further point about the *Dryad*. In a work as perceptive, authoritative and beautifully written as John Richardson's biog-raphy of Picasso, it is almost impossible to take issue with any of his judgements about the master. But a rare question mark hovers over his identification of the source of the *Dryad* as a print in a sixteenth-century book by Vesalius on the musculature of the human body. I once spent several weeks with the version of the *Dryad* illustrated on p. 245 hanging in my office, and in the end I decided that what counts with her figure is its pelvic thrust forward, which gives momentum to the composition. There is a sexual aggression to her pose that is original and characteristic

83. Georges Braque, *Cubist Landscape*, 1908

of Picasso and totally absent from the Renaissance prototype. I would doubt whether Vesalius had much to do with this particular nymph.

What Braque painted in the south of France in the summer of 1908 finally left Fauvism behind. Inspired by Cézanne, Braque now did battle with conventional Renaissance perspective – 'a ghastly mistake which it has taken four centuries to redress,' he decided. A jumble of trees, houses and hills crowd in on each other in the landscapes of low-keyed colour that Braque concocted this summer. But there remains an ambiguity, because Braque's painting still exploits the eye's natural inclination to read planes and masses by means of a residual perspective, which is implicit to the practice of modelling: how else can you perceive a painted cube? What Braque has removed is the consistency of an overall perspectival viewpoint. And just as important as the multiplication of points of perspective is the multiplication also being introduced of sources of light. Perspective still operates in order to give the illusion of depth, but it does so unpredictably and irrationally. Here was the beginning of 'passage', defined by Alfred Barr as 'the merging of planes with space by leaving one edge unpainted or light in tone'. 'Passage' creates a new pictorial phenomenon: Cubist space.

Picasso finally gave in to the heat of the city and spent August in a village outside Paris, La Rue des Bois, also turning his attention to painting landscapes. Kahnweiler, writing in 1915, remembered what happened that summer of 1908 when Picasso was in La Rue des Bois and Braque at the other end of France in L'Estaque. 'No connection existed between the two artists,' he recalled. However, 'by an entirely different route Braque arrived at the same point as Picasso ... Separated by distance and working independently, the two artists devoted their most intense effort to paintings which share an extraordinary resemblance.' Both independently 'began with objects of the simplest sort: in landscape, with cylindrical tree trunks and rectangular houses; in still life with plates, symmetrical vessels, round fruits, and one or two nude figures. They sought to make their objects as plastic as possible, and to define their position in space.' 'The first object of cubist exploration,' confirmed Braque, was 'the exploration of space'. This involved 'the materialisation, the translation into matter, of that new space which I felt'.

Back came Braque to Paris in early September in time to submit his new landscapes to the jury of the Salon d'Automne. They were all rejected, by a selection committee that included Matisse. But Kahnweiler stepped into the breach: in November, he gave Braque an exhibition at his gallery, including his most recent work of the summer. Apollinaire wrote an introduction in which he said: 'In his valleys the bees of youth hum and plunder, and the happiness of innocence reposes on his civilised terraces', which is a by no means unique example of the poet's willingness to rhapsodise outstripping his artistic understanding. But elsewhere in the introduction he wrote, rather more perceptively: 'For the painter, for the poet, for artists (this is what differentiates them from other men and particularly from scientists) every work becomes a new universe with its own particular laws.' And it was allegedly Matisse who now described Braque's L'Estaque landscapes as being built up out of 'petites cubes'. It was the beginning of the word Cubism, a term which in the years that followed expanded to embrace such a wide variety of artistic innovation that it confused more people than it enlightened, becoming synonymous with anything revolutionary that the public didn't understand. Still, it was an important moment for the wily Kahnweiler. In giving Braque this exhibition – twenty-seven recent paintings crammed into his tiny gallery – he was tacking his colours to a very specific modernist mast, one that was to stand him and his artists in good stead for the rest of his long life.

Elsewhere there were resettings in the modernist kaleidoscope. At the Bateau-Lavoir it was Juan Gris, with the encouragement of his fellow Spaniard Picasso, who now took over the quarters vacated by the van Dongen family and reinvented himself as an avant-garde artist in 1908. He gave up his work as a caricaturist in order to commit full time to the new art. But it may be that this graphic work turned to his advantage. The figurative distortion that caricature involved, often in order to make a subversive point, chimed with the direction of modernist art. It was a good apprenticeship for the ruptures and revolutions of Cubism. But now he was trying to make people think rather than make them laugh.

Another recalibration took place early in 1909 when Sonia Terk, temporarily Mrs Sonia von Uhde, met the young modern painter Robert Delaunay in her husband's gallery. They became lovers in April. Von Uhde probably wasn't too upset. He had done his bit for modern art by marrying her in the first place and thus enabling her to stay in Paris rather than return to her native Russia. In 1909 Delaunay began his series of paintings of the Eiffel Tower, the first of the studies for which he dedicated to Sonia with the words 'The tower calls out to the Universe/ Movement/ Depth 1909/France – Russia'. It was the beginning of a fruitful – and colourful – marital collaboration.

What was Delaunay up to? In 1909 he and other young paint-ers such as Jean Metzinger (who, like Delaunay, had recently emerged from his obligatory Pointillist phase), were struggling to respond to various different stimuli. They were driven by their growing awareness of the dynamism of modern life, emphasised in February by Marinetti's Futurist declaration. They sought means of expressing this dynamism; and their initial approaches were conditioned by their recent experience of Cézanne. So their forms became increasingly faceted, analysed from simultaneous different viewpoints. The Eiffel Tower, reaching 300 metres into the sky and built for the Exposition Universale in 1889, was a spectacular symbol of modernity and scientific aspiration and inspired Delaunay to paint a series of views deconstructing the famous landmark, creating fragmented images of vertiginous power. A new visual language was now evolving among Delau-nay and his friends, distinct from what Braque and Picasso were separately inventing.

In fact a curtain of secrecy descended on the work of Picasso and Braque in the course of 1909: they both ceased exhibiting at any of the Paris salons. Braque's Cubist landscape in the Salon des Indépendants in April was the last opportunity to see work by either of them in public for a considerable time. It was only visible in the next two years either in their studios by invitation, or in the small gallery of Kahnweiler, who carefully controlled access to it. Braque's landscape in the Salon des Indépendants eliminated space 'to a point of contradiction', in fact to such an extent that it laid down a challenge to Picasso, who set off to Horta for the summer, determined to catch up by focusing further on landscape painting himself.

Self-isolation in his Pyrenean refuge this year proved pro-ductive and dramatic. At one point he found it necessary to fire

84. Picasso, *Tête de Fernande*, 1909

a gun from his balcony in order to disperse the local women who had assembled in the street in protest at his blatant cohabitation with the unmarried Fernande. This sort of primeval village prejudice was a less acceptable aspect of the ideal of Primitivism. But meanwhile he made significant progress with his Horta landscapes. He advanced his geometricisation of form until he, too, achieved that homogenisation of human and landscape elements that eliminates space and creates that distinctive Cubist airlessness. Then he turned to Fernande and painted a memorable head of her, employing the same technique in such a sculptural way that he followed it up back in Paris with an actual plaster version that proved to be one of the first great Cubist sculptures.

Gratifyingly that autumn Gertrude and Leo Stein came through again as patrons, buying three works painted in Horta by Picasso, two landscapes and a head of Fernande. They also took the plunge and finally acquired Picasso's *Three Women*, a Primitivist experiment of 1908, which was to hang, massive and imposing, in the Steins' rue Fleurus studio till 1913. This influx of cash gave Picasso the financial confidence to move out of the Bateau-Lavoir into a more commodious residence. He and Fernande even took on a maid. The soufflé-cook, about which Picasso and Braque had once joked as being the ultimate symbol of arrival in society, was only just round the corner.

According to Kahnweiler, during that summer of 1909, which Picasso spent painting in Horta and Braque in La Roche-Guyon, 'the new language of form was further augmented and enriched, but left essentially unchanged'. It was from the autumn of 1909 that the great period of Cubism began, when Picasso and Braque – in one of the most famous metaphors of art history – operated roped together like mountaineers. 'The first object of cubist exploration,' said Braque later, was 'the exploration of space.' This involved 'the materialisation, the translation into matter, of that new space which I felt'. Space was now constructed with the same rigorous faceting of form as the depicted objects themselves. One of the dangers that the two mountaineers had to guard against was a false step that would precipitate them into abstraction and mere decoration. The consequence was a new focus on still life, a subject matter that anchored them securely to recognisable objects but left them free to experiment with the materialisation of space and resultant effects such as 'smoke so solid that it has to be cut with a knife'.

Braque and Picasso continued their development of Cubism throughout 1910, again largely out of the public eye. Braque spent his summer in L'Estaque, while Picasso and Fernande, together with their maid and their dog Frika, set off in bourgeois splendour for Cadaques on the north-eastern Spanish coast. During his stay at Cadaques Picasso's compositions, whether of nudes or fishing boats, were increasingly created by the interpenetration of unfolding forms, almost monochrome, carefully crafted, subtly lit. By the end of the year Braque, like Picasso, had also ceased to facet forms and was breaking them down into flatter, more irregular, less opaque elements. And Derain? He was in Cadaques too, but he still hadn't thrown off Cézanne. Five years earlier he had come to the south of France at the summons of Matisse, and painted Fauve landscapes that fully matched the intensity and daring of his illustrious colleague. Now, working alongside Picasso, it was clear how far behind he had fallen in the march of modernism. He was still painting through the prism – or prison – of Cézanne.

Having warmed up with a more realistic proto-Cubist portrait of Clovis Sagot the previous year, in 1910 Picasso decided to paint his three major dealers. They followed one another in a series of gathering Cubist intensity. First came Vollard, then Wilhelm von Uhde (who held a small exhibition of Picasso's work at his Galerie Notre Dame des Champs in May), and finally Kahnweiler, in September (see p. 302). The subsequent histories of these paintings tell us something about the dealers portrayed: Kahnweiler bought his and it remained in his private collection until confiscated by the French authorities in the First World War as the property of an enemy alien. The same fate befell von Uhde's portrait: he was unable to extricate it from Paris with his other possessions at the outbreak of hostilities. But Vollard was happy to sell his on to Ivan Morozov a year later for 3,000 francs.

When Picasso got back to Paris in late August, Kahnweiler annoyed him by suggesting that most of the works he had produced in Cadaques were unfinished. This was a constant source of contention between Picasso and his main dealer. When Picasso finally signed a contract with Kahnweiler in 1912, one of the stipulations in the agreement was that Picasso reserved the right to decide whether a picture of his was finished. On this occasion the opportunist Vollard, despite not really understanding them, nonetheless stepped in and bought most of the Cadaques production.

Picasso, a regular visitor to the Salon d'Automne although he no longer exhibited there, was entranced by a Corot retrospective that year which focused on the artist as a figure painter, particularly of women with musical instruments. These were the unlikely stimulus for a series of Cubist 'figure studies' of women with mandolins. One of these, painted by Braque, was the first work in oval format, an innovation introduced in order to counter the problem of corners, those insistent right angles that often lay awkwardly in analytical Cubist compositions. It was also confirmation that the Cubism of Braque and Picasso was driven as much by aesthetics as by philosophy or science.

In the same Salon d'Automne it was possible to see works by Le Fauconnier, Metzinger and Gleizes all by chance grouped in the same room. These three, in loose association with Léger and Delaunay, were continuing their independent development towards a style of painting that was diminishingly colourful and increasingly volumetric. But their Cubism was more scientific than that of Braque and Picasso. They craved theoretical justification and mathematical foundation for their formal experiments. The fourth dimension began to be much discussed among them, as it was in scientific circles at this time. Could it be that this was the visual promised land into which they were about to break through? More was revealed about the development of Cubism in the exhibition of the Salon des Indépendants in spring 1911. The group of radical young painters, who had first noticed sympathies and similarities in each other's work in the Salon d'Automne of 1910, now managed to organise themselves so as to take over an entire room in the Indépendants. There was no total uniformity in their approaches to Cubism, but anyone visiting Room 41 would have seen that something new and striking was happening. There was now a discernible group that became known as the 'Salon Cubists', those painters who were happy to reveal the progress of their work in public exhibitions. On the other hand, operating largely below the radar in Paris, were the secret Cubists, Braque and Picasso.

As the history of Cubism has accumulated its massive literature, opinion has ebbed and flowed as to the relative importance

85. Braque, *Woman with Mandolin*, 1910

in the development of the movement of the Salon Cubists on the one hand and Braque and Picasso on the other. It is clear in retrospect that Braque and Picasso took Cubism in directions beyond the capacity of the Salon Cubists; but it is also clear that, from the perspective of the year 1911, Cubism would have been understood as largely the creation of the Salon Cubists. Almost no one had yet set eyes on the *Demoiselles d'Avignon*. And what Picasso and Braque were r ow up to was known only to a small circle.

There was no let-up in theoretical discussion among the exhibitors in Room 41. Their focus was still mathematics and the investigation of the fourth dimension by pictorial means. Their common ground was their awareness of Cézanne. This was particularly the case with the young Ferdinand Léger, whose *Nudes in the Forest* was one of the most striking images in Room

86. Léger, *Nudes in the Forest*, 1910–11

41. He has taken Cézanne's original prescription, to see nature in terms of the cylinder, the sphere and the cone, to its literal limits: trees and human figures and bits of landscape blend into each other in an airless mix of pipes and mechanical parts. A disdainful critic in *Paris-Midi* dismissed it as 'not painting but plumbing'. But Kahnweiler and Picasso, discreet visitors to the show, were intrigued. They could see something different and worthwhile in Léger. The press called Léger a 'Tubist'. 'This boy must have something,' said Picasso to Kahnweiler. 'They don't even give him the same name as us.' Beneath the mocking tone was an admiration. That's why Kahnweiler signed him up a year later as one of his gallery artists.

Not all the exhibits were masterpieces. Le Fauconnier showed an oppressively awkward picture called *Abondance,* a heavily faceted naked mother and child in a heavily faceted landscape which made its impact largely by virtue of enormous scale. There was nothing new about this subject matter: it was simply an academic set piece with a fashionable Cézannesque Cubist

87. Le Fauconnier, *Abondance*, 1910

make-over. Still, Le Fauconnier, who had in 1908 complained about the lack of intelligent art criticism devoted to advanced art, must have been gratified by the fact that Apollinaire, André Salmon and the young Roger Allard all wrote serious reviews of Room 41 in the press.

Cubist Paris was a fascinating and confusing place in the spring and summer of 1911. Critics were struggling to get a grip on what was happening: Apollinaire had been inclined to dismiss the Cubism of Metzinger and Gleizes as intrinsically inferior to the work of Picasso and Braque, to whose secrets he was privy. But gradually, with guidance from Apollinaire, the Salon Cubists began to get wind of what was going on in the studios of Picasso and Braque. Léger said later, 'if Apollinaire and Max Jacob had not come to see us we would not even have known what was happening in Montmartre. They told us to go to Kahnweiler's, and there we saw, with the great Delaunay, what the Cubists were doing. And Delaunay, who was surprised to see their grey canvases, exclaimed, "But these fellows paint with spiders' webs."' Metzinger was also aware of Picasso and Braque, and by the summer their influence was becoming more evident in his work and that of other Salon Cubists.

When they exhibited together again at the 1911 Salon d'Automne (this time in Room 8), the Cubists were even more numerous. Artists who had recently joined the Cubist movement included Archipenko, La Fresnaye, Picabia, Marie Laurencin and the Duchamp brothers. There had been developments in their approach. Forms and spaces were increasingly fragmented, and there was more juxtaposition of different viewpoints. But there remained major differences from what Picasso and Braque were doing. The exhibits in Room 8 showed little or no interest in African and Oceanic art. They were heavily geometric. For instance Metzinger's *Le Goûter* – saluted by Salmon as 'The Giaconda of Cubism' – was no more than a conventional portrait of a woman fragmented into a geometry that still periodically obeyed the laws of perspective. Nonetheless, Apollinaire was now taking a more favourable view of the Salon Cubists. One factor was Delaunay, with whom Apollinaire felt a growing sympathy. On top of that, there had been a cooling of relations with Picasso, for personal reasons to do with the scandal of the theft of the *Mona Lisa* in which the two of them had become embroiled (see p. 374). So now Apollinaire reviewed the Salon d'Automne in positive terms: 'Cubism,' he wrote in October 1911, 'is the most noble undertaking in French art today.' The Salon Cubists are to be taken seriously. No longer are they 'Jackdaws in Peacocks' Feathers', as he had described them in 1910 in relation to Picasso and Braque.

Picasso and Braque, however, were working on a very different Cubism in 1911 from the perspectival geometry of Metzinger and his associates. Their territory was the intersecting area of what one remembers and what one sees – the view of an object created by one's mind, and the view of an object created by one's eye. This makes the essence of a Cubist picture an experience of extended duration, more contemplative than the snapshot immediacy of, say, an Impressionist picture. Thus the Cubist painter does not depict 'the chair' or 'the wineglass' but indulges in visual ruminations on 'chair-ness' or 'wineglass-ness'. By now traditional perspective had been jettisoned as no longer useful and space had been reinvented. Shortly Braque and Picasso would go further and would reach the conclusion that paint by itself was an inadequate medium for their purposes. They would expand into collage: newspaper, wallpaper and sand would be variously employed on the picture surface as means of expressing the multiplicity of associations that their visual rumination threw up. These were advances into realms previously unimagined, and beyond the scope of the Salon Cubists. They were the exclusive innovations of Picasso and Braque.

So in Paris in 1911 the two of them – the solitary mountaineers – worked more closely than ever. Picasso later told Francois Gilot: 'Almost every evening either I went to Braque's studio or Braque came to mine. Each of us *had* to see what the other had done during the day. We criticised each other's work. A canvas wasn't finished unless both of us felt it was.' Picasso set off to spend the summer in Spain – Ceret this time – but without Fernande. Their relationship was in an advanced stage of disintegration, and she stayed in Paris. In mid August Braque joined Picasso in Ceret and their close collaboration resumed. Three magical weeks ensued when, in the words of Golding, 'a moment of poise and equilibrium' was achieved, or as Richardson has it, the summit of Cubism was conquered by a combination of 'Spanish duende and French poésie'. It is not easy to differentiate between the work of Picasso and Braque in the summer of 1911. Each was painting still lives and figure subjects, often involving musical instruments. Kahnweiler had the best idea of what was going on, because he got their periodic letters from Spain.

88. Braque, *Le Portugais*, 1911

What was the moment of 'poise and equilibrium' that constituted the peak of analytical Cubism? It consists of the disintegration of solid structures into looser overlapping planes that are variously opaque, transparent or reflective of light. Lines are superimposed on the composition not in order to define contours but as a kind of pictorial scaffolding that suggests spatial movement. But the whole never quite tips into abstraction: there remain oblique references to real objects. Just as it seemed that this phase of Cubism had been taken about as far as it could go, an innovation of Braque's revealed a new direction. His crucial breakthrough, in the second half of 1911, was the introduction of stencilled numbers and letters to the surface of his Cubist compositions. In the words of Daix, 'this use of standardised forms, which owes nothing to painting by hand, completely objectivizes these references, turning them into signs which are external to the composition. They become intrusions of actual reality outside the picture. The idea of collage is close at hand ...' By the end of the year Braque, retrieving a skill familiar from his father's painting and decorating trade, had also introduced into the surface of his painting areas of *faux bois* technique. Here is the beginning of the second phase of the movement: synthetic Cubism.

A photograph taken in autumn 1911 shows Marie Laurencin standing in Picasso's studio, in front of his half-finished *L'homme à la Mandoline*. It provides fascinating evidence of how Picasso painted his great analytical Cubist compositions. The outline is sketched in, not so much as a basis for experiment – he is past that stage – but as a reminder of challenges already met and questions resolved. So once he starts painting he knows exactly where he is going. He begins at the top and works meticulously and definitively downwards. That's not to say that Picasso is a prisoner of rationality. 'Despite the strong intellectual and rational strain that characterises Cubism,' says Golding, 'the painting of Picasso and Braque remained markedly unscientific. The method of both artists was throughout primarily intuitive ... the painter's liberty has become absolute.' What this

89. Marie Laurencin in Picasso's studio, 1911

photograph does confirm, however, is that the complex intellectual and visual elements of the composition have been arrived
at intuitively in advance, and once Picasso starts painting there
is not just very little opportunity for revision but also very little
call for it. When he resumes work (once Marie Laurencin gets
out of the way) he will just continue on down.

By 1911 Cubism had taken over in Paris. Young aspirant modernists arrived in the city and were immediately swept up by
it. Marc Chagall, fresh from Russia, settled into a studio in La
Ruche where his neighbours included Léger and the sculptors

Archipenko and Henri Laurens, who were already engaged in their Cubist experiments. Next door was an abbatoir, and Chagall recorded that he began painting Cubist still lives to the sound of the slaughtering of cattle. Another to come to Paris in 1911, in the spring, was Lyonel Feininger, an American who had settled in Germany and exhibited at the Berlin Secession. He wrote: 'I had gone to Paris for two weeks and found the art world agog with cubism, a thing I had never heard even mentioned before but which I had already, entirely intuitively, striven after for years.' Mondrian paid his first visit this year, as did the Futurists, eager to find out what they needed to do to become truly modern. For Mondrian, the Futurists, Chagall and Feininger, Cubism was a common catalyst in 1911, but they each made something different of it. For the Futurists, Cubism offered a new language in which to express the dynamism of modern life; for Chagall the subversive element in Cubism gave an extra edge to his disposition to fantasy; for Feininger, seeing the work of Delaunay recast his own highly individual vision into a system of semi-transparent planes and prismatic intersections; and for Mondrian, the encounter with analytical Cubism was an important stepping stone on his progress to abstraction.

And Cubism gained some sort of toehold in London, too. The Camden Town Group, a formation of modernist British artists catalysed by exhibiting together at the Allied Artists, held its first exhibition in June 1911. They had come together under the leadership of Walter Sickert (who had finally broken free of his obsession with bedsteads) and painted everyday life in styles that owed various debts to French post-Impressionism. Percy Wyndham Lewis, who had spent time in Paris and was at this point one of the very few British artists with some inkling of the latest avant-garde movements there, was the most advanced. He showed *Smiling Woman Ascending a Stair*, a figure subject painted in a kind of ornamental Cubist style, but given edge by a hint of absurdist subversion. In November he was back in Paris visiting the Salon d'Automne. The most interesting artists in the exhibition, he reported, were Gleizes, Léger and Metzinger. Around this time, perhaps in order to acquire a greater modernist credibility, he dropped 'Percy' from his name. It was probably the right decision.

The Cubist debate continued to be fought out in Paris throughout 1912. Futurism had announced itself to considerable excitement in its first Paris exhibition at Bernheim in February. The Cubists felt the need to defend themselves from this alien incursion. In the Salon des Indépendants, which opened in March, the young Marcel Duchamp's *Nude Descending a Staircase* (see p. 279) was deemed too Futurist for exhibition. In the same show, Juan Gris showed Cubist paintings for the first time, in apparent alignment with Gleizes and Metzinger as a Salon Cubist. However, one of his exhibits was entitled *Homage to Pablo Picasso*. This was a picture that the critic Vauxcelles called mockingly 'Portrait of Père Ubu-Kub', but it was nonetheless acknowledgement of Picasso as a Cubist entity deserving of homage. Delaunay's vast *City of Paris* was also a prominent feature of the exhibition. Here the Three Graces were rendered in a kind of Cubist space which faded in and out of a deconstructed view of Paris. Delaunay was adamant that there was no affinity with Futurism in his art; but the intelligent modern art lover would have been reminded of the dynamic Italian modernism that had been on view in Bernheim-Jeune the month before.

In the April 1912 edition of the magazine *Je Sais Tout*, Jacques de Gachon wrote an article on *La peinture d'après demain*. He interviewed Kahnweiler. What was Cubism all about? It was a joke, wasn't it? Kahnweiler assured him that Messrs Picasso and Braque were not to be laughed at; they were innovators of great integrity:

> 'I understand that deciphering the most recent works of Picasso and Braque is difficult. I have been initiated since I witnessed the evolution of these paintings. I know the artists' intention. For instance, this is a painting of "The Poet".'

The journalist thought he had been looking at a landscape.

'Yes, he is seated,' continued Kahnweiler. 'This is his brow, here the arm, this is a leg.'

'What about this line here, slanting down?'

'It doesn't correspond to anything concrete, but notice how expressive it is since it immediately caught your attention. His hands ... '

'Where are the poet's hands?'

'Here's one hand.'

'How strange.'

'Isn't it?

The journalist was convinced at least of the strength of Kahnweiler's conviction. He compared him to a great couturier speaking with fluency and enthusiasm about his latest creation.[32]

That summer in the south of France Picasso and Braque took their work in new and extraordinary directions, rather beyond the scope of the readership of *Je Sais Tout*. 'Picasso and I discussed things which nobody will ever discuss again, which nobody else would know how to discuss, which nobody else would know how to understand,' Braque wrote later. Historically, 1912 is characterised as the year when the Cubism of Braque and Picasso transmuted from the analytical to the synthetic. What did that mean? The synthetic reconstruction of reality involved the employment of all sorts of new and revolutionary techniques and materials. First had come the stencilled numbers and letters applied to the picture surface which – in Daix's words – had ruptured 'the homogeneity of painting'. There was experimentation with the household paint Ripolin, whose prosaic functionality by contrast with traditional 'fine art' oil paint was part of the same rupture. There was the addition of sand to paint to create interesting new surface effects, along with *faux bois* episodes. What were being produced were no longer paintings but 'assemblages of methods and of codes'.

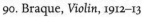

90. Braque, *Violin*, 1912–13   91. Picasso, *Guitar*, 1912–13

The next step was the addition of further extraneous matter to the surface of the painting in the form of *papier collé* and collage. Bits of newspaper were cut into shapes and incorporated into the composition. Braque's letters to Kahnweiler that summer are a breathless catalogue of unprecedented innovation: in fact Picasso took to calling Braque 'Wilbourg' after Wilbur Wright the aviator, because he was so inventive. Soon objects created in wood, paper and cardboard – guitars were a favourite theme – start to emerge in their own right, transcending the pretext of a painting on a two-dimensional support. Picasso's natural talents as an artisan and 'gadgeteer' were now fully engaged. In another life he would have made rather a good household handyman, the sort who comes round to mend a leaking pipe and stays to knock up a cat flap out of a cigar box and a door lock from a bit of wire and a clothes peg. From 1912 onwards improvised constructions in three dimensions become part of the Picasso–Braque repertoire.

Looking back on synthetic Cubism later, Picasso remembered:

> the purpose was to give the idea that different textures can enter into a composition to become the reality in the painting that competes with the reality in nature ... If a piece of newspaper can become a bottle, that gives us something to think about in connection with both newspapers and bottles, too. This displaced object has entered a universe for which it was not made and where it retains, in a measure, its strangeness. And this strangeness was what we wanted to make people think about because we were quite aware that our world was becoming very strange and not exactly reassuring.[33]

This was the first summer that Picasso spent with his new girl-friend Eva, while Braque brought along his live-in lover Marcelle Lapré, whom he married in 1912. Collage was thereby given extra piquancy: it was also a slang expression for two people shacking up together.

Meanwhile Gleizes and Metzinger spent the summer writing their own account and explanation of Cubism. It was a deeply serious essay, published in the autumn. Not many people entirely understood it, perhaps not even the authors. It was heavy with theory, placing the Bergsonian idea of artistic intuition and unmeasurable duration at the centre of what the movement was all about. The fourth dimension was also invoked, sometimes as a geometric space and sometimes as a spiritual one. The authors' insistent theorising was anathema to Picasso and Braque, and to Kahnweiler (although he would write his own occasionally impenetrable analysis of Cubism some years later). If you believed, as Kahnweiler did, that modern art was all about feeling and intuition, then these were exactly the qualities that the Salon Cubists were jeopardising in their absurd formula-icising and geometricisation. The essay was padded out with statements such as 'it is by setting fire to the heart of the star for our intimate joy that we shall exalt the universe', whatever that means. And it concluded that 'the artist who abstains from any concessions, who does not explain himself and who tells nothing, builds up an internal strength whose radiance shines all around.' Picasso and Braque might legitimately have read this as vindication of their own taciturnity. Picasso was always wary of artists who talked too much, maintaining that 'in painting an idea will not be pure if it can be expressed in a language other than its own, painting'.

But Gleizes and Metzinger were tireless agitators for their own version of Cubism, and in October they mounted a big exhibition of the group that, together with Jacques Villon, they had brought into existence called, with a certain mystico-mathematical flourish, the Section d'Or. Over 200 works were included. It was intended to show – even explain – recent developments in avant-garde art in Paris. Despite the fact that Picasso and Braque had excluded themselves, the exhibition was a success. It gave a platform to some interesting Cubist sculpture. Cubist painters had learned to express space in the shape of solid form – smoke or fog that only a knife could cut. Now here were sculptors like Archipenko expressing form in the shape of empty space – sculptures with holes in them. And by the end of the year Archipenko had pushed back the bounds even further: his *Medrano*, a seated figure representing a circus performer, was constructed of a challenging range of different materials, and had an adjustable arm. Here indeed is a wave to the future.

The Section d'Or also offered a glimpse of what might lie ahead in the constantly evolving avant-garde art that went under the catch-all name of Cubism. New adherents emerged. Apart from Duchamp there were others, like Francis Picabia and Frantisek Kupka, for whom Cubism was a temporary rite of passage, a catalyst in their development towards different goals. Picabia – having in recent years passed through the obligatory stages of Impressionism, Pointillism and Fauvism – was now inventing a metallic and highly coloured Cubism steeped in symbols, illogicality and eroticism. Kupka, who had arrived in Paris in 1896 from his native Slovakia, went through phases of mystical symbolism heavily influenced by art nouveau; as a sideline he also operated as a spiritualist medium. Now, in works like *Amorpha, Fugue in two Colours*, which comprised a heady mixture of occult science, the study of light and movement and the forms of art nouveau, he too approached very closely to pure abstraction.

At the same time, Delaunay was ushering in his new move-ment, christened Orphism by Apollinaire. Delaunay had spent the summer developing his *Fenêtres* series (see p. 199), composi-tions concentrating simply on the power of colour, rendered in a succession of planes that even flow off the edge of the canvas and on to the frame. Apollinaire gave a lecture at the Section d'Or on 11 October in which he announced that Orphism was the most advanced category of Cubism. He defined it in words that sound like Delaunay's: 'It's the art of painting new *ensembles* with elements borrowed not from visual reality but entirely created by [the artist] and endowed by him with their own pow-erful reality.'

Picasso kept a beady eye on proceedings. He was not obliv-ious to the efforts of the Salon Cubists, nor did he necessarily disapprove of everything they did. A fascinating list, written in the artist's own hand, indicates which Cubist artists he felt were at the forefront of the broader movement in autumn 1912. It was prepared for the Americans visiting Paris in search of exam-ples of the most modern Parisian art for the Armory Show they would shortly mount in New York; Picasso scribbled it on a piece of scrap paper, possibly with a visit to the Section d'Or fresh in his memory. It reads: Juan Gris, Metzinger, Léger, Duchamp, Delaunay, Le Fauconnier, Marie Laurencin, De la Fresnaye; and Braque, added almost as an afterthought.

While Picasso was intrigued by the Section d'Or exhibition, the majority were of course horrified. It created a particular ferment of anxiety among conservative art lovers in the autumn of 1912. Was the world going mad? This Cubist mania was beyond a joke. In an open letter in the *Mercure de France* on 16 October, a Paris city councillor, Pierre Lampue, described those artists who had succumbed to the movement's insidious influence as a 'gang of criminals who behave in the art world like yobs and delinquents'. Conservatives in the Chamber of Deputies were also up in arms against the use of the Grand Palais – a public monument – for the exhibition of Cubist monstrosities in the Salon d'Automne. 'It is unacceptable,' said Jean-Louis Breton, 'that our state-owned historic buildings should be used for events of a character that is so clearly anti-artistic and anti-national.' Cubism continued to polarise opinion. 'I consider the modern school of painting to be the most daring that ever existed,' declared Apollinaire in 1913. 'You can paint with whatever you like, with pipes, postage stamps, postcards, candalabras, pieces of oilcloth, shirt collars, wallpaper or newspapers.' This certainly didn't please the critic of *Gil Blas*. Louis Vauxcelles in his article on the Salon d'Automne that year was still not converted to the new art: 'Every room of the exhibition has its Cubist,' he observed, 'the way every hospital ward has a dangerous psychopath.'

Apollinaire was everywhere in these crucial years of Cubism; its advocate, interpreter and evaluator. As a writer on art he was uniquely equipped to keep up with the breakneck speed of modernist developments in Paris. He was a poet, which – according to Baudelaire – was the best qualification for an art critic, and as a central member of the 'Picasso Gang' he was an insider well placed to report from the front line of the artistic avant-garde. He had his finger closer to the pulse of Cubism than anyone. He was capable of pronouncements of extraordinary insight, of gnomic impenetrability and of deliberate absurdism. Occasionally he foundered out of his depth in front of art that he did not yet understand, but that didn't stop him from taking a view and expressing it in high-flown language. Confronted with an example of Léger's *Contrastes de Forme*, he cannot help himself, rhapsodising irrelevantly 'this painting is liquid, like the sea, blood, rivers, rain, a glass of water and our tears too, with sweat from times of great effort and exhaustion, and wet with kisses.' It is hard to imagine what Léger made of this. Chagall, more irreverently, observed of the portly Apollinaire, 'he carried his stomach like a volume of collected works'. But Cubism owes a lot to that stomach.

By 1913 Juan Gris had moved on from Salon Cubism and into the orbit of Kahnweiler. His command of colour married to a distinctive geometrical vision of Cubism was probably enough to persuade the dealer to sign him up to his gallery, although the decisive factor may have been Gris's remarkably early experiments with collage: among his exhibits at the Section d'Or in October 1912 were *Le Lavabo*, to which he attached a piece of mirror, and *La Montre* whose surface bore a fragment of printed paper. In 1914 Gris reached his high point, producing Cubist collages that were as innovative and imaginative as anyone's. While they admired Gris, Picasso and Braque were sometimes suspicious of what they saw as his excessive harnessing of mathematical calculation to Cubism. 'Watch out,' Braque told him, 'or you're going to find yourself trying to fit two fruit dishes into a single apple.' Picasso said of him, a trifle patronisingly, that 'he kept the accounts of Cubism'.

At the Salon des Indépendants of 1914, which opened on 1 March, all the usual suspects exhibited. The Salon Cubists were there en masse, led by Gleizes and Metzinger. Apollinaire, in his review of the show, discerned a certain lassitude in the ranks. He feared that the sort of Cubism being produced by the followers of the movement had become routine, even conventional in its anti-conventionality. 'L'art pompier', so-called because of the resemblance of the helmets of Paris's fire brigade to those of the heroes of antiquity, had been the sort of classically inspired nineteenth-century academic painting against which the modernists had been rebelling. Now Apollinaire identified a 'pompierism' of anti-academicism, just as stagnant as the original 'pompierism' of the Academy. It was a salutary thought to

92. Gris, *Landscape at Ceret*, 1913

carry away from the last Salon des Indépendants before world war broke out, that even rebellion could become routine.

At the end of 1913 Picasso painted his synthetic Cubist masterpiece *Femme en Chemise* (see p. 7), as an erotic tribute to Eva. As 1914 unfolded, things were looking bright for him: he was happily having his cake and eating it, as he had tried to do most of his life. He enjoyed playing the radical subversive but simultaneously took pleasure in banking cheques. His self-confessed aim was to 'live like a poor man with a lot of money', to paint pictures that pushed artistic boundaries but at the same time produced for him the wherewithal to employ maids and the legendary soufflé-cook. Picasso was now indeed financially well established. The years of penury were over, underlined by the success that year of the Peau d'Ours sale in which his work was perceived to have jumped dramatically in price. He was confident enough to undermine his own revolution by toying with minute representationalism again. He painted an ultra-realistic apple for Gertrude Stein in compensation for the Cézanne still life that Leo had taken in the Steins' messy sibling divorce. The apple was an act of subversion against the subversion of Cubism.

The years 1907–14 were the most important in Picasso's career. Of course he had a constantly inventive future ahead of him after the First World War, one that took him in many new directions. But the visual language he brought into being in the Cubist years became thereafter his lingua franca, his default mode of expression in the depiction of figures and objects. The distortions that he practised on the form of Marie-Thérèse in the 1930s, on the tomato plants and the fighting cats of the 1940s, on the *Femmes d'Algers* series of the 1950s or the eroticisms of the 1960s all derived from the fragmentations and the multiple viewpoints of Cubism.

CHAPTER TWENTY-SEVEN

Futurism: Beautiful Ideas that Kill

F. T. Marinetti, the Italian poet and polemicist, loved fast cars. He was speeding along the road near Milan in June 1908 when he swerved to avoid two cyclists and ended up in the ditch. 'O maternal ditch, almost half full of muddy water', he rhapsodised afterwards. 'Fair factory drain! I gulped down your nourishing sludge; and I remembered the blessed black breast of my Sudanese nurse.' This was Marinetti's moment of truth: he emerged from the wreckage galvanised, inspired, by his own account 'a new man'. Those two absent-minded cyclists are indirectly responsible for Futurism.

On 20 February 1909, the staider readership of *Le Figaro* in Paris would have been bemused by an announcement on the newspaper's front page signed by Marinetti, under the heading of 'Initial Manifesto of Futurism'. It was an incendiary document, heralding the beginning of a movement whose name became in the next five years a shorthand for outrageous modernism as cogent as the dreaded Cubism. At this point Marinetti's manifesto was primarily addressed to poets, but there was a strong visual imagery running through it which might have alerted artists too. It was a hymn to energy and danger, to strife and speed. In a famous declaration Marinetti asserts that the racing motor car is more beautiful than the *Victory of Samothrace*. An echo of the all-pervasive voice of Nietzsche exhorts the poet to 'give himself with frenzy'. In a vividly visual passage Marinetti speaks of the dynamism of the modern city, of the nocturnal vibration of arsenals and workshops beneath their violent electric moons; of the greedy stations swallowing smoking snakes; of factories suspended from the clouds by their strings of smoke; of bridges leaping like gymnasts over the diabolical cutlery of sunbathed rivers.[34]

The past must be abandoned, Marinetti thundered on, and Italy must be freed from the baleful influence of museums and 'second-hand dealers'. He continued: 'To admire an old picture is to pour our sensitiveness into a funeral urn, instead of casting it forward in violent gushes of creation and action.' Messrs Duveen, Agnew, von Bode and Berenson, old master specialists who had been pouring their sensitiveness into funeral urns for most of their professional lives, must have felt their foundations wobble. Marinetti pulled no punches: he wanted to make Italy great again and that meant War, 'the only health-giver of the world'. Beauty was everything. 'N'est-ce pas beau comme la littérature?' had been Jarry's justification of any sort of extreme behaviour. 'What do the victims matter,' demanded Marinetti now, 'if the gesture is beautiful?'

The year 1910 saw the Futurist bandwagon really start to roll. In the recollection of the Futurist painter Gino Severini, it was probably the most important year of the first quarter of the twentieth century. 'I recall an extraordinary feeling of dynamism that year ... an inexpressible appetite for innovation and adventure.' The indefatigable Marinetti's international schedule of Futurist performances across the continent in 1910 was prodigious: on 12 January he conducted a Futurist evening in Trieste, in which he asserted that 'the living must be freed from the dead', and 'poets, painters, musicians and sculptors must rid themselves once and for all from the cult of the past'. A satisfactorily animated response from the audience was provoked and violent protests ensued. This was followed by a Futurist evening held in Turin in March, when it was the turn of the painters: Umberto Boccioni, Carlo Carra and Luigi Russolo lined up on stage alongside Marinetti for a first reading of the

Manifesto of Futurist Painting that they had just put together. 'The way pictures are constructed is stupidly traditional,' they declared. 'Painters have always shown us things and persons as if set directly in front of us. We however will put the *viewer* himself in the centre of the picture.' Further, the Futurists asserted that 'all subjects previously used must be swept aside in order to express our whirling life of steel, of pride, of fever, and of speed'. Oh, and there was to be no more nude painting, not for ten years anyway. Nude painting had become monotonous in the hands of artists 'obsessed with the desire to expose the bodies of their mistresses' who had thereby 'transformed the Salons into arrays of unwholesome flesh'. The Futurists' announcements provoked huge uproar in Turin that evening. People fought with fists and sticks and the police intervened. It was a pattern that was to become familiar: from 1910–14 the same taste for hooligan violence that was satisfied in the 1980s in football stadiums was met on a smaller scale but with similar zest in Italy at Futurist events. Apollinaire commented, a trifle patronisingly, that the violence of the movement was 'a stimulant, good for the weakened senses of the Italians'.

The Futurists exhibited their work in Milan later in March, to a reaction of simmering hostility. The manifesto, as published in tract form on 11 April, was signed by Boccioni, Carra and Russolo, plus Balla from Rome and Severini from Paris. On 20 April, Boccioni read it out on stage to an audience in Naples. Marinetti, meanwhile, visited London in April. His first event was an address to an all-female gathering, in the Lyceum Club, Piccadilly, which was audacious of him in view of the 'contempt for women' that he had publicly professed the year before. At least one other man infiltrated the meeting, the intrepid Wyndham Lewis. A few days later Marinetti gave a 'Futurist Speech to the English', praising English individualism and passion for boxing, and criticising traditionalism and love for aristocracy.

In June Marinetti published his *Proclama futurista a los Espanoles*, then returned his attention to Italy where he lectured in Naples, Parma and Milan on 'The Necessity and Beauty of

Violence'. The summer culminated in a particularly exciting Futurist event in Venice: a proclamation entitled *Contro Venezia passatista* (Against Venice, Prisoner of its Past) was printed on leaflets, 800,000 of which were dropped from the top of the clock tower in St Mark's Square in the late afternoon of Sunday 8 July. It was vintage Marinetti: a declaration to 'cure and heal this putrefying city, magnificent sore from the past', and refashion it as 'an industrial and military Venice to dominate the Adriatic Sea, that great Italian lake'. Baffled tourists were informed of the need to 'burn the gondolas, rocking chairs for cretins' and to 'fill in the little reeking canals with the shards of leprous, crumbling palaces'. The distribution of leaflets was followed by an improvised 'Speech to the Venetians'. And proceedings ended in a very satisfactory fist fight between Futurists – Boccioni, Russola and Carra were among those trading blows – and Venetian 'Prisoners of the Past'.

Marinetti certainly knew how to create a spectacle. He was one of the great publicists of the twentieth century. Simultaneous with his aesthetic rabble-rousing around the country, he was also being tried in Milan that summer on a charge of 'affronting public decency'. The prosecution arose out of his recently published novel *Mafarka the Futurist*, and he succeeded in turning the court case into a public platform for the dissemination of Futurist views. In December Marinetti was back in London, lecturing once again at the Lyceum Club on 'Futurism and Woman'. If there had been air miles in 1910, he would have been a gold card holder.

What the Futurist artists were painting in spring and summer 1910, however, hadn't yet caught up with their theory. They whirled along gamely in a style that remained essentially divisionist, an Italian version of the dots of pure colour of Pointillism. But later in the year Boccioni painted two increasingly dynamic works: *Riot in the Galleria*, and then *The City Rises*, a composition full of energy, dissonance and fragmentation. It is a painting all about horse power: maddened steeds surge along the urban street, sweeping human beings along in their

93. Boccioni, *The City Rises*, 1910

slipstream. 'It comes out of all my pores ... ' wrote Boccioni. 'I feel I am really creating something, and the work comes to me now with a fever.' Meanwhile in Paris Severini – closer to the latest Cubist developments – was coming up with increasingly fragmented and forceful treatments of dancers in the bars and cabarets of the city.

Marinetti's pace around Europe did not slacken in 1911, stirring up excitement, violence and subversion wherever he went. On 2 March there was a tempestuous Futurist event at La Scala in Milan, where Marinetti launched his manifesto *Against La Scala: Pompeii of Italian Theatre*. On 9 March he was in Paris, lecturing on Futurism at the Maison des Étudiants. There were further Futurist evenings in Ferrara, Mantua and Como over the next month; the one planned at the university of Parma was banned, which led to violent student protests and Marinetti's own arrest. In June he was in the police station again in Florence after another good Futurist brawl, as result of which, in the later words of Apollinaire, 'there were injuries and one or two hats

were rendered useless'. In October Marinetti took on an assign-
ment as war correspondent of *L'Intransigeant* and went to the
Libyan front to report on the Italo-Turkish war. Here at last was
a genuine conflict to witness, albeit as an observer rather than
a participant.

But Futurist painting, despite its noise and its fury, still hadn't
totally broken its divisionist moorings and established itself as
the transformative force that its rhetoric proclaimed it to be.
When Gino Severini arrived in Milan in the summer of 1911 on
a visit from Paris, he was shocked to find that the works of his
fellow Futurists in Italy so little resembled the paintings of his
avant-garde friends in Paris. He looked at what Carra, Russolo,
Balla and even Boccioni were painting and realised they had to
catch up. It was a matter of particular concern to Severini, who
was helping to arrange a major exhibition of Italian Futurism,
scheduled for the Bernheim Gallery in Paris in early 1912. For its
impact to be maximised, Severini decided that his languishing
fellow countrymen needed first-hand experience of Cubism.
So in the autumn a band of Italian Futurists led by Boccioni
and Carra set off from Milan on a fact-finding mission to Paris.
The Italians visited Kahnweiler's gallery, met Picasso, and one
of them then slept with Picasso's mistress for good measure,
thus precipitating Fernande's exit from the Picasso household
and putting an early Futurist marker down in the coming rivalry
with Cubism.

After their crash course in Cubism the Futurists bounded
forward. The long-prepared and much vaunted exhibition of
Italian Futurism was finally held at Bernheim-Jeune in Paris from
5–24 February 1912. The preface to the exhibition catalogue,
probably written by Boccioni, announced: 'In order to make
the spectator live in the centre of the picture, the picture must
be a synthesis of WHAT ONE REMEMBERS and WHAT ONE
SEES.' He goes on to articulate a very Bergsonian statement of
intent: 'The gesture that we would reproduce on canvas shall
no longer be a fixed moment in universal dynamism. It shall
simply be the dynamic sensation itself. Indeed all things move,

94. Boccioni, *The Farewells*

95. Boccioni, *Those Who Go*

96. Boccioni, *Those Who Stay*

all things run, all things are rapidly changing.' Here is the beginning of a controversial artistic concept, that of Simultaneism, the proprietory rights to which would be disputed by Cubists, Futurists and Orphists in the years to come. Objects, memories, landscapes, and emotions are all thrown together simultaneously in the same painting. First space has been reinvented by the avant-garde; now time is collapsed and redefined.

Boccioni was triumphant about the impact on Paris of the show generally, and of his own work in particular. He was especially delighted by the reception of his *States of Mind* triptych: 'My states of mind ... are being talked about in all the artistic and literary centres in Paris,' he reported. 'The French are dumbfounded that in a little provincial city like Milan something could be said that leaves them speechless.' The triptych takes as its subject a train journey, its three parts comprising *The Farewells, Those Who Go* and *Those who Stay*. In fact Boccioni had begun to work on the idea the previous year, but recast it in the light of what he learned in Paris in autumn 1911, imbuing it with appreciably more physical and emotional dynamism. Trains were understandably dear to the hearts of the Futurists, symbolising the speed, drama and beauty of modern life. In its recharged form, the *States of Mind* triptych constitutes three remarkable visual and psychic documents combining the energy of train travel with the emotions that its experience evokes. In the drama of *Farewells* diagonals prevail; in the speed of *Those Who Go* horizontals predominate; and the anti-climactic pedestrian melancholy of *Those Who Stay* is emphasised by a composition heavy with verticals.

Other Futurist works particularly singled out for attention by the Parisian critics included Carra's *Funeral of the Anarchist Galli*, a dynamic street scene full of fields of force, and Severini's huge *Pan-Pan at the Monico*, a wild and colourful evocation of a dance hall. It was the sheer energy of Futurism that made the impact. The exhibition demanded a response from French critics. Salmon, in the *Paris-Journal*, gave it as his opinion that the Italian Futurists showed 'agility' rather than 'dexterity', a very

97. Duchamp, *Nude Descending a Staircase*, 1912

nice distinction; Kahn, in the *Mercure de France*, paid tribute to their 'enthusiasm and brilliance'. There was an ever-expanding literature of Futurist theory for confused reviewers to dip into for elucidation. Boccioni had written in 1911 of the 'archaism' of the 'immobility' of a picture set against 'the vertiginous movement of human life'. Now he went further: the paintings of the future, he predicted, would be 'swirling musical compositions of great coloured gases ... which will move and electrify the complex soul of a crowd that we cannot yet conceive of.' Unnerved by this vision, the critic of the *Journal* suggested that a better understanding of it might be achieved with the help of 'a young psychiatrist'.

The Futurist invasion of Paris in early 1912 provoked a lingering hysteria in the French capital. It started with the incendiary address that Marinetti gave in the exhibition itself at Bernheim on 15 February. The podium was stormed and the police were called. This sort of physical manifestation of conflict and energy was, of course, an inseparable part of the Futurist message, and the febrility simmered on: in June Valentine de St Point added to the controversy with her *Futurist Manifesto of Lust*, eulogising lust in terms that set already over-active pulses racing. That Futurism had touched a nerve in the Paris avant-garde as an alien threat to the purity of French Cubism was confirmed as early as March, when the Salon des Indépendants opened. Marcel Duchamp submitted his *Nude Descending a Staircase*, a powerfully energised elaboration of a figure in motion. Although Duchamp claimed he had painted it before being aware of Italian Futurism, in an unusual act of censorship he was forced to take it down. Gleizes and Villon rejected it as being too Futurist. But such was the pace of the internationalisation of the avant-garde in 1912 that it did find wall space in Barcelona in April, where the Dalmau Gallery included it – thanks to the efficiency of the railway system – in its 'Exposicio d'art cubista'.

The Italian Futurist exhibition drew to a close at Bernheim in Paris on 24 February and then moved on in March to London where it was shown at the Sackville Gallery. The aggressively dynamic artistic position of the Futurists was reinforced in their English catalogue preface. The autumn before they had been keen to learn from the Cubists in Paris, but now these same Cubists were criticised for painting 'objects motionless, frozen, and all the static aspects of nature', thereby betraying 'an obstinate attachment to the past'. 'We, on the contrary, with points of view pertaining essentially to the future, seek for a style of motion, a thing that has never been attempted before.' The reaction of the London art world to works by Boccioni, Carra, Russolo, Severini and Balla was bemusement and shock, but the exotic visitors found the stoic locals less provokable into violence than the excitable French and Italians. Boccioni wrote disparagingly of English complacency on 15 March in a letter to his friend Vico Baer: 'London, beautiful, monstrous, elegant, well-fed, well-dressed but with brains as heavy as steaks.' While in town Boccioni – having given up hope of art-induced rioting – instead joined a suffragist demonstration where a number of umbrellas were broken and hats rendered unwearable.

The next stop in the Futurist tour of Europe was Berlin, and here the roadshow met its entrepreneurial match in Herwarth Walden. Walden commandeered the operation, mounting the exhibition at his Der Sturm Gallery from 12 April to 15 May. On his own initiative he added in three works by Robert Delaunay, the French artist whose position at the dynamic end of the Cubist spectrum was a better fit with Futurism. So far so good, and the show attracted considerable public interest. Walden's wife Nell recorded excitedly: 'Sometimes there were a thousand visitors a day. The press could complain as much as they wanted – which they did – but everyone wanted to see the exhibition. It was fashionable to have been there.' A German translation of the Futurist Manifesto was included in the catalogue; the inevitable Marinetti was in attendance and distributed flyers of the manifesto widely about the city. Franz Marc saw the show and wrote an article on Die Futuristen in *Der Sturm* magazine in which he said they 'would mark the history of modern art. We shall envy Italy her sons and we shall hang their works in our Galleries'.

The exhibition's impact on German modernism was not limited to Marc. Lyonel Feininger's powerful *Trompetenbläser* of 1912 shows distinct Futurist influence. Feininger wrote that year: 'I believe firmly that every picture that deserves the name must be an absolute synthesis of rhythm, form, perspective, and colour, and even that is not good enough if it is *not expressive*.' In fact what Feininger has achieved in *Trompetenbläser* is a successful synthesis of just about every current modernist tendency: his own German Expressionist heritage is given plastic weight by the Cubism he experienced the previous year in Paris, and energised by the Futurism he could see in Berlin.

Despite the public interest generated by the Italian Futurist exhibition wherever it went, its high profile was not yet matched

98. Feininger, *Trompetenbläser*, 1912

by sales. At this point Walden's entrepreneurial flair took over. He persuaded Albert Borchardt, a German collector with a speculating instinct, to buy twenty-four of the thirty-five exhibits for a total of 11,650 marks. Actually selling their work was a novel and intoxicating experience for the Futurists, so they jumped at the deal. But they were less delighted when they found Walden recycling Borchardt's purchases to mount his own Futurist exhibitions, with rather higher asking prices, over the following months. Upon sober reflection, Severini felt that the sum he had received for his chef-d'oeuvre *Pan-Pan* was particularly niggardly, especially after the gross figure of 2,000 marks was significantly shrunk by deduction of transport costs (all those railway journeys across Europe) and Walden's commission. Balla, intrigued by Germany, stayed on in Dusseldorf where, in

99. Boccioni, *Testa + Luce + Ambiente*, 1912

mid July, he spent the proceeds of his own sales in designing his first Futurist menswear, an asymmetrical black suit with white stripes.

Animosity between Futurists and Cubists smouldered on through the summer. The fraught nuances of the relationship between the two movements are illustrated by another Boccioni of 1912. It is a painting directly stimulated by the Picasso sculpture *Tête de Fernande*, that Boccioni must have seen either on his exploratory mission to Paris in autumn 1911 or when he was there for the exhibition in February 1912. He called his painting *Head, Light and Air* (*Testa + Luce + Ambiente*). The head is wholly subsumed into its surroundings so that there is simultaneous perception of window and fruit bowl and table and figure and face. It is not just a fusion of Cubist fragmentation

of form and Futurist energy and colour; more than that Boccioni's painting is an implicit attack on Picasso, an attempt to
animate the immobility of objects and space that the Futurists
found so leaden in Cubism. It is not entirely successful. It's as if
the 'swirling musical compositions of great coloured gases' that
Boccioni envisaged as the future of painting have escaped too
early, before Boccioni fully understood what he was unleashing.
Perhaps in acknowledgement that all was not yet well with his
painting, Boccioni now veered more towards sculpture and the
challenge of inducing energy into three-dimensional form.

Meanwhile Futurism was spreading east, and by 1913 had
reached Moscow and St Petersburg. 'We rang for room service
and the year 1913 answered,' declared the Russian writer Velimar
Khlebnikov. 'It gave Planet Earth a valiant new race of people,
the heroic Futurians.' The Russian avant-garde took to Futurism
with enthusiasm and were keen to assert the independence of
their own version from that of the Italians. The painter brothers
Vladimir and David Burliuk, and the writers Mayakowsky and
Kamenski, went on a travelling crusade round seventeen cities in
Russia to spread propaganda for their movement. The message
was as iconoclastic as anything the Italians promulgated, with
the same scorn for the art of the past. 'A museum of Russian
street signs would be a hundred times more interesting than the
Hermitage,' announced David Burliuk.

The same year there was sedition in Paris, where the French
painter Felix del Marle became a recruit to Italian Futurism. He
rallied to the flag with all the fervour of a religious convert, and
on 10 July launched a 'Futurist Manifesto Against Montmartre'
in which he exhorted the 'Intrepid Wreckers' to 'Get Out the
Picks – Montmartre Must Be Destroyed'. This was a declaration of war against Cubism, which was understood to have
originated in that area of Paris. At the same time he acknowledged Futurism's debt to Bergson, quoting with approval the
philosopher's dictum that 'Everything is change and flight'. It
was indeed. Nothing stood still. As Malevich warned in Moscow
that year, 'Hurry or you'll miss us'. For the first time in history

(but not the last) an avant-garde had come into being rendered neurotic by Fear of Missing Out.

One thing was clear in Paris in 1913: if you were a pure Cubist you couldn't be a Futurist, and if you were a pure Futurist you couldn't be a Cubist. On top of that, the vexed question of Simultanism continued to be fought over by Orphists and Futurists. On 9 March 1913 Apollinaire announced in the magazine *Montjoie!* that 'the reign of Orpheus' was just beginning. Orphism, according to Apollinaire, was an art 'which not only vibrates with the contrast of complementary colours discovered by Seurat, but in every shade calls forth and is illuminated by all the other colours of the prism. This is simultaneity.' So far so good for Delaunay. But then Apollinaire propounded the view that 'simultaneity' was ultimately a creation of the Futurists. This was to tread on the soul of Delaunay, who saw himself as its originator. Delaunay was angry beyond words. Apollinaire wavered. In the feverish atmosphere of conflicting -isms in Paris in the last years before the great war, realignments and reinterpretations happened overnight. But the controversy of whether Orphism was plagiarising Futurism or vice versa rolled on: underlying it were broader conflicts of French nationalism pitted against Italian nationalism. Between November 1913 and June 1914, Boccioni, Apollinaire, Delaunay, Carra, Papini and Sofici all published articles on whether Simultanism was the invention of Orphists or Futurists.

In November 1913 Marinetti was in London again, holding a series of Futurist evenings. A group of young avant-garde British artists declared themselves his adherents, notably Etchells, Wadsworth, Nevinson and Wyndham Lewis, and on 18 November Marinetti's London friends gave a dinner for him at the Florence restaurant in Soho. Marinetti, who as a correspondent in the first Balkan war the year before had witnessed the Siege of Adrianople, declaimed a 'sound poem' he had composed to commemorate the experience entitled *Zang Tumb Tumb*. Nevinson recalled the evening, to which about sixty of London's intelligentsia had been invited, in his autobiography:

100. Larionov and Gontcharova engaged in a
piece of Futurist Performance Art, 1914

Marinetti recited a poem about the Siege of Adrianople,
with various kinds of onomatopoeic noises and crashes
in free verse, while all the time a band downstairs played
'You made me love you. I didn't want to do it, but still you
made me do it.' The tinkling band, who only seemed to
know that one song, continued reprising it throughout the
evening.[35]

In 1914 Moscow saw Larionov, Gontcharova and Malevich
all in their different ways proclaiming themselves Futurists and
engaging in initiatives of Futurist subversion. Sensing action,
Marinetti arrived in Moscow in January bursting to add to the
debate. But he immediately encountered opposition to his Italian

version of the movement. The Russian Futurists were less keen on the Italians' rapturous adoration of technology and speed and their dreams of war and conquest; the Russian emphasis was on a more complex restructuring of society and culture. From their different versions of Futurism in 1914, a far-seeing commentator might have predicted the two countries' post-war political destinations, to Fascism and Soviet Communism respectively. For the time being Larionov's considered response to Marinetti was that he 'should have rotten eggs thrown at him'. Marinetti moved on to St Petersburg, but met hostility here, too, from Russian Futurists. Lishvits suspected that there was a colonialist purpose to Marinetti's visit, 'betraying the first step of Russian art on the path of liberty and honour and bending the noble neck of Asia under the yoke of Europe'.

By February the naturally fractious condition of Italian Futurism was manifesting itself in widening internal divisions at home. The magazine *Lacerba* carried a succession of articles: first, 'The Circle is Closing' by the Florentine critic Giovanni Papini; then one by Boccioni speaking for Milan, 'The Circle is not closing!'; followed by Papini responding with 'Open Circles'. Undismayed, Marinetti moved west again. In April he organised a second expanded Futurist exhibition in London at the Doré Gallery, with works by Boccioni, Balla, Carra, Russolo and Severini. Their reappearance in England drove Wyndham Lewis into a frenzy of conflicting feelings. 'I am not a Futurist,' he told Marinetti in April. 'I hate the movement which displaces lines.' Then in May he was hailing Marinetti as producing art that 'distils in beings the importance of the present, the importance of life', and was calling him the 'Cromwell of our times'. But by June he had formed his own movement, Vorticism, in opposition to Marinetti's Futurism, for which only Nevinson was still declaring himself. Thus London was set up for a summer of artistic violence, of modernist posturing and counter-posturing, of punches being thrown between Futurists and Vorticists. One of the qualifications for a place in the vanguard of cutting-edge artistic modernism was a certain pugilistic ability. It was a little

101. Wyndham Lewis, *Vorticist Composition*, 1914

gentle practice for the real battlefields that awaited many of them later in the year.

Vorticism was the brainchild of Wyndham Lewis. While it owed something to the energy of Futurism, it had its own jealously guarded agenda which included elements of spiritualism and the occult. At first sight its forms looked geometric and mechanical, but an underlying mysticism connected it with the 'cosmic' concerns of Kandinsky. The new movement provided an excuse for a new manifesto and in July, masterminded by Lewis, Vorticism's aims were proclaimed in the first issue of a magazine called *Blast*. It is a wonderfully self-indulgent document, composed from a peculiarly British point of view. It comes out firmly against the English climate, English loutishness, English mildness, the Bishop of London and the unfortunate Henry Tonks, director of the Slade School of Art. 'England is just as unkind and inimical to Art as the Arctic zone is to Life,' it declares. 'This is the Siberia of the Mind.' There is a long and arbitrary list of people that it 'blasts', and a long and arbitrary list of people that it 'blesses', extending even to cricketers: the patrician batsman C. B. Fry is blasted; the honest, industrious, working-class Yorkshire bowler George Hirst is blessed. 'Amateurs', 'Journalists' and 'Art-Pimps' (possibly the first recorded use of the term) are also firmly rejected. *Blast* mocks the 'automobilism' of the Futurists, and their immersion in flux. Vorticism is for 'essential movement' and 'activity' as opposed to the 'fuss and hysterics' of the Futurists; but Cubism isn't the answer, either: Vorticist 'activity' runs counter to the 'tasteful passivity' of Picasso. Wyndham Lewis summed it all up: 'At the heart of the whirlpool is a great silent place where all the energy is concentrated. And there, at the point of concentration, is the Vorticist.'

CHAPTER TWENTY-EIGHT

Pioneers of modernism:
Dealers and Collectors of New Art

The new art that came into being at the beginning of the twentieth century was nurtured by the efforts of a small but energetic band of sympathetic critics, museum directors, collectors, dealers and indeed speculators. A few stand out as the Impresarios of modernism, those who relentlessly advocated, explained and publicised advanced art and ensured, through giving lectures, writing articles in the press and mounting exhibitions, that the word spread – and prices rose. The first rank of these movers and shakers were identified in the Introduction to this book: they included critics and proselytisers such as Apollinaire, Diaghilev, Marinetti and Fry, dealers such as Vollard, Kahnweiler, Cassirer and Walden, and collectors such as the Steins and Sergei Shchukin. Other significant pioneers emerged alongside them: Harry Kessler, Wilhelm von Uhde, Karl Osthaus, Bernhard Koehler, Alfred Flechtheim, Hugo von Tschudi and Georg Swarzenski in Germany, Félix Fénéon, Paul Guillaume, André Level, and Gustave Fayet in France, Ivan Morozov and Nikolai Ryabushinsky in Russia, and Victor Kramar in Czechoslovakia. What motivated them? What is the attraction of revolutionary art – and art was never more revolutionary than in 1905–14 – to its advocates and consumers?

Dealers in New Art

In his promotion of the Impressionists Paul Durand-Ruel had set a template for the successful handling of difficult new art. You had to find young revolutionary artists you believed in. You had to be prepared to support them financially. And you had to be patient: it might be years before you could make profitable sales. It was only now, in the early years of the twentieth century, that the work of the shocking new rebels whom Durand-Ruel had championed since the 1870s was becoming sought after.

A new auction record for Monet was established in 1905 when his *Lavacourt, Soleil et Neige* of 1881 sold in Paris for 27,100 francs. In the 1870s, when Durand-Ruel first began supporting him as an artist, you could buy a Monet landscape for 200 francs. Now all that had changed: Durand-Ruel's clientele – which included Americans, Germans and Japanese – queued up for his work. Monet was still in full production, and for the rest of his long life (he died in 1926) he barely moved from the lily pond that he created in his own garden at Giverny in order to provide the right sort of 'natural' subject matter for his painting. His late work developed Impressionism almost as far as it would go, and in the example illustrated on p. 295, painted in 1907, he concentrates solely on the surface of the water, with its horizontal lilies set against the more vertical reflections of sky and foliage. The intensity of Monet's observation, the freedom of his brush-stroke and the extraordinary sensitivity of his eye creates an almost dreamlike effect. It also propels the composition several steps closer to abstraction. Paris was largely acclimatised to Monet now, and Impressionism was no longer problematic to any but the most conservative art lover. The popular eye needs educating, and familiarising: what had outraged the bourgeoisie a generation earlier was now reasonably acceptable. Just as long as you didn't stand too close.

In Paris a new generation of dealers was now emerging whose aim was to orchestrate a repeat of the Durand-Ruel strategy with the young and as yet undiscovered masters of the early twentieth century. These were men like the morose but far-seeing Ambroise Vollard, the photographer and restauranteur Eugène Druet, and the flexibly principled Clovis Sagot; there was also a lone, heroic lady gallerist, Berthe Weill. Loitering in the

102. Monet, *Waterlilies*, 1907

margins were ambiguous figures like Wilhelm von Uhde, part collector and part merchant. And there were longer-established dealers like Bernheim who were now eyeing contemporary art as an area for development. In 1905 prices were desperately low for the avant-garde, and dealers were not above exploiting the situation. On his return to Paris from a trip to Holland in August, Picasso was once again hard-pressed financially. He asked Clovis Sagot to come to his studio to look at his work. According to Fernande, Sagot's behaviour was unscrupulous even by the standards of the art trade. He made an offer of 700 francs on three works, including a life-size full-length nude *Girl with Basket of Flowers*. Picasso turned it down. Fernande takes up the story:

> After a few days we still desperately needed money, so Pablo decided to go back to Sagot and accept his offer. But Sagot said he had thought it over and that 500 francs was really the most he could give for the three pictures. Pablo was furious and came back to the studio having refused the offer. A few days later they went through the same performance, except that Sagot's offer was now down to 300 francs and Pablo had to accept.[36]

All that can be said in favour of Sagot is that in the dog days of August he was the only dealer left in Paris with the imagination to see that Picasso's work was worth anything at all.

That same month of August, Matisse was immersed in his momentous invention of Fauvism in Collioure. But even in the midst of his excitement, part of Matisse remained wary, conscious of the need to appease the art trade and make some sales. He feared his new style was too outlandish to prove marketable. 'In spite of myself I must consult the views of dealers so as to return to Paris with some saleable merchandise in hand,' he wrote regretfully. This explains the occasional reversion to a Pointillist technique in his paintings of this summer, a retreat for commercial reasons. A man had to feed his family.

At this point Vollard was ahead of a rather limited field, the dealer most likely to risk expenditure on difficult modern art. For those few collectors in search of the work of the avant-garde, his gallery was the place to go. His premises were notoriously disorganised and chaotic, but if you looked you could find works by Cézanne, van Gogh, and Gauguin, plus Matisse, Picasso, Derain and Vlaminck. In February 1907, however, the young German who was to become one of the most important art dealers of the twentieth century arrived in Paris to rival, and indeed overtake, Vollard in his promotion of the most advanced line of modernism. Brought up in Mannheim, Daniel-Henri Kahnweiler had been expected to join the family bank. But he chose to open a modest gallery in the rue Vignon instead, at a rent of 2,400 francs a year. Coming from a financial background, he may have been uneasily aware of the stock market slump that panicked investors through much of the year. But he was not deterred: he deployed the relatively meagre funding that he had begged and borrowed from his family to start buying stock at once for his new venture. His first purchases were from the Salon des Indépendants of that year and included works by Signac, Vlaminck, Derain and Friesz, painters at that intersection of Pointillism and Fauvism which constituted most people's understanding of advanced art that spring.

As a character Kahnweiler was serious to the point of dourness and thick-skinned to the point of armour plating; but what he lacked in sense of humour he made up for with his huge conviction: first, that his mission as an art dealer did not concern dead artists but was 'to fight for the painters of my age', and second, that he had the eye to identify the ones that were going to make it. Kahnweiler understood that, having first spotted the up and coming star, your next move should be to get him under contract to your gallery so that you could reap the benefit of the price rises for his work that you then orchestrated. Vollard, on the other hand, was too much of a curmudgeon to bother with the effort of actually managing living artists on a day-to-day basis.

One of the first painters whom Kahnweiler considered signing up was van Dongen. Dealers liked van Dongen. He thought commercially. But there was something about van Dongen's artistic pragmatism that put Kahnweiler off. Van Dongen claimed, in the words of Assouline, that he could visualise every detail of the painting before he began. This was too calculating for Kahnweiler. As we saw earlier, he preferred the slower, more instinctive method of evolving their work that he found in Picasso and Braque, whom he had met that summer. In 1907 prices were still low for the new modern artists of the twentieth century, but they were about to ease upwards: later in the year Picasso, for instance, would sell a work for 1,000 francs for the first time. In this case it was a transaction made directly from his studio rather than through a dealer. But as Kahnweiler gradually grew closer to Picasso and Braque in the years to come, he wrought a transformation. He increasingly managed their art – and more significantly their prices – coaxing and encouraging them through the unprecedented challenges of inventing Cubism. And he made another important innovation: from early on in his career Kahnweiler understood (like Durand-Ruel and Vollard) the importance of photographing the works he handled. These images were initially deployed as selling tools to tempt the small circle of buyers from abroad that Kahnweiler gathered to him. But later they became invaluable archive material for art historians, proof of authenticity for which succeeding generations of dealers and collectors would become eternally grateful. As the year progressed, Kahnweiler's first important clients materialised, led by Hermann Rupf, a Swiss, and Roger Dutilleul, a Frenchman. The thoughtful Dutilleul described the process of buying modern art from Kahnweiler in quasi-religious terms: he became Kahnweiler's 'disciple'. The artists remained the deities, but Kahnweiler was the high priest.

In 1909, when Matisse decided that his interests were best served by entering into a permanent arrangement with an art dealer, he signed a contract with Bernheim. Gertrude Stein mocked his choice as 'a very middle class' gallery; but what tipped the balance was Félix Fénéon, the deeply eccentric ex-terrorist and former cycling correspondent of *La Revue Blanche*, who now ran Bernheim's contemporary art department with the flair and unpredictability of a lifelong rebel. Anarchism was as good a preparation as any for the challenge of persuading rich patrons to spend their money on avant-garde art. Instead of planting bombs among the bourgeoisie, Fénéon was now planting Matisses. He did it with increasing success.

Modern art dealers varied from the rapacious to the self-sacrificing. We have already seen the act of heroism performed in 1908 by Wilhelm von Uhde, the pioneer collector of modern art who had recently opened his own gallery in Paris. He met Sonia Terk, a young Russian woman painter of avant-garde instincts, and in order to extend the time the authorities would allow her to stay and study in France, he married her. Given that he was not the marrying kind, this represented an initiative of some nobility, a *beau-idéal* of the lengths to which the dealer/collector should be prepared to go in order to smooth the artist's path and facilitate art. He even introduced her to Robert Delaunay, for whom she left von Uhde in 1909. There was a sigh of relief all round.

Young artists who tried to manage their own affairs and act as their own dealers tended to flounder. Modigliani, for instance, had only a hazy sense of financial matters at the best of times. After the unexpected sale of a painting, he and Vlaminck took the cash and went on a three-day drinking spree. What money they didn't drink they folded into paper aeroplanes and sent gliding into the trees along Boulevard Raspail. Thus even by 1911 Modigliani's prices were still very modest indeed. Edward Roworth, a South African artist in Paris, bought one of Modigliani's magnificent carved heads that year and paid just 100 francs for it. An oil painting would go for as little as 60 francs. The drawings that Modigliani notoriously exchanged in the bars of Montparnasse in payment for his drinks bills had a value of 5 francs, sometimes even less depending on the urgency of his need for a drink and the tight-fistedness of the bar owner.

Modigliani's prices only began to rise when he was taken up by the young Parisian dealer, Paul Guillaume, in 1912–13.

In Germany there were a growing number of dealers and commercial galleries handling advanced art. Paul Cassirer was the leader of the pack. His sympathies were Parisian, and he mounted influential exhibitions of the great French post-Impressionists at his gallery in Berlin. Early on he established close relations with the leading French dealers who supplied him; he in turn would ship on the exhibitions he mounted in Berlin to other dealers sympathetic to modernism across the German-speaking world, including Cometer in Hamburg, Galerie Arnold in Dresden and Miethke in Vienna. In his manipulative hands, prices for works by van Gogh in particular were persuaded ever upwards. At the beginning of 1905, Cassirer was buying from the van Gogh family at about 1,500 marks per canvas, and aiming to sell on at prices between 2,000 and 3,000 marks. That year, Cassirer sold twenty works by van Gogh, almost all of them to German buyers. By 1908 van Gogh prices had just about tripled. Cassirer that year sold *Roses* and *Vase of Irises* to the bankers Robert von Mendelssohn and Fritz Oppenheim respectively for 9,000 marks each. By 1913 Cassirer's missionary work had borne fruit across Europe, and the young Paris-based German art dealer Alfred Flechtheim, a natural entrepreneur and showman, now managed to sell a van Gogh to the Dusseldorf Museum for 40,000 marks. The brand was most emphatically established.

Cassirer's antennae continued to tune themselves most acutely to developments in Paris, and he gave Matisse his first exhibition in Germany in 1909. Other Berlin dealers were emerging to challenge Cassirer, however, dealers more focused on the new German art. The Galerie Fritz Gurlitt gave early exhibiting opportunities to Die Brücke and were particularly supportive of Max Pechstein. But the most go-ahead dealer in Berlin was Herwarth Walden, whose Der Sturm Gallery was highly cutting edge. When Italian Futurism hit Berlin in 1912, it was a sign of the natural sympathies of the respective proprietors that the exhibition was shown at Der Sturm, not Cassirer.

In Munich the leading modernist dealer was Thannhauser, in whose gallery the artists of the Blaue Reiter found exhibition space. But Thannhauser was a cautious operator. He lent his premises for a Futurist exhibition, but put up a notice absolving the gallery from responsibility for its contents. Here was the dilemma for the dealer in difficult modern art: go too far and you alienate your consumer base. It was the same dilemma that had worried Matisse in Collioure in 1905, further up the supply chain: go too far, and no dealer will touch your work.

By 1912, goods wagons packed with modernist paintings were now criss-crossing the railway systems of Europe in ever increasing numbers, as if in rehearsal for the movement of troops. Led by the mammoth Sondebund in Cologne, international exhibitions proliferated, mounted in different cities across the continent by pioneering dealers, go-ahead critics and groups of revolutionary artists. To what end? To break new boundaries, to shock, to educate, to make nationalistic points, to change society; but most importantly, to open up new markets. Dealers found that the internationalisation of modernism was good for sales. Germans were certainly buying avant-garde French art, as were some Russians, Eastern Europeans and Scandinavians. What was harder to orchestrate was foreign buying of German or Russian advanced art, or Italian or Spanish buying of any sort of foreign modernism. Except for the odd isolated Englishman like Michael Sadleir, who had acquired his minor Kandinsky at the Allied Artists Exhibition, there was not yet much activity in London, either. But with the help of the railway system, heroic attempts were being made to get new art in front of new eyes. And the opportunities created for the expression of local outrage at foreign artistic excess sold a few newspapers too.

The increasing internationalisation of advanced art, plus his own desire to stay in control of what he saw as true Cubism, now persuaded Kahnweiler to get his own favoured artists under contract to himself. Braque was the first to sign up, in an agreement dated 30 November 1912. His prices were established at 60 to 400

103. Picasso, *Portrait of Kahnweiler*, 1910

francs per painting, according to size. Derain was recruited on 6 December, and the same month Kahnweiler finally reeled in his star catch, Picasso. His work was to be priced dramatically higher than the other two, at 250 to 3,000 francs for paintings. This was when Picasso inserted the significant proviso that it should be up to him (not Kahnweiler) to judge when a painting was finished. In February 1913, Gris – who had made huge strides as a Cubist – would sign up to the Kahnweiler stable, to be followed by Léger in October that year. At that point the dealer felt he had assembled his dream team and secured his own position on the right side of history. All would have been well if it hadn't been for the First World War.

Kahnweiler spent 1913 spreading the fame of his gallery artists far and wide by means of loans of their work not just across Europe but even to the other side of the Atlantic. There was particular focus on Picasso. In February Kahnweiler lent most of the 114 paintings and works on paper that comprised a major retrospective of the artist's work held by Thannhauser in Munich. It was well attended but did not yet result in a cascade of sales. Undeterred, Kahnweiler intensified his efforts. He had never before been so active in foreign markets as in early 1913: besides Munich, galleries in Cologne, Moscow, Prague, Berlin, Dusseldorf, Dresden, Frankfurt and New York were all recipients of loans of works by Kahnweiler artists.

Herwarth Walden was also particularly busy in 1913. In September he opened the first German Autumn Salon at his Der Sturm Gallery in Berlin, in emulation of the Salon d'Automne in Paris. Walden travelled with huge speed and energy round the European capitals that summer, from Budapest to Paris, and assembled 366 paintings and sculptures by ninety artists from twelve countries. He was aided and abetted by Marc and Macke, who corralled the international avant-garde. Lectures were given by the inevitable Marinetti and Apollinaire. The September edition of the *Der Sturm* magazine pumped up the excitement, carrying an article by Blaise Cendrars, the Belgian poet, which was in itself a bit of a manifesto. He wrote, 'I love legends, dialects, grammatical errors, detective novels, the flesh of whores, the sun, the Eiffel Tower, Apaches …'. Exhibitors included Archipenko, Delaunay, Léger, Severini, Carra, Boccioni, Jawlensky, Münter, Klee, Chagall, Kandinsky, Marc, Macke and Picabia. The *Hamburger Nachrichten* called it 'The art gallery of a lunatic asylum'. Kokoschka, writing to Walden in 1913, had totally bought into Walden's self-professed image as an idealist, not a merchant. 'Let the dealers peddle in pictures, you are too great-spirited and out of the ordinary for that', he told him. It was just as well that Bernhard Koehler, Macke's uncle by marriage, had agreed to underwrite the exhibition, because despite its glittering cast list of modernist exhibitors it made a thumping loss.

What were the modernist art dealers of 1905–14 actually selling? What was their sales pitch to prospective buyers? For some the emphasis was on opportunities for speculation: look at what happened to the Impressionists – now here's the latest artistic gravy train, and here's your chance to board it early. But at the other extreme they were offering participation in a glorious new art unlike anything that had gone before, the chance to link your wagon to the future before anyone else. You too could become a superman, by binding yourself to an art that had advanced as far beyond its traditional limitations as technology had advanced in the twentieth century. Here was the artistic equivalent of the aeroplane, the racing car; and of the nervous breakdown.

Collectors of New Art

'I put down my colours without a preconceived plan. I discovered the quality of colours in a purely instinctive way.' This was Matisse's account of how he painted the revolutionary *Woman with a Hat* (see p. 6) in 1905. And here is the reaction to the painting of its buyer, Leo Stein, when he first stood in front of it: 'It was a tremendous effort on his [Matisse's] part, a thing brilliant and powerful, but the nastiest smear of paint I had ever seen. It was what I was unknowingly waiting for.' Perhaps recognising suddenly something you have been unknowingly waiting for is the crucial element in the process of a contemporary collector acquiring art at the cutting edge. Leo and his sister Gertrude decided to buy it. 'It was very strange in its colour and in its anatomy,' Gertrude says. 'People were roaring with laughter at the picture and scratching at it ... but this picture by Matisse seemed perfectly natural and [I] could not understand why it infuriated everybody.' Instinct, when it is revealed to you, can be shocking, like a nasty smear of paint. But it is a revelation which answers a need in you that you weren't aware of until it hit you in the face. In order to appreciate the new art, you had to be in touch with your own instincts, like the artist who created it.

Leo and Gertrude Stein had recently arrived in Paris. They were indeed in touch with their own instincts. They were eccentrics, and wore regrettable sandals: Gertrude's apparently had 'toes like the prow of a gondola'. But they were committed to modern art. In 1904 they had bought a Cézanne, which was a firm statement of modernist intent. Now they decided to buy *Woman in a Hat*. What neither Leo nor Gertrude had reckoned with, however, was the inflexibility of Madame Matisse when it came to negotiating the sale. The Steins offered 300 francs for *Woman in a Hat*. The price set by Matisse was 500 francs. Despite the fact that they were totally broke, and this was the only painting by her husband either in the Salon d'Automne or anywhere else in Paris in which anyone was showing any interest, Amélie Matisse held out for the full asking price. 'As for me, I'm in my element when the house burns down,' she once observed. She was made of the right material for the wife of a struggling artist. The Steins paid the full 500 francs. Sometimes this sort of intransigence over the price of a work of new art acts as a validation of its importance. Had the Matisses been prepared to go down, the picture might have struck the Steins as less desirable. They could afford it, just. They were not millionaires, but they had about $150 (750 francs) available each month to spend on books and pictures, which made them powerful (and often solitary) players in the market for advanced contemporary art. Later Gertrude explained to Ernest Hemingway how they maximised the financial resources available to them: 'You can either buy clothes or buy pictures,' she said. 'It's that simple. No one who is not very rich can do both.' The Steins' notably ungainly style of dress is testament to this prioritisation.

John Richardson sees Leo as the driving force early on: 'Between 1905 and 1907 Leo Stein was unquestionably the most adventurous and discerning collector of twentieth-century painting in the world.' In late October, soon after his audacious purchase of Matisse's *Woman in a Hat*, Leo went to Sagot and bought Picasso's *Harlequin Family with an Ape*. Gertrude wasn't sure she liked the ape. A few days after that, Leo and Gertrude returned to Sagot to look at *Girl with Basket of Flowers*, the full-length nude that was one of the paintings bought by the dealer from Picasso that summer at such a shamefully low price. Gertrude said she liked the top part of the picture, but not the legs. Sagot, ever inventive, suggested chopping off the bits of canvas that displeased her, which is an early example of the art trade striving to enhance the client experience. In the end the Steins took the canvas intact. And gradually Gertrude was won over to Picasso. That autumn he began painting her portrait. Gertrude claims that she sat ninety times. Certainly, sittings continued through the depth of winter, and still the work remained unfinished. Picasso was fascinated by this cumbersome, eccentric, serious-minded and strong-willed woman whose ambition – thankfully only fitfully fulfilled – was to write dense and very long experimental novels.

Who else, apart from the Steins, was buying truly avant-garde art in late 1905? One of the few was Wilhelm von Uhde, the rich young aesthete, who flitted between Parisian studios and galleries making occasional daring purchases. It is significant that he was from Germany, where there was a growing number of advanced collectors already buying French post-Impressionism: Karl Osthaus, for instance, in Hagen, still in his thirties, was forming a major collection of modern French art, as were Oscar Schmitz, Carl Sternheim and Paul Mendelsohn-Bartholdy in Berlin. Generally these early collectors were liberal, cosmopolitan intellectuals. But at this point, while they might buy van Gogh or Gauguin, they were not yet ready for Picasso or Matisse.

Osthaus also bought German modern art. His name was included in the forty-eight subscribers who, in return for a small annual fee, were regularly supplied with woodcuts and other prints by the artists of Die Brücke. Nolde paid tribute to three particular patrons at this stage:

> The early first true friends of my art were Hans Fehr, Karl
> Ernst Osthaus and Gustav Schiefler. These friendships filled
> Ada and me with pride that these strong, dear people held
> my art in such high esteem, and their friendship accom-
> panied us throughout our lives. During the early, grey times
> their letters and visits had a warming effect on us just like
> rays of sunshine.[37]

Osthaus was exceptionally rich, but the other two were professional men without huge resources. Hans Fehr, a professor of
law, was an early supporter of German Expressionism in general
and Nolde in particular, and for a time, besides buying his work,
also sent him 50 marks a month to keep him going. Fehr shared
with Nolde a keen interest in folklore and – in Nolde's words –
'all things primal'. He later also saved Kirchner's life by rescuing
him in 1915 from the military service to which he was deeply
unsuited. Schiefler, too, was a lawyer, based in Hamburg, and an
early collector of Munch. All these German collectors of modernism were serious, earnest and convinced that their country
was in need of a redemption by modern art.

In the Salon des Indépendants of 1906, Matisse's most controversial exhibit was *Le Bonheur de Vivre*. It found an admirer in the
rich Russian textile merchant, Sergei Shchukin, who happened
to be in Paris on business, but he was not yet ready to buy something so advanced. Once again it was Leo Stein who stepped
up. He took it home with him when the exhibition closed on
30 April. Having established that it would hang happily in the
context of the rest of his collection, he bought it. Initially he
hadn't liked it. It had taken him the full run of the exhibition to
get its point. It is fascinating the way that new and revolutionary
art can take its time fully to impinge even on those most geared
to understanding it.

Picasso had put on hold the continuing struggle to get
his portrait of Gertrude Stein right. He had tried everything,
including taking up boxing, so in the spring he painted out the
face and left it for the time being. A resentment, fuelled by the

104. Photo of the Steins' apartment with Picasso's *Girl with Basket of Flowers* (left) and his portrait of Gertrude (centre of image)

frustrations of the portrait and perhaps by Leo Stein's decision to buy Matisse's *Le Bonheur de Vivre*, turned him temporarily against the Steins. He decided they were ridiculous. And they weren't sexy. His jaundiced verdict on them was, 'Ils sont pas des hommes, ils sont pas des femmes. Ils sont americains'. Of course once they started buying his pictures again, he forgot his reservations.

Michael and Sarah Stein, Leo's brother and sister-in-law, were in Paris too, and were particularly drawn to Matisse. Sarah became especially close to him and began collecting his work. Indeed she was Matisse's chief supporter as he moved into his phase of large figure subjects from 1906 onwards. In the web of connections between expatriate art-loving Americans at large in Europe, one of the more interesting is that between Sarah and Bernard Berenson. A few years earlier Berenson had actually been persuaded to buy a Matisse, a pre-Fauve landscape. But in 1907, urged by Sarah to admire the *Blue Nude, Memories of*

Biskra, his modernist sympathies hit the buffers. 'If you can ever convince me of any beauty in that toad,' he told her, 'I'll believe in Matisse.' For Berenson, this was the jump too far.

In autumn 1906 Matisse arrived back in Paris after his summer in southern climes to find that his stock was rising. There was gratifying competition for his work not just between the two dealers Vollard and Druet, but also among private collectors. The Steins (Leo, and Michael and Sarah) were joined by the French collector Gustave Fayet as owners of Matisses. It was a very busy summer for Fayet: his first passion had been for Gauguin, but he was one of those buyers at the cutting edge of art who was always prepared to move on, to sell an old obsession (if the price was right) in order to finance a new one. So this year he got rid of his Gauguins at a considerable profit and replaced them with Matisses, several of which he bought via Druet off the walls of the Salon d'Automne. This was the same Salon d'Automne where Fayet had helped organise the splendid retrospective of Gauguin's work that opened the eyes of artistic Paris still further to that mixture of colour and Primitivism which Gauguin so thrillingly represented. Fayet was a step ahead of the game.

Who bought Fayet's Gauguins? The major purchaser (he took eleven) was Sergei Shchukin, who by the late summer had become a competitive player in the nascent market for more advanced contemporary art. There was no holding Shchukin when he got an idea in his head, and for a while Gauguin dominated everything. In November Shchukin bought three further works by the artist, for one of which (*On l'appelle Vairamuti*) he paid 25,000 francs. These were canvases that Vollard had been buying for 250 francs each a few years earlier. It is an early instance of a now familiar story: how a major retrospective can inflate the prices of an artist's work.

Sergei Shchukin was the merchant prince par excellence in a golden age of Russian mercantile risk and reward. At the same time as American captains of industry were amassing wealth beyond dreams – the late nineteenth and early twentieth centuries – so Shchukin, and his friend and fellow collector Ivan Morozov, were making fortunes in Moscow on a similar scale to those of Frick, Huntingdon, J. P. Morgan and Widener. 'I never encountered anything to equal the lavishness of the Russian merchant', wrote Feodor Chaliapin. 'I do not believe that Europeans could have any idea of its scale.' In the years leading up to the First World War Shchukin decided to deploy that lavishness in acquiring the most cutting-edge avant-garde art in Paris with which to decorate his opulent Moscow palace. Unlike their American equivalents, who splashed huge sums on the great masters of the past, Shchukin, and to a lesser extent Morozov, were buying the work of unproven young men like Matisse and Picasso. So it was not so much a financial lavishness as a lavishness of daring, of confidence in his own judgement of the new, something that his American equivalents were conspicuously lacking.

Shchukin's first foray into modern art had involved the Impressionists. Between 1899 and 1904, buying largely from Durand-Ruel in Paris, he put together a collection including works by Pissarro, Renoir and Degas, as well as eleven Monets. And then came a pause. In 1905, Shchukin bought nothing. He was distracted by events in his home country. In Russia the year 1905 was book-ended by political upheaval and violence on the streets: Sunday 9 January saw the Winter Palace massacre in St Petersburg when the army opened fire on unarmed striking workers. In May Ivan Morozov's liberal-thinking cousin Savva shot himself. Then in the Moscow uprising in December there was more bloodshed. In between, Shchukin took advantage of the situation to corner the textile market, to his considerable financial advantage. But in December in Moscow, his moody seventeen-year-old son Sergei Sergeivich went missing. It was not till March 1906 that his son's body was pulled from the Moskva river. The boy's apparent suicide was the first of a succession of family tragedies that scarred the great collector's life. One of the unanswered questions about Shchukin is what influence these tragedies had on his collecting. Did he turn to buying contemporary art as an escape from his horrors, or as an expiation of them? Within a month of his son's death, Shchukin was in Paris, being powerfully moved by *Le Bonheur de Vivre,* which he saw at the Salon des Indépendants. He was too late to buy it, but he sought out Matisse in his studio and acquired three works on paper from him.

Then in January 1907 Shchukin's wife died. This blow put another temporary stop to his modernist collecting. But Ivan Morozov did buy in a major way in Paris this year: he appeared at the sale of the pictures of Georges Viau – one of the great early French collections of Impressionism – and carried off Renoir's *Under the Arbour at the Moulin de la Galette* of 1875 for 25,000 francs. While Morozov was still Impressionist-orientated, Shchukin was moving on, although for the time being his absence from the market left the field clear for the Steins. Matisse showed *Le Luxe* at the Salon d'Automne, where it baffled and outraged; critics had problems with its lack of finish. Sarah and Michael Stein acquired it but took it on loan first. The fact that they didn't buy it immediately may have been simply a matter of lack of cash. But it may have been another instance of the way that even for the most advanced collectors, some novelties could not immediately be stomached. Time was needed to live with and assimilate before committing.

The year 1908 started badly for Shchukin with yet another violent death in his family: the suicide, on New Year's Day, of his brother Ivan. Ivan was a collector of old masters, an intellectual, an aesthete, a bit of a poser and a spender rather than a maker of money. He lived permanently and extravagantly in Paris, and – confronted with an ever-growing pile of unpayable bills – retreated to his study and shot himself. Having weathered his latest personal tragedy Shchukin emerged again in the spring to buy modern art with redoubled vigour. For the time being it was Gauguin who continued to obsess Shchukin. He was now consumed with a passion for the climactic Tahitian period of the artist, and conceived the idea of a whole wall of exploding south seas colours for his Moscow mansion. So, in the course of the next twelve months, ten more Gauguins were acquired, crowned by the purchase of Gustave Fayet's prize example, *La Femme du Roi*. 'I didn't want to sell it,' recounted Fayet afterwards. He turned down 15,000 francs for it. Then Shchukin, who had by now learned the lesson that if you could afford the best, money was a secondary consideration, offered him 30,000. Fayet couldn't refuse. It was Shchukin at his most determined and irresistible; he was now the possessor of probably the best Gauguin collection in the world. And Gauguin prices had been moved up to a new level. Leonid Pasternak recounts how Shchukin showed him the Gauguin *La Femme du Roi* soon after he had borne it back in triumph to Moscow. Shchukin, who never quite conquered a childhood stutter, told Pasternak wryly: 'A m-madman painted it, and another m-madman bought it.' True enough: Shchukin has identified an important link between the painter and the collector of modern art. Their seeming shared madness is actually their mutual communication at an instinctive level.

But even as the marvellous assemblage of Gauguins reached completion, Shchukin was already thinking ahead. His taste was moving forward. In Paris he was introduced to the Steins, and saw the extraordinary collections of both branches of this eccentric family, that of Gertrude and Leo, and that of Michael and Sarah. The impact of the experience must have been considerable. Nowhere else in Europe was it possible to view so many major avant-garde Picassos and Matisses in the same room. It must have been overwhelming to someone like Shchukin, who now commissioned Matisse – for 4,000 francs – to paint a *Harmonie en Bleu*, which turned into a *Harmonie en Rouge* and was exhibited at the Salon d'Automne in 1908 before Shchukin actually took possession of it. What seems to have caught Shchukin's imagination was that it originated – in its blue form – from a piece of fabric that Matisse kept in his studio as a colour stimulus: the artist was speaking to the textile entrepreneur. Shchukin's exceptional eye for modern art was based on an extraordinary sensitivity to colour, a sensitivity deployed in parallel on the fabrics that he often chose personally for his highly successful family business. Since the early twentieth century there have been submarine currents running between those who make money in textiles, the fashion world and the seething waters of contemporary art. Shchukin was one of the first to stand in the tide of these connections.

That autumn, Matisse took Shchukin to Picasso's studio for the first time. Neither Picasso nor Fernande were particularly impressed by him. Fernande remembered 'a small, wan figure with a heavyset, hoggish head and a terrible stutter. He found it very difficult to make himself understood, which made him ill at ease.' Although Shchukin bought nothing immediately from Picasso, a seed had been sown. In the next six years Shchukin would become his prime patron, assembling an unmatched collection of his Cubist works.

In January 1909, however, his focus was trained entirely on Matisse. He now had fifteen Matisses and that month he bought another, the *Nymph and Satyr*. But he was dreaming of even bigger things, which he discussed with Matisse over lunch at Larue on the Place de la Madeleine. His friendly rival Morozov was taking delivery of seven large panels by the Nabi painter Maurice Denis on the theme of the story of Psyche for his Moscow house. They had been exhibited at the Salon d'Automne three months earlier. Shchukin said that they were too decorative (and, by implication, insipid) for his taste. Would Matisse consider producing a counter-blast, a volley of the cannon to scatter the starlings once and for all? Shchukin rhapsodised about the *Harmonie en Rouge*: 'That's what a museum of modern art should be all about,' he said, formulating in words for the first time his own ambitions. 'We have a once-in-a-lifetime opportunity to do something.' One piece of news that would have reassured Shchukin was that Hugo von Tschudi – free of the stifling atmosphere of the Berlin museum world – had commissioned a still life from Matisse on the same scale as *Harmonie en Rouge* for his own private collection in Munich. So Shchukin asked Matisse to paint what turned into *Dance* and *Music*, the greatest works of the artist's career.

For the next year and a half, the project involved most of Matisse's time and energy.

In November 1909 Shchukin took the decision to open his collection to the Russian public, which created an important point of access to modernist French art for Russian artists. But not everyone in Moscow was attuned to what they saw. The reaction was a mixture of enchantment, bafflement and downright fury. This year one visitor was rendered indignant enough by the sight of a Monet landscape to attack it with a pencil. While a pencil seems a curiously inadequate weapon to choose with which to do damage, it was a symbolic – and perhaps peculiarly Russian – expression of neurosis about the new. Scherbatov remembers how, when Shchukin opened his house to the public, 'Youths stood with mouths agape before the canvases of artists of the most extreme tendencies, like eskimos listening to a gramophone.'

In Moscow, just three days into 1910, another of Shchukin's sons committed suicide. It was the fourth time in five years that his new year had been marked by an appalling bereavement, and the third time that someone very close to him had taken their own life. January was the cruellest month, particularly in Russia, which was anyway widely acknowledged as the home of neurasthenia. Only Vienna rivalled Moscow as the European capital of suicide. The death by his own hand of a second Shchukin son prompted unkind critics in Russia to suggest that the frequency with which the Shchukins took their own lives was connected to Sergei's love of decadent French painting. Did his family go mad and shoot themselves because of the modernist pictures in the house, or were the large number of modernist pictures in the house there because its occupants were mad and thus liable to shoot themselves? Cause or symptom, modern art was dangerous to the health.

Or could it be that modern art was actually Shchukin's salvation? That spring in Moscow, as a distraction from his family tragedies, he thought obsessively about the decorations he was commissioning. Early in the month Matisse sent him sketches for what he called 'Composition 1' (on the theme of dance) and 'Composition 2' (on the theme of music). Shchukin agonised over them for a new reason. He explained in a letter of 16 March why he felt he couldn't go forward on the scale originally envisaged: 'After the death of one of my relatives I took into my house three young girls (of 8, 9, and 10 years of age), and here in Russia (remember we Russians have one foot in the Orient) one cannot show pictures of nudes in the sight of young girls.' After more painful deliberation, Shchukin sent a letter on 27 March to ask Matisse for a smaller version of *Dance*, not for the staircase, but to go in his bedroom. He'd pay the same price, he said. But the same evening the final sketch for *Dance* arrived in Moscow, and Shchukin was bowled over by it. Next day he sent a telegram to Matisse saying disregard my letter. Go for it as originally planned. He explained in a further letter of 31 March: 'I find your panel of *Dance* to be of such nobility that I have resolved to defy Russian bourgeois opinion and install a painting with naked figures in my main staircase.' Nobility is an interesting word for Shchukin to use of *Dance*; he was looking for something that would trump the nudity, a moral detergent to wash it clean, even for young girls.

So the commission proceeded as first conceived. Shchukin was determined to reject the theory that his collecting of French modern art had anything to do with the prevalence of suicide in his family. But in May, just to cover all angles, he made a substantial donation to psychiatric research.

Dance and *Music* were first exhibited at the Salon d'Automne in 1910. Public and critical reaction was predictably hostile. Shchukin arrived in Paris on 1 November 1910 and was immediately made aware of the controversy that the paintings he had commissioned were generating. At this point his resolve wavered: could it be that the cruel voices in Moscow were right, and the acquisition of such revolutionary objects would precipitate more disasters in his personal life? He veered towards the idea of cancelling the project and installing a large work by Puvis de Chavannes on his stairs instead. The Bernheim

105. *Dance* hanging in Shchukin's palace

brothers, eager only to do a deal, encouraged him to take the safer option of the Puvis, with which they could also supply him. History does not relate what position Fénéon took in this moment of crisis, but presumably, in view of his rapport with Matisse, his was a lone voice urging Shchukin to stick to his original scheme.

On 8 November Shchukin set off back to Russia. The train journey from Paris to Moscow took three days, ample time for tortured reflection. The passing telegraph poles changed his mind again and stiffened his resolve. He would take *Dance* and *Music* after all, of course he would. He sent a telegram to Matisse from Warsaw station to say he was ashamed of his 'weakness and cowardice'. So the panels arrived in Moscow and were installed on 4 December. Shchukin was pleased with them, but still nervous of their impact in one respect. On 5 January 1911 he himself surreptitiously retouched with gouache a detail on one of the dancers, so as to diminish the prominence of their private parts.

Shchukin's assimilation of a work of advanced art always involved a process of ordeal. According to Matisse, Shchukin told him: 'I buy it [the picture], but I'll have to keep it at home for several days, and if I can bear it and keep interested in it, I'll keep it.' Elsewhere he elaborated further: 'You have to live with a picture for at least a year to understand it fully. Very often the first time you see a picture you don't like it, but even so you find yourself going back to see it again and again. And eventually it opens up to you.' There are echoes of Leo Stein's experience here. And of Rilke, grappling with Cézanne for the first time in 1907: 'The puzzlement and insecurity of one's own first confrontation ... And then for a long time nothing and suddenly one has the right eyes.'

So *Dance* and *Music* grew on Shchukin over the year. On 5 January 1911 (the same day that he surreptitiously overpainted the private parts of one of the figures in *Dance*) he wrote to Matisse: 'I am beginning to contemplate *Dance* with genuine pleasure. As to *Music*, the same thing will happen in time.' Ten months later, in October, he was telling friends, 'Look at the colours! The panels illuminate the entire staircase ... don't view them as pictures. Look at them as you would porcelain dishes, or ceramic tiles, with painted marks that delight the eye. Come on! Isn't it marvellous? Isn't it magnificent? What subtlety in the association of colours ... what taste, what consummate daring.'

At the same time as the Matisse drama, Shchukin's thoughts were beginning to encompass Picasso. Intriguingly, it was Kandinsky – according to Kandinsky – who helped push him in this direction. On 21 November 1910 Kandinsky wrote to Gabriele Münter from Moscow:

I was in the Shchukin gallery yesterday for nearly two hours. There were other people there as well. The gallery is capital: Monet, Pissaro, Renfrelli [sic], Degas etc., big selection of Gauguin, a few good van Goghs, marvellous Cézannes & finally a lot of Matisses, even very recent ones. I spoke a bit & all right. I also convinced Sh. that he *must* buy some of the very latest Picassos, which he was reluctant to do. He thought it over & said very kindly, 'You are right.'[38]

Shchukin had visited the artist's studio and already owned at least one Picasso, *Portrait of a Lady with a Fan*; but he was not yet committed to the artist in the way that he was to Matisse, and had not yet bought anything totally Cubist. Kandinsky's fervent recommendation of Picasso must have resulted from the second exhibition, in Munich in September, of the Neue Kunstler Vereinigung, with its impressive representation of new art from Paris including several Picassos. So Kandinsky arrived in Moscow with the memory of Picasso fresh in his mind. His enthusiasm had its effect on Shchukin, who reacted typically: initially reluctant, and then – after reflection – persuaded.

It is impossible to be precise about when Shchukin bought his first challenging Picasso, but it must have been about now, in late 1910 or early 1911. He afterwards recounted how he hung it at home, in a dark passage that he walked through on his way to the dining room.

After about a month I found that if I didn't look at it I felt something was lacking when I sat down to lunch. After that I started to look more closely and for longer; at first it felt like stuffing pieces of broken glass into my mouth. Then I started going at other times and not just on my way through. The day came when I was vanquished.[39]

It's an even more extreme version of the process already described by Leo Stein in connection with Matisse's 'distorted drawing', which acts like vinegar or lemon on the palate: sour at first, but once you're used to them they enhance your pleasure. So the even more jagged dissonance of Cubism was initially like eating broken glass; but in time that too developed its piquancy.

You started missing it when you didn't get it. In fact conventional painting became impossibly anodyne by comparison.

Shchukin continued to build his Picasso collection: in the spring, he bought *Composition with Skull* for 10,000 francs from Kahnweiler. Skulls being emblematic of the brevity of human life, the subject matter may have touched a chord in the Russian's sorely tried soul. Kandinsky, arriving in Moscow in November, was peeved. He had urged Shchukin to buy Picasso twelve months earlier, it was true, but what about a few Kandinskys? Why wasn't Shchukin buying his work, he complained in a letter back to Münter, when it was 'just as good as Matisse's panels'? It's an interesting question: perhaps in the end Kandinsky was just too Russian for Shchukin, too spiritual. It was the relative sensuality of the Parisians Matisse and Picasso that appealed to the textile magnate. And the family man who had experienced the recent suicides of two of his sons perhaps felt safer with the underlying structure of Picasso – and indeed Matisse – than with the volatility of Kandinsky. So Shchukin also continued to buy Matisse in a big way in 1912. He came to Paris in July and acquired five of the paintings that Matisse had recently finished, inspired by a winter visit to Tangier.

But Shchukin did not have a monopoly on Picasso and Matisse. New collectors were emerging from elsewhere in Europe. For instance, the Czech art historian Vincenz Kramar became a Kahnweiler disciple, and began buying Picasso in 1910. He was a serious scholar, and after the First World War he would become director of the National Galleries in Prague. Now, alerted by Kahnweiler that there were new works by Picasso in the gallery, he would take the first train from Prague to Paris to see them. He provided an additional line of communication between Czech Cubists and the latest developments in Paris; and similarly he also brought photographs of works by avant-garde Czech artists to show to Kahnweiler. Like three other eminent art historians of the time who had modernist sympathies – von Tschudi, Swarzenski and Worringer – Kramar had initially been a specialist in Gothic art. The connection first articulated by Worringer between Gothic art and the urge to abstraction must have rung bells for them all, as did Worringer's thesis that the Gothic answers a specific need in humanity, one which expresses man's insecurity and alienation and addresses his spiritual anguish. As an analysis of the appeal of the modern art of the early twentieth century, Worringer's definition of the Gothic was remarkably relevant.

Meanwhile, what of the Steins? On 13 February 1912 Boccioni and Severini took advantage of their presence in Paris for the Italian Futurist Exhibition at Bernheim to visit Leo at Rue de Fleurus. They found him, stripped to the waist, furiously exercising on a rowing machine. Boccioni was trying so hard not to laugh that the artists had to leave. Perhaps this was the moment when Leo abrogated his position as a serious patron of the avant-garde. The sad reality was that by now Leo and Gertrude were breaking up. The increasing closeness of his sister's relationship with Alice B. Toklas was making Leo uneasy. The publication the previous year of her impenetrable 925-page novel *The Making of Americans* had not mustered in him any great enthusiasm, either. He sought refuge in his rowing machine and in Renoir, to whose rosy carnality he found himself increasingly attracted. Gertrude, meanwhile, was not giving up on Picasso. She made her first independent purchase of a work by him, the *Architect's Table*. She initially saw the picture – a transitional work between analytic and synthetic Cubism – on a visit to the studio in February. As the artist was out she left her card, which Picasso then craftily incorporated into the lower right-hand side of the design. Now that the work literally had her name on it, Gertrude decided she must have it. But Picasso wavered regretfully, saying that Kahnweiler had told him that Kramar was interested. So he got the full asking price out of her. It was an insight into Picasso's growing confidence not just in the rising value of his art but also his own ability to sell it.

What Leo and Gertrude Stein had to negotiate in 1913 was thus a kind of divorce. They exchanged curt and hurt notes about the dispersal of the art they had assembled together. Sales ensued. The final agreement was that Leo would keep all the Renoirs and Matisses, and Gertrude would have most of the Picassos. As for the remaining Cézannes, they would split them. They nearly came to blows over a little Cézanne still life of apples, however. Leo won it, describing the victory, a shade provocatively, as 'an act of God'. In compensation Picasso painted Gertrude a substitute Cézanne, an extraordinarily naturalistic study of an apple. Three major Picassos – *Young Acrobat on A Ball* (1905), *Nu à la draperie* (1907) and *Three Women* (1908) – were earmarked for sale, and in October the ever-obliging Kahnweiler gave the Steins 20,000 francs for them, plus a recent Picasso *Man with Guitar*. Kahnweiler didn't hang around. He quickly sold *Young Acrobat* to Morozov for 16,000 francs, and the other two to Shchukin at levels which probably doubled their cost prices. In April 1914 Leo, leaving Paris to live near Florence, offered a rueful assessment of the situation. He described himself as 'a simple-minded person of the "Old School" without a single Picasso, hardly any Matisses, only two Cézanne paintings and some aquarelles, & 16 Renoirs. Rather an amusing baggage for a leader in the great modern fight.' The truth was that from 1908 onwards Leo had become increasingly disenchanted with Picasso; he now couldn't see the point of what he was doing, which he described as 'cubico-futuristic tommy-rotting'.

Morozov, meanwhile, was burning on a slower fuse than Shchukin. He remained enchanted by Impressionism for much longer. In 1910, the year Shchukin took delivery of *Dance* and *Music*, the most expensive picture that Morozov acquired was a Renoir *Young Woman with Fan* (1881), for which he paid 25,000 francs. In 1913 Morozov showed the two sides of his collecting persona in his purchases at Vollard. The less adventurous, more decorative instinct was evident in the 42,000 francs he splashed out to buy Renoir's *Child with Whip*. But he also bought a Picasso, and got himself a bargain. He paid just 3,000 francs for Picasso's portrait of Vollard. Why did Vollard let it go? Perhaps because he never really understood Cubism, and lacked confidence in the durability of its market. A sale was a sale, after all, even when the painting was a portrait of yourself. Later in life Marguerite Matisse, the artist's daughter, gave her recollection of the difference between Shchukin and Morozov. Morozov, she said, was forceful ('plein de force'), while Shchukin was more acute ('plus aigu'). In the end, Shchukin had the greater confidence in his own judgement: when Morozov went to Vollard he would say, 'I want to see a very beautiful Cézanne'; but when Shchukin called he would ask to see all the Cézannes available and make his own choice.

Shchukin continued to buy the latest Matisse and Picasso voraciously. Indeed in the three years leading up to the outbreak of the First World War, Shchukin bought an average of ten Picassos a year. He was now something of a legend as a collector of the avant-garde, and his fame had spread internationally. On 10 October 1913 he reported to Matisse that in the last two weeks he had been visited in Moscow by the following museum directors: Osthaus (twice), Tessen of Berlin, von Trenkmold of Frankfurt, Hampe of Nuremburg, Polaczek of Strasburg, Sanerman of Flensburg, Stelliner of Hamburg, Bach of Darmstadt, Sauerland of Halle and Thiis of Oslo. There were no British visitors, however; not one museum director, critic, artist or dealer.

As 1914 unfolded Shchukin was still in touch with Picasso and Matisse from Moscow, and he was still in a mood to buy. His Picasso room now comprised fifty major works. 'What we saw was a jumble of cubes, cones, cylinders and other shapes', reported the painter Mikhail Nesterov after a visit to his palace. 'This chaos of carpentry seemed to hypnotise Sergei Ivanovich.' Shchukin also wanted to complete his Matisse room by adding four more pictures to the upper line. There seemed to be no slackening of energy. But war and revolution intervened and ended his collecting for good.

There was a remarkable acceleration in art prices in the three years leading up to the war. The American artist William Glackens reported from Paris in 1912: 'You can't touch a Cézanne for under $3,000 and that for a small landscape.' Morozov pushed prices even higher in 1912 when he bought a Cézanne, *Blue Land-scape*, from Vollard for 35,000 francs ($7,000). Meanwhile Rodin was offered 125,000 francs ($25,000) to sculpt the kaiser, a commission he was financially secure enough to turn down. One benefit of his suffocating affair with the widow Choiseul was that she took command of his finances. When she first came into his life he was only earning $12,000 a year. By now she claimed she had raised his annual income closer to $80,000. On 10 December 1912 the market for Impressionist paintings attained new heights with the auction in Paris of the collection of Henri Rouart. The American pioneer Impressionist collector Louisine Havemeyer paid an amazing 489,500 francs (nearly £20,000) for a Degas, *Dancers Practising at the Barre*. This made Degas the most expensive living artist, though how much pleasure this gave him, living out his last years in morose near blindness, is a moot point.

How far did this heating up of the market extend into advanced modern art? The answer was supplied on 2 March 1914, when the Peau d'Ours collection came under the hammer at the Hotel Drouot. The Peau d'Ours was the first art fund, set up by the Parisian lawyer and collector André Level in 1904. Thirteen investors contributed a modest 250 francs a year for ten years, and the plan was to put the money into new art, into works by artists who hadn't arrived yet. The sale of the 145 works of contemporary art that the fund had amassed provided a remarkably clear measure of how demand had developed during the past decade. It was a great success. And the high prices had a further effect: they sanctified the importance of these new artists in a way that the public art market, in the form of a well-publicised auction, is uniquely equipped to do. It was certainly well publicised, orchestrated by Level. He ensured that a large number of potential buyers were in attendance, glamorous socialites as well as journalists, collectors and dealers with interests in avant-garde art. It wasn't just French buyers who crowded into the room: there were significant Germans, too. And even a couple of curators from the Louvre, Paul Jamot and Léon-Jacques Blocq, although they didn't buy anything.

Things moved fast in the ten years before the First World War, so the collection was already to a certain extent dated: the Matisses were early ones, with nothing fully Fauvist by the master. And the only work by Picasso that was painted after 1905 was an early Cubist still life of 1908. But nonetheless the financial returns were impressive. An overall investment of 27,500 francs produced sale proceeds of 116,545 francs. A Gauguin for which the fund had paid 300 francs in 1904 now fetched 4,400. But the star lot of the sale was Picasso's *Family of Saltimbanques* (see p. 77) – representational in technique and elegiac in mood – for which in 1907 Level had pushed the boat out and paid 1,000 francs. This now realised 12,650 francs. It was bought by the German art dealer Thannhauser, who promptly announced – shamelessly deploying the oldest trick in the dealer's repertoire – that he had bought it remarkably cheaply and had expected to pay double. It would not have escaped beadier market observers that Thannhauser, who had held a large Picasso exhibition in Munich in 1913, was a frequent business partner of Kahnweiler.

Picasso came out of the Peau d'Ours sale pretty well. On 4 April 1914 he received a cheque for 3,978.85 francs from Level. It was an act of pure altruism on Level's part: six years before *droit de suite* was introduced as a legal obligation in France, he took it upon himself voluntarily to pay 20 per cent of the profits realised by the fund to the artists concerned, provided they were still alive. As a project, Level's fund was enlightened and ahead of its time. The fact that it showed such good returns over such a short period was a reflection of the dynamic pace of change in the years 1905–14. Over no previous decade in history would such profits have been possible through investment in avant-garde art. There is always an element of gut instinct in successful investment. Perhaps when the commodity being invested in – the new art of the early twentieth century – was itself the product of instinct, the synergy provided extra fruitfulness.

PART V

KEEPING CONTROL

CHAPTER TWENTY-NINE

Call the Police:
Academicism and Conservative Taste

In one of the more unlikely episodes of the previous artistic generation, the arch conservative and academic painter Jean Louis Ernest Meissonnier was persuaded to experiment with hashish. What visions were unleashed within him? The mid nineteenth-century mood of Baudelairean individualism, which under the influence of opium and hashish dreamed dreams of unbridled sensuality and exoticism, could not have been further from the spirit of the doggedly principled academician. All he reported seeing was regular symmetric designs, like a garden by Le Nôtre. There was no hope for him. While the avant-garde of the early twentieth century was empowered by releasing control and following instinct, conservative artistic taste and academic practice was still very much governed by the exercise of control and the rigid application of traditional, 'civilised' rules. This created an almost catatonically restrictive mindset.

Meissonier died in 1891, but his spirit lived on at the conventional Paris Salon well into the twentieth century. His speciality, meticulous reconstructions of historical domestic life, was enthusiastically replicated by a band of followers. Adolphe Alexandre Lesrel was one of the most successful. His *The Connoisseurs* of 1909 would have been much sought after in bourgeois art circles. Six overdressed cavaliers are assembled in an elegant seventeenth-century Flemish interior, looking at prints in a knowledgeable kind of way. Three of the cavaliers are arrayed in splendid red costumes which ravish the eye of the viewer and animate the composition. The whole thing is

106. A .A. Lesrel, *The Connoisseurs*, 1909

rendered in fantastically detailed realism. The artist is saying to the spectator, Want to own this picture? If so, you're a connoisseur too, in the great tradition of these sophisticated gentlemen. For every lonely patron of the avant-garde to be found in Europe in 1909 – isolated forward-thinking spirits dotted sparsely across the continent – there were still many thousands of unapologetically bourgeois art lovers whose aesthetic taste aspired to ownership of the sort of picture exemplified by a classic Lesrel.

Or a classic Alma-Tadema. The Edwardian era was still a golden age for those traditionalist painters who served up their tried and trusted mixture of heroic or sentimental narrative pictures to the delight of an admiring public. Sir Lawrence Alma-Tadema's prices were denominated in the thousands of pounds. *Ask Me No More, For At A Touch I Yield* was the title of his

107. Alma-Tadema, *Ask Me No More For At a Touch I Yield*, 1906

108. Rouault, *In the Brothel*, 1906

exhibit at the 1906 Royal Academy exhibition in London. It was a piece to send Edwardian pulses racing. The encounter between a young woman and her suitor is set on some marbled terrace in antiquity, but the sentiment – female frailty tested against determined male wooing – is eternal. The models look suspiciously like Victorians in toga fancy dress, but that ambiguity only enhanced the spectator's pleasure. To tangle the emotional mood further with a strand of Pre-Raphaelite romance, the title is a quotation from Tennyson.

In Paris in 1906, by contrast, there was plenty of female yielding to male touches. The sort of women that Georges Rouault was depicting this year, from vantage points in assorted houses of ill repute, would no doubt have eaten Alma-Tadema's polite young suitor for breakfast. Rouault was an artist in the Matisse circle who was marrying Expressionist technique to a brutal realism. Whereas Alma-Tadema's everyday-life classicism was an insipid attempt to redeem Victorian ugliness by bathing it in the beauty of an ersatz antiquity, on the other side of the channel the avant-garde was turning away from classical ideals to the art of primitive people, to the rough rather than the smooth, to instinct rather than reason.

Conservative taste took its tone from the top: paintings such as the Rouault would have horrified the Royal families of Europe. Most of them were out and out traditionalists. The kaiser found it difficult to conceal his outrage at the incursion of French Impressionism into German museums. He pronounced sourly that the French Impressionism he encountered in the National Gallery – works by Manet, Monet, Pissarro and Renoir – 'lacked interest'. He ordered that they be relegated to a less prominent position on the second floor. What particularly upset him was their imprecision of technique. The gallery director von Tschudi gamely countered with the argument that 'not all painters in the 17th century, for example Rubens and Rembrandt, had drawn so exactly'. 'If I had been Emperor in the 17th century,' declared the kaiser, 'Rembrandt would have painted differently.'

In Austria, the Archduke Franz Ferdinand's expressed desire to break all the bones in Oskar Kokoschka's body was prompted by fear of the anarchism that was implicit in the work of the young avant-garde. Edward VII might occasionally be persuaded to take an interest in an old master, particularly if it featured female nudity, but his attitude to anything more modern would have been equally hostile and uncomprehending. Only in Stockholm was there a glimmer of sympathy from the royal palace: Prince Eugen, son of King Oscar II, became a full-time artist himself. His moody, symbolist Nordic landscapes are evidence of a considerable artistic sensibility. But he was the exception. Most royalty would have privately concurred with the view that in a well-ordered society, artists, like prostitutes, should be subjected to regular health checks in order to avoid infections of the public's visual imagination.

Who was to carry out this surveillance? The police, of course. Art history is inclined to underestimate the police as a factor in the development of modernism, but they had considerable influence over what artists of the avant-garde actually got to show publicly in these years. There was no great consistency in official restrictions, and prosecutions or suppressions were often initiated at the whim of individual officers. But prohibitive action in art galleries was not uncommon, particularly in Germany, where the forbidding figure of the kaiser loomed threateningly at people's shoulders.

Indeed, you had to tread carefully in Germany at the turn of the twentieth century. Sexual liberty was under threat from the draconian Lex Heinse, introduced after the conviction of a notorious Berlin pimp of that name and intended to crack down on public immorality. In its most extreme form it led to the banning from exhibition at the Leipzig Museum of an innocuous Cranach nude. The poster selected to advertise the first Die Brücke show in 1906 was a print by Fritz Bleyle showing a spindly female nude rendered entirely in blocks of shadow. It, too, was banned from public display by the police on the grounds of indecency. It was probably not so much the eroticism of the image as its uncompromising ugliness which caused the upset. Nudity was fine as long as it was set in antiquity and partook of idealisation; the bourgeoisie only felt threatened and in need of police protection when it was ugly, and therefore more real. Or, and here was another alarm signal, when the nudity was horizontal. Ferdinand Hodler's painting *Love* (see p. 88) when exhibited at the Zurich Kunstlerhaus in 1909 might normally have escaped censure because it was allegoric; but it showed a naked man and woman, clearly modern rather than classical, in a horizontal embrace. Lying down was dangerous. Had he kept his nude figures vertical, Hodler would have been on safer ground. As it was, the Swiss police hovered uncertainly. Fortunately the young collector Josef Muller, who was to become an important Hodler patron, stepped in and bought the work. With some relief it was taken down from view.

In the same year Max Liebermann was drawn into a dispute over some dirty postcards. The Berlin police were prosecuting an unfortunate entrepreneur who was selling reproductions of exhibits at the conventional Paris Salon, involving the sort of saucy nudity exemplified by Comerre's *Leda*, which was acceptable in French academic practice because it was classical. Liebermann was turned to as an artist of standing who could define what was and wasn't immoral in art. In the end he came up with the casuistical argument that while the original painting was not obscene, its image on a postcard was, and the police got their conviction. A useful precedent was thereby set in the legal struggle to protect law-abiding citizens from art, and in 1911 the Berlin police managed to get another German art dealer called Huckser fined 20 marks for peddling pornography in the form of postcards of nudes by Anders Zorn.

A rather more problematic case for the police, however, arose the same year, this time involving Paul Cassirer. Cassirer published in his art magazine *Pan* some particularly steamy excerpts from Flaubert's Egyptian diary, which were deemed obscene by the Berlin police chief Traugott von Jagow. Copies of *Pan* were confiscated and Cassirer fined 50 marks. Not long after, in his relentless mission to root out pornography, von Jagow accompanied the Berlin censor of plays to a rehearsal of Carl Sternheim's farce *Die Hose*. There his eye fell upon a rather pretty actress, Tilla Durieux. It may not have been regular police procedure, but he sent her a note asking for a private meeting the following Sunday. Tilla Durieux showed the note to her husband. Her husband was Paul Cassirer, who challenged the police chief to a duel. The police chief apologised, and the awkwardness was smoothed over. But the gap between public and private morality had been exposed; and the irony of an official on the one hand banning the French writer's diary as pornographic, and on the other using his position to attempt the seduction of an actress, might have amused Flaubert himself.

The artists of Die Brücke spent much of the summer of 1910 disporting naked in the Moritzburg lakes with their female models, at least one of whom – Franzi – was well below the age of consent. Modern scholars have speculated that Heckel and Kirchner may have had sex with Franzi. If that was so, the last person they wanted to see was a policeman. Unfortunately one turned up unexpectedly, to interrupt the sylvan idyll. We don't know exactly how the conversation went between the artists and the guardian of the law. Possibly the nudists argued that they were asserting their right to live in nature unfettered by convention, and that as non-conforming artists they had the licence to follow their instincts and fly in the face of society's arbitrary norms. The policeman, unsure of his ground, confiscated a canvas that Pechstein was painting as evidence of immorality, and withdrew.

A rather different work also painted in Germany that year was entitled *Steht dir gut!* (*Suits you!*), a typically winsome production of the popular Bavarian genre painter Hugo Kauffmann. A German in official uniform, possibly a policeman, flirts in a cosy inn with a couple of cheeky village wenches, allowing one of them to try on his hat. Could it be that the hard-pressed officer who had such a perplexing experience with a bunch of modern artists in the Moritzburg lakes relaxed the

109. Hugo Wilhelm Kauffmann, *Suits You!*, 1910

same evening in similar surroundings? Did he perhaps even titillate the girls with accounts of the antics of Kirchner and his friends? The Kauffmann, like so many Munich school paintings of the time, is the essence of *gemütlichkeit* (cosiness). Here indeed is an elemental clash of mood and culture: however else one might characterise the work of Die Brücke in 1910, it certainly wasn't *gemütlich*. In the event, the Dresden state prosecutor took no further action against Kirchner and his colleagues. The artists breathed a sigh of relief and Pechstein was allowed to retrieve his painting from the police station. He noted that while in custody it had dried out quite well. Thus the September exhibition of Die Brücke at Dresden's Galerie Arnold was able to go ahead. But it is hard to avoid the conclusion that the German police, ponderously vigilant against indecency elsewhere, missed a trick here. A potential paedophile ring was penetrated by an officer of the law, yet in the confusion no prosecution resulted.

The Die Brücke artists continued to dance on the precipice. Relocating to Berlin in the autumn of 1911 they established their own art school, the MUIM-Institut (Modern Instruction in Painting). Its enticing prospectus offered 'lessons with new methods in a new way' and, most joyous of all, 'in summer open air nudes at the sea'. Would they never learn? The document caught the shocked eye of that arch conservative Anton von Werner, the director of the Royal Academy of Fine Arts and the kaiser's favourite painter. He immediately informed the police and urged them to investigate. In the end the prosecution never got to court, largely because there was so little take-up of the course that opportunities for the propagation of immorality were judged to be negligible.

In Austria, Egon Schiele's brushes with the police were to be expected, given the erotic nature of many of his drawings. In February 1910 there was a controversial exhibition in Prague to which Schiele had contributed a number of drawings of female nudes with particular emphasis on their genitalia. The police moved quickly to order the removal of fourteen of these drawings. But then, in one of the occasional compromises that emerged between the forces of the law and the forces of avant-garde art, the police softened their position. They suggested that the fourteen offending drawings might be viewed in the gallery if shown in a portfolio rather than on the walls. Schiele was of course not so lucky in 1912, when he served twenty-four days in jail for corrupting minors, having been found guilty of allowing them into a room in his house where an indecent drawing was hanging. He should have kept it in its folder.

The Paris Salon d'Automne, no stranger to controversy, was the scene of a police raid when it opened in September 1913. Their object was the removal of an indecent picture hanging in the exhibition, a large nude by van Dongen called, a trifle disingenuously, *Le Châle Espagnol*. The critic Delcourt, who now made rather a speciality of spluttering effusions against avant-garde art, wrote in *Paris-Midi* on 15 November: 'In the context of the civilisation of Watteau, Fragonard, Lautrec, Musset, Baudelaire

110. Van Dongen, *Le Châle Espagnol*, 1913

and Mallarmé, this painting is no better than excrement and its painter a barbarian of the most primitive talent.' At first sight, the naked model, with her Klimtian background formed by the shawl, doesn't look too shocking. There had been equally flagrant nudity in the Academic Salon, under the soapy cover of a setting in antiquity. But what made the difference seems to have been the area of pubic hair at the very centre of van Dongen's composition. You could get away with an awful lot of nudity if you didn't show pubic hair. You could even get away with quite a lot of pubic hair if it didn't figure too prominently. But once you put pubic hair at the very centre of the composition, alarm bells rang in police stations across Paris.

Of course all police leave tended to be cancelled in the vicinity of any Italian Futurist exhibition or event. But the intervention of the forces of the law in these situations was less an assertion of traditional values in art than an exercise in keeping the peace between warring factions of Futurists. Breaking up a fight was a more straightforward challenge than choosing which works of art should be removed from public sight for society's own good. Through all the noise, calmer voices could occasionally be heard. When in 1912 reactionary members of the French parliament demanded that Cubism should be banned from exhibition in state buildings, Maurice Sembat, a socialist member of parliament and a friend of Matisse, struck a more balanced note: 'When a picture seems bad to you,' he countered, 'you have an indisputable right not to look at it and go and see other works. But one doesn't call in the police.'

In London, the police were kept less active by art galleries. They were more likely to be called out to deal with suffragette outrages against works of art rather than with works of art that outraged public decency. The power was still with the conventional art world. The George MacCulloch sale at Christie's as late as May 1913 was evidence of the continuing popularity of art painted to please rather than to challenge. Huge prices were realised for the heroes of the Royal Academy. MacCulloch was a man blithely unaware of Fauvism, Cubism or Futurism, a collector for whom Impressionism held no attraction. Legend had it that he won the Broken Hill gold mine in Australia, the basis of his future wealth, in a game of penny nap. He was prodigiously rich. And he spent his money on traditional contemporary art, by English painters like Millais, Burne-Jones, Alma-Tadema, Leighton, and continental masters such as Jacob Maris, Bastien-Lepage and Rosa Bonheur. He liked hard-edged realism; he liked pictures that told a story; he liked undemanding romance. And even more to the point, there were still plenty of people in London who liked them too, who were prepared to pay thousands of pounds for these 'old-fashioned' artists. The sale of his collection brought extraordinary results, and totalled £136,859. The John Everett Millais of *St Isumbras at the Ford* fetched £8,190, and a Jacob Maris Dutch Hague school landscape made £6,930; for comparison, the highest price paid at auction for a van Gogh by 1913 was £1,450.

But there was an intimation of changing taste at the Royal Academy. Alma-Tadema having died in 1912, the Royal Academy decided to devote their winter exhibition in 1913 to a retrospective of his work. The last time they had paid this sort of tribute to a recently dead colossus had been in 1905, when the oeuvre of the late George Frederick Watts had been celebrated. Then 60,000 people had flocked through the doors. Now the number attending the Alma-Tadema retrospective was a disappointing 17,000. Alma-Tadema's appeal is often described as 'cinematic'. Perhaps the explanation lies in the fact that in 1905 there were eight cinemas in London, and in 1913 nearly 200. The public were beginning to prefer the real thing to Alma-Tadema's version of it.

In January 1910 the Seine flooded, trapping Apollinaire in his house. He was rescued by a friendly sewage worker who carried him to safety, no mean feat considering the poet's bulk. The flood unleashed strange fantasies in the imagination of the conventional salon painter Louis Béroud, who produced an extraordinary large-scale work that year called *Les Joies d'Inondation*. It shows an elegant gentleman-artist in the Galerie de

III. Louis Béroud, *Les Joies d'Inondation*, 1910

Medici in the Louvre, who has set up his easel in front of Rubens'
Disembarkation of Marie de' Medici at Marseilles in order to make a
copy of a detail. The work depicts Marie upon her marriage to
Henry IV, being greeted by an allegorical figure of France while
a trumpeting angel of Fame flies above, and Neptune and his
muscular, fish-tailed naiads rise from the sea. The copyist is at
work on a study of the left-hand naiad when all at once the trio
of girls burst out of the imaginary space of the picture and into
the real space of the museum, swept forward by a gush of sea-
water. The title playfully suggests that the joy of this particular

inundation will be the physical encounter with the nude girls in prospect for the surprised artist, but you get the feeling that the effetely dapper copyist will stand no chance once hit by the wall of water and the combined mass of the three rather bulky females.

Several elements are in play here: Belle Époque sauciness; the topicality of the flooding Seine; and a Pygmalion-like pleasure in the static beauties of the painted Rubens being brought to palpitating real life in the galleries of the Louvre (but even that is a delusion because the 'real-life' girls are themselves only a painting by Béroud). A decade or two before their time, Béroud is thus contriving the layers of contradiction that the Surrealists thought they had invented. But perhaps it is also an expression of deeper unease in the face of all the disconcerting new developments of the young twentieth century, social, scientific and artistic. Perhaps Béroud's picture actually depicts the moment when Paula Modersohn-Becker's loose screw finally gives way and the deluge follows. Art is finally unchecked, control is lost, instinct is unfettered and the old certainties are swept away.

CHAPTER THIRTY

Wriggle-and-Chiffon: Fashionable Portraitists

The early twentieth century was a glamorous era, and a number of highly successful international portraitists flourished in Europe recording that glamour. These included artists such as Paul Helleu, Jacques-Émile Blanche, Vittorio Corcos, François Flameng and Philip de Laszlo; but the four leaders in the field were Giovanni Boldini (in Italy and France), John Singer Sargent (in England and America), Joaquin Sorolla (in Spain and South America), and Anders Zorn (in Scandinavia and America). The very rich adored being painted by them. They shared an excitingly impressionistic style: flashy, flattering, often very sexy, but in the end not so advanced as to frighten many horses. It was Sickert who in 1910 christened them the 'Wriggle-and-Chiffon School'. The extravagance of their brushstroke gave the appearance of spontaneity, creating the illusion that their response to the sitter was immediate and instinctive, but actually their method, based on exceptional technical facility, was highly measured and calculating. They inhabited a territory closer to the convention of the academy than to the outlandishness of the avant-garde, but enjoyed a degree of success that annoyed both conservatives and rebels.

The unreconstructed academicians thought their brushstroke was dangerously free. Lord Redesdale, chairman of the National Gallery trustees in London, railed against the devilish facility of Sargent: 'With almost demonic cleverness he makes a splash or two of paint do duty for a hand, an ear, a fan, or what not, sparing himself the tedium of detail.' In Redesdale's

112. Sargent, *Siesta*, 1905

opinion, there was something shabby about this cutting of corners. Great art should take pains, show evidence of labour. The avant-garde, on the other hand, dismissed artists like Boldini or Sorolla as being shamelessly commercial. Kandinsky distinguished between 'inner necessity', whose expression was the essence of the true work of art, and 'outer necessity', art motivated only by ambition and greed. The fashionable portraitists showed very little of the former but were arch exponents of the latter.

Sargent and Boldini were pretty much aligned in terms of the price they would ask for a full-length portrait. To be painted by Sargent was the acme of social aspiration among Edwardians on both sides of the Atlantic, while Boldini's desirability was particularly intense in fashionable Parisian circles. By the middle of the first decade of the twentieth century, Sargent was charging £1,000 or $5,000, and Boldini was on a par at 25,000 francs (that was what he asked for painting *Madame Georges*

113. Boldini, *Princess Bibesco*, 1911

Victor-Hugo Taking Tea in 1904). When Boldini painted a portrait of the renowned beauty and socialite Princess Bibesco in 1911, the sitter was so delighted with this image of herself shot through with sensuality, glamour and nervous dynamism that she assured the artist, 'I should have been pleased to pay for your work with the price of my great emerald necklace and with all the pearls there are in the world.' The extravagance of the valuation might have persuaded Boldini that there was scope for raising his prices further. Zorn's going rate was a shade lower, but not much: in the early 1900s he was charging $4,000 for a major portrait. Sorolla, as his popularity in America grew through the decade, found he could command closer to $10,000. Price points were rigorously enforced. Hugh Lane's admirers clubbed together to get Sargent to paint a full-length portrait of the Irishman in 1906. But there was a slight shortfall in funding. Sargent was regretful but adamant: what they had raised was only enough for a half-length, which was what he painted.

This same year Boldini was brought over to London to paint the gorgeous Consuela, Duchess of Marlborough. The Marlboroughs had already been elaborately portrayed by Sargent. To add the Boldini version to their collection was the equivalent of being depicted by both Reynolds and Gainsborough, or perhaps of supplementing your Rolls Royce with a Ferrari. Boldini was a show-off, and distinctly racy. In 1907 Sargent, whose flashy, impressionistic style of painting was so at variance with the awkward taciturnity of his personality, complained morosely: 'Painting a portrait would be quite amusing if one were not forced to talk while working ... What a nuisance having to entertain the sitter and to look happy when one feels wretched.' Boldini took a rather different line. He relished entertaining his fashionable lady sitters, particularly if they were youngish and nubile, as most of them were. The conversation that accompanied his portrait sittings was often an elaborate campaign of seduction. The Duchess of Marlborough describes her experience of sitting to the Maestro. She only agreed to his painting her, she said, provided his behaviour remained exemplary, for he had a salacious reputation with women. In the sittings that followed it was difficult for him to restrain the sallies that his Bohemian nature inspired. When the temptation became too strong, he would look at me with a humorous smile and, wagging his monstrous head, ejaculate, 'Ah, La Divina, La Divina!'[40]

Other accounts confirm that physical pursuit round the studio was not an unknown hazard of sitting to Boldini; but once his advances had been rejected, poses would be resumed – a trifle breathlessly – and dresses rearranged. Presumably when Boldini took up his brush again it was in a state of Freudian sublimation, much to the benefit of the ultimate portrait.

Sickert identified Boldini as the 'nonpareil parent' of the Wriggle-and-Chiffon school. In the ten years before the First World War, Boldini was at the peak of his fashionability, particularly in Paris and New York. The secret of his success was the dynamic elegance with which he endowed his sitters. It was unleashed by a prodigious facility of brushstroke which, when brought to bear on attractive female subjects, produced effects that bordered on the orgasmic. Boldini's women, according to his friend the caricaturist Sem, were 'contracted, arched … nervous wrecks, fatigued by this troubled century … These dazzling, zigzagging visions like radiations of heat, these shudders, these tremors, these contractions, they are all in keeping with this age of neurosis.' The novelty of Boldini's line and brushstroke also elicited admiration from an unexpected source. 'When times have established values at their correct places,' wrote Gertrude Stein, 'Boldini will be recognised as the greatest painter of the last century. All the new school is born of him, since he first simplified the line and the planes.' Not everyone would have agreed with her assessment, but perhaps she nursed a secret hankering to be painted by the Italian master. Or was he more of a modernist than he is given credit for? There are parallels between the energy of his technique and the lines of force of the Futurists four years later. Boccioni, Severini and Balla may have written the manifestoes, but did Boldini actually get there first? Not in any meaningful sense. He just shared with them a very Italian pleasure in showing off. Boldini's modernist credentials are set in a clearer context by a comparison of his portrait of Princess Bibesco with Braque's Cubist *Le Portugais* (see p. 260). also painted in 1911. A visitor from Mars shown the two pictures together and told they were both representations of human beings painted in the same city in the same year might indeed have concluded that there were two parallel realities on Earth.

The artist described as the greatest living Spanish painter had a major retrospective in Paris in the summer of 1906. That's how he was billed by the glamorous art dealer Georges Petit who mounted the exhibition in his gallery. It wasn't Picasso to whom Petit was throwing open his walls, but Joaquin Sorolla. Arriving triumphantly in the city for his show in June, Sorolla would not have been aware of the existence of Picasso. Picasso was probably not aware of the Sorolla show, either, or if he was he would have disdained it as laughably bourgeois: Sorolla was representative of high fashionability, both in his subject matter – sun-drenched Mediterranean beaches, elegant women in lovely white dresses – and in his style, a modish naturalistic Impressionism that gave his admirers an exciting whiff of a modernism, but the modernism of thirty years earlier now rendered safe by familiarity. Over time, generally about a generation, the eye gets conditioned to new artistic developments.

Thus the art-appreciating public were now attuned to the broad brushstrokes and thrilling light effects to be found in Sorolla's work. The sort of paintings that they might have looked at with dismay in 1880 were admired in 1906. The critic Camille Mauclair identified what people now found exciting about Sorolla's exhibition: 'In these 200 paintings and 300 sketches there is not a trace of hesitation: tones are recorded once and for all, without any afterthought, and with a strange infallibility.' 'Posez, laissez', Baron Gerard had told his pupils in

114. Sorolla, *On the Beach*, 1906

Paris a hundred years earlier. Don't rework: your first touch is the true one, because it is spontaneous and sincere. It is another instance of the instinctive being preferred to the calculated, although the irony was that, with artists like Sorolla, a huge amount of surreptitious calculation underlay their apparent freedom of brushstroke. The financial return on Sorolla's exhibition was impressive. Entry fees alone produced 50,000 francs; sales (of sixty-five works) amounted to 230,650 francs. Sorolla also picked up some remunerative portrait commissions from the international rich congregated in Paris.

From 17 May to 16 June that summer a rival exhibition was held at the premises of Durand-Ruel. It was a retrospective of the work of an artist of similar international appeal and flashy technique, this time from the other end of Europe: the Swede Anders Zorn. Zorn was already big in America, where he had made four successful visits and was highly sought after as a portraitist of grand sitters from the president downwards. His other great speciality was nudes. The nubile young women whom Zorn persuaded to shed their clothes and pose naked in the Swedish snow seem bursting with good health. The atmosphere was of the sauna in the nudist camp rather than of the boudoir in the brothel. But they were very sensual and much appreciated by worldly male clients of the artist on both sides of the Atlantic, and as we have seen in postcard form attracted the attention of the Berlin police. On one occasion in New York the line of distinction between Zorn's portraits of the rich and fashionable and his paintings of sensual female nudes blurred. Zorn made his way to 660 Park Avenue, the sumptuous town house of Miss Emilie Grigsby, the young friend of the American tycoon Charles Tyson Yerkes, under the impression that he was going to execute a remunerative portrait commission of another society beauty. But Miss Grigsby made it clear that, though she lived in some style, she could not afford Zorn's fees for a portrait. However, she was perfectly willing to pose as a model for him. The only problem was that she had something temporarily wrong with her leg which necessitated staying in bed that day. Within those constrictions, would Zorn still paint her? The resulting canvas indicates that the Swedish artist rather enjoyed the experience, and Yerkes's mistress was immortalised along with her bed linen.

Sorolla outsold Zorn that summer in Paris. The following year, after his success in France, Sorolla set his sights on Germany. Several German dealers proposed shows, and Sorolla opted to go with Eduard Schulte, who had large galleries in Berlin and equally well-appointed premises in Dusseldorf and Cologne, so there could be a tour. He sent off 280 works for the exhibition in February. But he had reckoned without Max Liebermann: the influential German Impressionist thundered in the *Berliner Tageblatt*: 'To bring to Berlin 300 works by a Spaniard who, although good, is not first-rate, is senseless. The fact that this is occurring nonetheless indicates the serious malady of our time, which should horrify everyone.' Liebermann may well have felt his

115. Zorn, *Miss Grigsby*, 1907

territory was being invaded by the flashier Sorolla. But he was right in one respect: there were almost no buyers in Germany for Sorolla, and his exhibitions there in 1907 were a commercial failure. Only one small work sold, and that for a desultory 1,000 francs. The explanation lies in the difference between Paris and Berlin in 1907. Paris was fashionable, rich, and frequented in the summer by a crowd of wealthy expatriate Spaniards and visiting South Americans eager to support the flamboyantly Hispanic Sorolla. Berlin was rich too, but Sorolla's lightness of touch failed in the more ponderous atmosphere of the German capital, where there was no Spanish community to speak of and excitable South Americans were thin on the ground.

Undaunted, Sorolla moved in on London in 1908. Never one to under-represent himself, he sent 278 of his works to a solo show mounted at the Grafton Galleries. Proceedings were opened by the Spanish ambassador on 4 May. Sargent and Zorn visited the exhibition in support of their colleague, and the Royal Academy threw a banquet in his honour. The last big international show at the Grafton had been Durand-Ruel's French Impressionists in 1905, which did not receive the same level of official support. In only three years, Impressionism had become more acceptable in London, and Sorolla's version of it was especially luscious. The pictures were admired, and, while the quantity of sales achieved in Paris in 1906 was not repeated, one important thing did happen: the exhibition was visited by the American Hispanist Archer M. Huntington, who proposed showing Sorolla's work in the United States. Doors were thus opened to what transpired to be Sorolla's most lucrative market of all, on the other side of the Atlantic. Sorolla's first triumphant show in New York at the Hispanic Society lasted from 4 February to 8 March 1909, and attracted tens of thousands of visitors. It moved on successfully to Buffalo and Boston. He sent 356 works to America, which is evidence of the sheer portability of works of art in pursuit of buyers in the early twentieth century. The financial results in the United States were impressive: Sorolla sold ninety-five works for a total of $181,760. Major individual works were selling for as much as $10,000. For comparison, Durand-Ruel's first New York Impressionist exhibition in 1886 made total sales of $17,000. As if in acclamation of his achievement and newly won status in America, Sorolla was invited to Washington in May to paint the portrait of the president, William Howard Taft.

This was Sorolla's apogee. Perhaps Boldini's came in 1911, when Princess Bibesco told him that his portrait of her was worth all the pearls in the world. Zorn's high point may have been his big retrospective exhibition in Stockholm in 1912, held to coincide with the Olympics. But things were beginning to change. Nineteen thousand people paid 100,000 kroner in entrance fees to attend Zorn's show, which were respectable but not sensational numbers. Advanced young Swedes were looking to Paris now, and some were even studying there under Matisse.

A suspicion was growing that Zorn's strappingly nubile nudes were no longer the most advanced point of modern art; indeed that they might be cavorting on the wrong side of history. And as for Sargent, his disaffection with the trials of portraiture increased as war approached. He kept at it, but the modern world was less and less comprehensible to him. On 16 January 1913, Lord Crawford records in his diary Sargent's attempts to paint the superstar dancer Nijinsky: 'Sargent … actually got him to the studio, but the man refused to sit and spent forty minutes blubbing like a child. Sargent was much puzzled at the cause for this demonstration, and ultimately discovered that Nijinsky was bewailing the loss of his pearl necklace!' Sargent and Nijinsky were probably not kindred spirits.

If you were rich and risk-averse you turned to Boldini, Sargent, Sorolla or Zorn to establish your wife as an icon of fashionability. But if you were rich and rather more daring, you could sometimes commission a modernist like Klimt or Munch to paint her. Both had been around long enough to establish surprisingly remunerative portrait practices, even though their modernism put them beyond what was acceptable for the conventional majority. Neither aspired to membership of the Wriggle-and-Chiffon school. Klimt's portraits in these years operate on a principle of realistic heads and hands set in broad expanses of fantastic mosaicised surfaces which blend dress into background. Ever since his first visit to Ravenna in 1903, he had been fascinated by the Byzantine mosaic technique he found there and had been assimilating it into his style. Klimt's extraordinary portrait of Adela Bloch-Bauer I, finished in 1907, is the culmination of this new inspiration. Here the gold-encrusted decoration takes over, so that it is impossible to assess even whether the lady is sitting or standing. It doesn't matter. She exists as 'a dream of bejewelled lust' as the Viennese critic Ludwig Hevesi noted admiringly at the time.

Almost Harry Kessler's last act before his enforced depart-ure from the directorship of the Weimar Museum in 1906 was to have himself painted by Edvard Munch (see p. 104). It was a good choice. What emerged was a marvellous full-length portrait, a timeless evocation of a great collector and man of the arts, pulsating with the palpability of a painting from life, in contrast with Munch's clunky posthumous rendering of Nietzsche of the same summer. As he worked, Munch let his hair down to Kessler. 'Perhaps my concentration on my art makes me fail to understand life,' he confessed. 'That's why I'm not good with money. But there comes a time when you say to yourself, I will let life take its course, I have better things to do.'

On the other hand painters like Boldini, Sargent, Sorolla and Zorn were notably good with money. They also understood rather more of life than Munch. For them it was indeed a Belle Époque.

CHAPTER THIRTY-ONE

Railroads and Rembrandts:
Dealers and Collectors of Old Art

At the end of 1905 there was excitement in Paris when the Cronier collection went on view prior to its auction on 2 December at the Georges Petit galleries. It was a collection of its time, heavily weighted in favour of the fashionable masters of the eighteenth century, including works by Gainsborough, Reynolds, Lawrence, Romney, Fragonard, Latour and Carpeaux, plus the obligatory tapestries and porcelain. The Louvre was rumoured to be contemplating a bid of 300,000 francs for the Fragonard. 'The whole collection,' commented Gide sniffily in his diary, 'has a flavour of the nouveau-riche.' He recorded various exchanges that he overheard in the course of the viewing, and was particularly galled by

> the insolent conversations of a group of sons of collectors, still without any down on their upper lip, calling Fragonard 'Frago' and saying: 'What *I* like in him, etc. ... etc. ... ' and this dialogue between two affected and very young men: 'But why doesn't anyone do things like this today?' And the other replies with a superior air: 'What do you expect, my dear fellow? No-one has the time! No-one has the time!'[41]

The insolent young men were right that the frenetic atmosphere of the beginning of the twentieth century had increased the pace and neurosis of life. There was an anxious feeling that control had been lost. For every Futurist who looked forward with excitement to an art of speed and sensation, there were a hundred traditionalist art lovers who looked back with nostalgia to the calm of past centuries when there had been the leisure to take pains, to create masterpieces of proven durability; they yearned for a time when life and art were stable and under control.

Some of these traditionalist art lovers were American. And some of these Americans were very rich indeed. Awareness of what a stupendous market existed for great old masters among American moguldom made European dealers hyperactive, thus further raising levels of freneticism. Whenever a major collector died, teams of market professionals sprang into action. In Paris in 1905 the legendary Rodolphe Kann breathed his last. He had made a fortune in gold and diamond mining in South Africa, and used it to assemble a collection that included ten major Rembrandts. It was an assembly of art that put the Cronier collection in the shade. The French dealers René Gimpel and Nathan Wildenstein were the first to move, and managed to obtain options on the paintings. But the young Joseph Duveen, just beginning to establish himself as a major player in the market, outmanoeuvred them. He ended up buying the whole collection for $4.2 million.

Ten Rembrandts were some prize. Henry Clay Frick made the telling observation that railroads were the Rembrandts of investment. It was indicative of the extent to which he had been brainwashed by Duveen's sales pitch that he put it this way round. Frick was one of a number of American tycoons rich enough to be able to afford just about any old master that came on the market if he decided he wanted it. And he decided he wanted quite a number of the major works that European dealers, particularly Duveen, sourced in the old continent. A Rembrandt was a rock-solid stock. The simple lesson that Duveen taught was the more expensive the painting, the greater its quality. You didn't need to be an aesthete to assess a work of art: you just had to look at its price tag. Thus ownership of a Rembrandt said good things about you socially, spiritually and financially.

The following year, the action moved to Berlin where the most tempting trophy that summer was the Oscar Hainauer collection. Hainauer, a rich banker who had put together an outstanding collection of Renaissance paintings, sculptures and tapestries, had actually died ten years earlier, but his estate was still in the hands of his widow. Wilhelm von Bode, the new director of the Kaiser Friedrich Museum and an old master paintings expert with a reputation that rivalled even Bernard Berenson's, wielded enormous power and influence in Germany. Von Bode was known to have the ear of the emperor, whose conservative stance on art he was happy to support. He had made it clear to the widow that he (and the emperor) expected the collection to be left to the museum. But she still hadn't actually handed it over. Bode decided that the prevarication had gone on long enough and put pressure on her to do the decent thing. She told him she needed money. Although the collection had already been valued at 3 million marks, Bode, in a lordly manner, made an offer of 1.25 million, then went off to London for a few weeks' holiday confident that he had secured the prize.

Thundering along the line in the other direction, from London to Berlin – perhaps their trains even crossed – travelled Joseph Duveen. The most successful art dealer of the early twentieth century was now coming into his own and beginning to show his legendary audacity, energy and fearlessness. He was acting on a tip-off that Mrs Hainauer was not happy and might be amenable to an offer. Despite the fact that he was already financially enmeshed in doing the Kann deal – which was costing him $4.2 million – Duveen had taken the precaution of arranging a $6 million overdraft on a London bank and now offered Mrs Hainauer 4 million marks for her collection. She succumbed to his blandishments and the deal went through. Before Bode realised what had happened, the collection was spirited away to London, and almost immediately Duveen was making sales to his eager American moguls. He was in profit fairly quickly, just by the sales of Renaissance sculpture to Benjamin Altman, P. A. B. Widener, and J. P. Morgan, which produced $5 million. Meanwhile Bode returned to Berlin for an uncomfortable interview with the emperor.

As the year 1906 unfolded, the art worlds of Paris, London and New York gradually became aware that Duveen had also bought the Kann collection. By August it was openly for sale, at a considerable mark-up from the substantial $4.2 million that Duveen had paid for it. In a brilliant piece of salesmanship, Duveen arranged for buyers to view the works in situ, in the Kann house itself, thus simultaneously emphasising the 'freshness' of the merchandise and subtly promoting the illusion that collectors were buying direct from the family. That summer 'the entire rich world trooped through the house' and many successful sales were concluded. Altman bagged four Rembrandts for $500,000, and Arabella Huntingdon, widow of Collis P. Huntingdon, the highly unpleasant railway magnate, committed to spending $2.5 million on various choice pieces of French furniture plus the most prized Rembrandt of all, *Titus Contemplating the Bust of Aristotle*. It was inspiring. It was exciting. It was even better than railroad stock.

The year 1906 was important for Duveen in another respect, too: in return for generous financial compensation, he secured the discreet services of the leading old master expert in the world, Bernard Berenson. It was the beginning of a legendary, morally ambiguous and extraordinarily profitable partnership. The top dealers were constantly on the alert for ways of getting ahead of the competition. Duveen already had an office in Paris, and in 1907 the leading London dealers Agnew's set one up too, an acknowledgement of the fact that old masters were still flowing out of France in shoals and needed to be fished further up the river in order to secure the best for their American clientele. A year later, following the money, Agnew's opened an office in Berlin. Duveen stayed focused on Paris. In May 1908 he opened a new gallery, called the Petit Trianon, in the Place Vendôme. Its glory and grandeur was testament to the huge amount of money that his firm was now making in France. In fact profit stood in the same sacred relation to these titans of the art trade as instinct did to the modern artist.

In 1909 Henry James wrote a timely novel, *The Outcry* (adapted into a play in 1911), which dealt with the dilemmas implicit in the sale of great paintings from Europe, and particularly Britain, to American moguls. The painting at issue is a work up until recently believed to be by a (mythical) Italian Renaissance artist called Moretto, but now excitingly reattributed to a much more important (mythical) artist called Mantovano. The aristocratic British owner is tempted to sell, despite the outcry from the public. James pulls no punches about the motives of his fellow countrymen. We are told that the prospective buyer, the obscenely rich Mr Beckenridge Bender, wants to acquire the painting simply because it is expensive. He comes from a country 'where the eagle screams like a thousand steam whistles and the newspapers flap like the leaves of the forest: there he'll be, if you'll only let him, the biggest thing going; since sound, in that air, seems to mean size and size to be all that counts'. Bender 'simply can't *afford* not to be cited and celebrated as the biggest buyer who ever lived'. Therefore he wants to buy the picture as a 'Mantovano' at £100,000 but is not interested in acquiring it as a 'Moretto' at £10,000.

The urge to own the best and to pay the most for it was driving up the market for old masters to boiling point. For those American buyers not quite sure that they were buying the best, Duveen had Berenson on hand to authenticate the 'Moretto' as a 'Mantovano'. Berenson's role was crucial, as the ultimate authority, the guarantor of authenticity. The money rolled in to such an extent that Duveen had to turn his attention to the age-old problem of how to shield his profits from the taxman. He had taken the decision to relocate out of London; by centring his operations in France, Duveen managed to achieve $13 million of business in Paris in 1909. It was a quite staggering amount of money. He was as agile on his feet as ever. Typical of his manoeuvring was his approach in 1909 to winning the collection of Maurice Kann, the brother of Rodolphe. Before actually making an offer for it, he managed to smuggle Baron Edmond de Rothschild into the Kann household so as to give him a surreptitious preview of the great Guardis and Bouchers and so pre-sell them. The same year something wonderful happened in the US: Congress amended the Revenue Act to provide exemption from import duty for works of art over 100 years old coming into the country. It was great news for Duveen. Everything seemed to be going his way. These are the dangerous moments in an art dealer's life, the moments when he starts to believe his own myth; 1910 would not be so kind to him.

In St Petersburg, meanwhile, there was a development in the old master world that trumped even the excitement of the Holbeins, Guardis and Bouchers available in London and Paris: the re-emergence of a lost Leonardo. The architect Leon Benois exhibited *The Madonna and Child with Flowers*, probably painted in 1478, as part of his father-in-law's collection. It caused a sensation and was widely accepted as genuine. Word travelled fast, and the international art-dealing fraternity, led by Duveen, began to circle. Here was a trophy that the Beckenridge Benders of this world would kill for. Duveen was determined to get his hands on it, but he was prepared to play a long game.

Old master art dealing in Edwardian London was taking on some of the intrigue and dering-do of a John Buchan novel. In May 1910 Roger Fry, *homo universalis* of the London art world, added to his roles as critic, painter, cultural entrepreneur, lecturer and modernist pioneer that of financially acute dealer. Later in the year he would be responsible for the single most important exhibition of advanced European art ever held in Britain. But now, in the early summer, he also found time to sell Rembrandt's *Polish Rider* to the American tycoon Henry Clay Frick, who had to liquidate large quantities of railroad stock to buy it. For Fry this involved a week's trip to Poland to negotiate with the owner, Count Tianowski, in Fry's words 'a rather stupid country gentleman who insists on selling the picture in his chateau; that's why I have to go and get it as I must see it before buying'. Out of the selling price of £60,000

116. Rembrandt, *The Polish Rider*

he took a personal commission of £3,000. So that at least made the journey worthwhile.

In November it was the turn of Morland Agnew, a partner in the London firm, to make his greatest coup. It involved a Velasquez, the half-length portrait of Philip IV in red and silver costume. This much-admired painting was apparently in the Dulwich Art Gallery. But it was doubted by the eminent Spanish expert Dr Beruete, who thought it was a copy of a lost picture. Privately Morland agreed with him. On 17 November Morland writes in his diary, 'Have to go to Vienna tomorrow on business – a great nuisance just now.' He travelled with Count Sala, Agnew's door-opener to middle-European aristocratic collections. Information had been received that the Velasquez in the possession of Prince Elias de Bourbon at Castle Schwartzou in

Austria was the lost prime version. On Sunday 20 November Morland Agnew's diary reads: 'Afternoon to see *the* Velasquez "Philip IV" in Palace. Decided to buy. Quiet dinner at hotel ... Feeding at Bristol very bad.' The next day: 'Called on Union Bank and made arrangements to pay and receive picture. Left 11.55 for London.'

The price paid was a hefty £60,000. Is it just a coincidence that this is the same price negotiated with Count Tianowsky by Roger Fry in Poland in May, when he bought the Tianowsky Rembrandt, also for Frick? In some freemasonry of middle-European aristocrats, did Tianowsky tip off de Bourbon that this was the going rate for masterpieces? Or is it an early example of the intuitive way prices for the unpriceable evolve in mysterious relation to each other, driven by nothing more definable than the spirit of the age?

The picture itself was then rushed by train across Europe to Madrid where it was immediately authenticated as the lost original by Beruete. Thereafter the sale to Frick was quickly accomplished; and Morland Agnew probably decided that the deprivation of having to endure Austrian food for a couple of nights had been worth the profit made. Just. It is unlikely that he also took in the exhibition of Klimt's erotic drawings then on view in Vienna at the Galerie Miethke.

That it was Agnew's who achieved this considerable coup with the Velasquez was partly the result of Duveen being distracted by trouble with the law. For a dealership that regularly sailed close to the wind, such things were an occupational hazard. But this one was serious. Just as the firm was congratulating itself on the previous year's relaxation of the US import regulations for art, which promised to create an era of even more spectacular profits, an aggrieved ex-employee put a spoke in the well-oiled turning of the firm's wheels. This ungrateful whistleblower revealed to the New York authorities several years' tax fraud in the firm's books prior to the 1909 exemption. On 18 October Duveen galleries were raided and $1 million of goods were seized in settlement of unpaid tax. For the next eighteen months much of the firm's energies were devoted to fighting the ruling.

Agnew's, meanwhile, were firing on all cylinders. They were into modern art, too, or at least into their idea of modern art. This same year they paid £190,000 for the Alexander Young collection, which comprised huge quantities of works by 'safe' Dutch Hague school and French Barbizon school painters. There were sixty-six Corots and fifty-nine Daubignys, plus numerous examples by Israels, Maris, Mauve, Tryon, Millet, Diaz, Harpignies, Boudin, Lépine and Whistler. For Agnew's and their clients, this was the closest they got to continental modern art: fisherfolk and lugubrious peasantry disporting in vaguely atmospheric landscapes. No Picasso, Matisse or van Dongen here.

The great art dealers move deftly and patiently, biding their time for the right moment to make a sale. In May 1906 Hugh Lane bought a painting at Christie's for £2,200. Art dealers have instincts too, and Lane's gut told him that this portrait of a man in a red cap was by Titian. He cleaned it, and what emerged once the thick varnish and dirt had been removed was a work of such high quality that the attribution was no longer to be doubted. Someone else's goose had once again been turned into Hugh Lane's swan. The other thing about the great dealers is that they are not afraid to price masterpieces aggressively. In 1911, the rich British banker Arthur Grenfell was persuaded to pay £30,000 for it, five years on from its acquisition for so much less. Did Grenfell suffer momentary doubt about the price he was paying? If so, Lane would have had persuasive arguments at the ready to reassure him: £2,200 had been what it was worth as a speculation in 1906; £30,000 was what it was worth now that its potential had been realised in its full glory. He might also have pointed out the current rate of increase in prices for the best old masters. They were in the midst of a boom that would continue until reaching its climax in 1914.

No boom is totally without its pockets of disappointment, however. On 26 June 1914 a familiar – perhaps now too familiar – picture came up for auction at Christie's as Lot 66 in the summer

117. Titian, *Man in a Red Cap*

old masters sale. Earlier in the year the banking firm of Chaplin, Milne, Grenfell and Co. had failed, so Arthur Grenfell, one of the partners, was obliged to put up for sale the Titian *Man in a Red Cap* that he had bought from Hugh Lane three years earlier for £30,000. Given the price he paid, the price now realised – £13,650 – might have struck him as a little disappointing, but he needed the cash. He would have been even more upset to discover the identity of the buyer: Hugh Lane. Worse, within a few months Lane had sold the Titian for a second time, on this occasion to the ubiquitous Henry Clay Frick. One can only hope that Grenfell never discovered the price Lane persuaded Frick to pay: £50,000. But triumph turned to tragedy the following year when Lane, returning from New York having completed his business with Frick, lost his life when the *Lusitania* was sunk by German naval action. Even art dealers cannot go on being lucky forever.

Through most of 1911 Duveen continued to be distracted by having to fight out in court the case brought against them by the New York tax authorities. Duveen had the resources to hire the very best in legal representation, and the firm had friends in high places – powerful people in the city who were very often already their clients – but it took time, energy and ingenuity to negotiate the significantly smaller fines that were ultimately levied. It also played to the temporary advantage of other European old master dealers in New York who hadn't been caught, firms such as Wildenstein and Seligman. But by the end of the year, unbound like Prometheus, Duveen launched themselves back into the market with a vengeance.

In 1912 Duveen and Berenson entered into a secret profit-sharing arrangement, to apply to every painting sold that Berenson authenticated. One work that Berenson did not get to inspect this year was the *Mona Lisa*, stolen from the Louvre in 1911. He might have, though: its temporary custodian Vincenzo Perruggia, having left behind the Leonardo still hidden in a box in his Paris lodgings, made a trip to see Duveen in London this year. His intention was presumably to assess the viability of some kind of sale of his trophy through the best-known and most successful old master dealer in Europe. But Duveen decided he was a hoaxer and sent him away.

The history of the art market in the twentieth century is the story of a gradually changing balance between old art and modern art. While prices for the former continued on a steady upward trajectory, demand for modern art accelerated even more strongly and began to outpace it; as the twenty-first century approached, a further surge in prices for modern and contemporary works meant that they for the first time achieved a larger share of the market than older art. These developments were prefigured by events in Paris in 1912. Two separate old master collectors – Paul Poiret and Jacques Doucet – independently decided they were no longer content, in Marinetti's words, 'to pour their sensitiveness into a funeral urn'. Instead they resolved, as Marinetti urged, to 'cast it forward in violent gushes of creation and action' by buying avant-garde art. This meant cashing in their collections of French eighteenth-century painting and decorative arts in order to buy modernism.

Poiret and Doucet were both eminent haute couturiers, a profession with particularly sensitive antennae to the art world. Poiret's change in direction saw him buy some early Picassos and a Cubist painting at the Peau d'Ours sale in 1914, and a *Maiastra* sculpture, one of Brancusi's first engagements with the subject of the bird in flight. Doucet was to develop into an even more important collector of contemporary art. First, he too had to clear the decks: the sale in Paris in 1912 of his eighteenth-century works was a highly successful and well-attended event. Prices realised reflected the remarkable boom that had resonated through the old master market over the past decade. His beautiful Chardin, a version of *The House of Cards*, for which he had paid 4,200 francs in 1903, now sold for an extraordinary 160,000. His Fragonard *Sacrifice au Minotaur* fetched even more: the hammer came down at 300,000. Most sought after of all was his *Portrait of Princesse Talleyrand* by Elisabeth Vigée-Lebrun, which made 350,000 francs. Needless to say, it ended up in the hands of Henry Clay Frick. These were not fire-sale prices: on the contrary, they showed that the old master market was stronger than ever. But for Doucet and Poiret the seductive brew of dynamic new art, now coming to the boil in the three years before the war, was growing irresistible. Over the following years Doucet acquired a number of fine Picassos including major Cubist works. In 1916 he would achieve his greatest coup of all, when he bought the *Demoiselles d'Avignon* for 25,000 francs.

Old master prices continued their surge through 1913. Major art dealers traversed the continent, engineering the passage of important paintings of the past from old European collections into new American ones. Hugh Lane, who darted like some elegant eel between Europe and America, sold Titian's portrait of Philip II to Mary Emery of Cincinatti for £60,000. Another Titian to change hands expensively (£36,000) was the portrait of Caterina Cornaro, which was bought by the plutocratic British art historian and collector Herbert Cook, who promptly reattributed it to Giorgione. Once again, the bulk of the year's major transactions involved Duveen, ably assisted by Bernard Berenson. Duveen managed to persuade the American tycoon Benjamin Altman to buy yet another Titian, a portrait of Ariosto, a work whose attribution Berenson had doubted in 1895 but now, with a bit of deft footwork, recommended as being by Giorgione. If you were very rich it was great to have a Titian, but Giorgione was even sexier, so if your early Titian could be reinvented as a Giorgione then you were made a happy man. It was all part of the Duveen service. After that Altman bought Rembrandt's *Bathsheba* at auction through Duveen for £50,000 (£44,000 plus Duveen's commission). Finally he agreed to pay Duveen £103,300 for a Mantegna, but then in October he most inconveniently died before the transaction could be completed.

Undaunted, Duveen turned his attention to other masters. He sold Velasquez's *Portrait of the Duke of Olivarez* to Mrs Collis Huntingdon for $400,000. Then Lord Michelham wanted a Romney, so Duveen sold him a portrait for £41,000. Frick wanted a Gainsborough so Duveen sold him one for $400,000.

Then there was the small *Cowper Madonna* by Raphael, which he sold to another American tycoon, P. A. B. Widener for $700,000 in January 1914. Even by Duveen's standards, it was quite a year.

Duveen did all he could to secure the Benois Leonardo, too. In early 1914 there were signs that it was now to be prised from the hands of the Benois family. But then the tsar stepped in and bought it. Duveen was not used to being thwarted, but even he could not compete with the tsar in Russia. He found consolation for the disappointment in a string of other high-priced deals over the rest of the year. He sold a van Dyck from the collection of the Duke of Abercorn to Frick for £81,000, and a portrait by Hoppner to E. T. Stotesbury of Philadelphia for £72,000 (famously Stotesbury's estate sold it again in 1944 when it fetched £2,500; but Duveen was no longer around to support prices). And Duveen's other consolation was that he had his ear rather closer to the ground than the tsar did: throughout the summer he was moving his stock out of Paris to London and New York in anticipation of war.

Chapter Thirty-two

Heritage, Museums and National Collections

By the beginning of the twentieth century, great old master pictures were disappearing across the Atlantic in numbers. This was all very well for their grateful sellers, European aristocrats otherwise unable to make ends meet. But the threat to the cultural heritage of Europe was recognised as becoming increasingly serious. If private owners had to sell major works, ways must be found of keeping them in the country, of guiding them into national public collections. How was this to be financed, in an era of rapidly rising art prices? Underlying these concerns was a nationalist agenda: the Louvre, the Hermitage, and the National Galleries of London and Berlin were increasingly perceived as expressions of national strength and pride. The respective glories of France, Russia, Britain and Germany were at stake. And at the same time those of advanced sympathies began to found museums of modern art, too. Debate ensued as to the criteria by which works should be included. Nationalism was in play here as well: were German museums, for instance, being overwhelmed by modern French art?

A high-profile case illustrating the risk to Britain's heritage loomed in London in the course of 1905, when Agnew's made a momentous acquisition. In 1820 John Morritt of Rokeby Hall in Yorkshire had bought a splendid painting by the then relatively unknown Spanish master, Velasquez. It was a sumptuous full-length reclining nude. Morritt referred to it fondly as 'my fine picture of Venus's backside' and hung it a little above eye height in his library, 'to spare the blushes of the ladies'. It was the painting now known as *The Rokeby Venus*. The landed aristocracy in

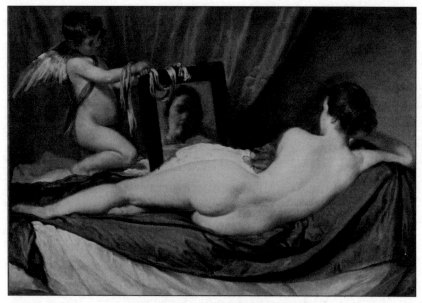

118. Velasquez, *The Rokeby Venus*

Britain had been in financial trouble for a generation. From the 1880s onwards they found themselves under pressure as a result of the agricultural glut created by the expansion of farming in the new world. Land was no longer producing the returns, so more and more treasures from old British art collections were appearing on the market, and more and more rich Americans were opening their capacious wallets in order to acquire the status that ownership of such works bestowed. Agnew's recognised the huge commercial potential the *Rokeby Venus* had to transatlantic moguldom, and happily paid the Morritt family £30,000 for it.

But they had reckoned without the heritage lobby now rearing its head in Britain. The painting was identified by the nascent National Arts Collection Fund as a treasure that must be saved from going abroad at all costs. The National Gallery in London should be its natural destination. But Agnew's – which was not a charity – was now asking considerably more for it than their purchase price; hefty offers had already been received from the Louvre and Berlin (according to Agnew's), not to mention a queue of American collectors. The acquisition budget for the National Gallery in London for the year was a paltry £5,000. The newly established National Art Collections Fund had done their best, but were some way short of the financial target, which Agnew's had set at £45,000. There was much hand-wringing, and letters to *The Times* bemoaning opportunities about to be lost.

Then help emerged from an unexpected source. In January 1906 King Edward VII made a private visit to Agnew's to see the picture. He spent half an hour in a room on his own with the Velasquez. Who knows what exactly happened in that time, what demons the king wrestled with? Certainly it was not the first occasion that Bertie had been alone in a room with a naked woman; nor indeed the first occasion that the encounter resulted in him parting with a conspicuously large amount of money. But in this case the result was thoroughly beneficial to the country. He guaranteed £8,000 to buy the painting, and pledged a further £5,000 as a loan for twelve months. He did it anonymously, and the identity of the royal benefactor did not come to light till 1996. But the painting was saved, and went on view in the National Gallery. The British press crowed: *The Times* rejoiced in the acquisition for the nation of what it described as 'perhaps the finest painting of the nude in the world'. Art was being deployed as a symbol of British might. In May 1906 the king became patron of the National Art Collections Fund.

One elderly and distinguished misanthrope in Paris had different ideas about museums. He maintained that too many people were going to them. Edgar Degas, at dinner at Vollard's in 1907, ranted against the popularisation of art and the swelling sea of exhibitions, pictures and artists engulfing France. Even the army was going under. 'Today everyone has to have taste the same way one has clothes!' he exclaimed in Kessler's hearing. 'It's shameful! It's come to the point where the garrison in Paris has ordered that each week a detachment of soldiers should visit the Louvre *under the supervision of an officer!*' This dragooning of the army into art appreciation had a motive that Degas may not totally have grasped. It was to deepen military understanding of French national heritage and thereby to make them better soldiers in its defence.

While there was increased awareness of the potency of a national art collection as a statement of national prestige and glory, there was still an unwillingness on the part of governments to use public money to pay for it. A fraught pattern emerged in the passage of national art treasures from private to public collections at the beginning of the twentieth century: niggardliness in official museum acquisition funds, followed by outrage as a major work came on the market and seemed to be escaping abroad, and then last-minute salvation through the patriotic generosity of rich individuals joining forces with newly established organisations such as the National Art Collections Fund. In the German museum world, big money was available: the Prussian budget for museums for 1906 was 2.6 million marks (£130,000), but a relatively small proportion of that was earmarked for acquisitions. The National Gallery in London, as we have seen, was allowed £5,000 per annum for buying works of art, and the French government gave the Louvre £8,000 for the same purpose. The funds provided by governments, while conspicuously more generous in Berlin than in London or Paris, did not – even in Germany – keep up with the prices for major old masters as dictated by the realities of the art market. In each country, the saving of great works for the nation was often dependent upon outside philanthropic sources of money. This did not just mean the intervention of rich individuals. The urge to philanthropy, and to the preservation of heritage, was more democratically channelled through organisations such as the National Art Collections Fund in London, which was paralleled by the Rembrandt Foundation in Amsterdam (set up in 1883 to help the Rijksmuseum fund purchases), Les Amis du Louvre in Paris (founded in 1897) and the Kaiser Friedrich Museums Verein in Berlin (also founded in 1897). Through these bodies the culturally aware prosperous middle class could make its contribution (although the Berlin Group, unlike the NACF, retained ownership of their purchases and made loans of them to the museum). Extreme cases prompted the occasional intervention of monarchs: the kaiser was ready to lend his financial muscle to the acquisition of special treasures to enhance the fatherland's international standing. It was perhaps a rivalrous awareness of his German cousin's spending that persuaded Bertie to open his cheque book in 1906.

Beneath the surface of relative financial plenty in the German museum world, internal battle lines were being drawn up in Berlin. On the conservative side, loyal to the emperor, the increasingly powerful Wilhelm von Bode headed the Kaiser Friedrich Museum and was on the prowl on behalf of the nation for major old master collections to enhance the glory of Germany. On the other hand, Hugo von Tschudi, director of the National Gallery, was a progressive with a significant sympathy for modern French art. In 1906 von Tschudi nailed his modernist colours to the mast and bought a second Gauguin for his own personal collection. He also orchestrated with the critic Julius Meier-Graefe an exhibition of German art from 1775–1875, held at the National Gallery in Berlin. This was an exercise in the manipulation of the past in order to promote an aesthetic value system of the present. The exhibition's emphasis on 'painterly' qualities in the art of the period prepared the ground for a view of contemporary art that embraced the aesthetic of French Impressionism. Von Tschudi was not alone: he was one of a generation of exceptionally enlightened German museum directors eyeing the great French post-Impressionists and manoeuvring to make acquisitions.

At the same time radical questions were being asked in Germany about museums themselves. Ludwig Pallat, writing in 1906 on the state of public art institutions, declared, 'Museums are too big, too diverse, and too exhausting'. One man doing his best to change that was Karl Osthaus, who was carefully hanging his recently established museum in Hagen with modern art, mostly French (although the tenacious Ada Nolde also persuaded him to buy her husband's *Springtime in the Garden* that summer). Osthaus called his museum the Folkwang, after the dwelling of Freya, goddess of beauty, in Valhalla. It was a different sort of museum, the interior of which has been designed by Kessler's friend the art nouveau architect Henry van de Velde. The exhibition rooms were studiedly neutral. Gertrude Osthaus, the collector's wife, explained, 'a well-arranged distribution and sequence of spaces, together with a rhythmic blend of their proportions and colours, creates an almost imperceptible but vital atmosphere in which each object can freely release its power'. The breath of change was beginning to waft through some of the older museums, too. In 1906 Georg Swarzenski was appointed director of the Städel Museum, Frankfurt. He was the pioneer of an approach that he articulated in a musical analogy. Instead of being a storehouse of objects, the museum was to be 'like a concert hall' where works of art could be orchestrated 'to transmit artistic experience as perfectly and directly as possible'.

When it came to modern art, Britain moved more slowly. In 1905 the Tate Gallery, having missed the opportunity to buy any number of great French Impressionist pictures at the Durand-Ruel show in January, roused itself to pay £2,000 for Whistler's *Old Battersea Bridge* (which in 1886 had only fetched £63 at Christie's). They had barely got off the starting line and would have to await the era of Samuel Courtauld between the wars before doing some catching up. The man most committed to setting up a museum of modern art in Britain was actually Hugh Lane, who aimed to do it in Dublin. Lane was continuing to put together a fine collection of French Impressionists for the purpose. And he was continuing to finance it by astute purchases in his day job as a dealer in old master pictures. Lane's eye was legendary in the London sale rooms: simply by being seen inspecting a lot on view at Christie's he could materially increase the price that it sold for.

Meanwhile the war between modernists and traditionalists continued to be fought out in the halls of the German museums. This year the emperor paid an official visit to the National Gallery in Berlin. Here was the moment of reckoning for von Tschudi, the director who had discreetly infiltrated into the collection a 'fifth column' of French modernist paintings. At the last moment von Tschudi felt misgivings about the Cézanne and removed it from the wall. But he was only delaying the inevitable. A year later he was dismissed from the National Gallery in Berlin by the emperor, whose belief that military painting was the highest form of art, and that ultimate responsibility for enforcement of standards of morality in public exhibitions lay with the police force, was a serious obstacle to their mutual understanding. But von Tschudi soon found a new job as director of the Munich Museum, where his modernist sympathies were more acceptable. For von Tschudi, like Swarzenski, it wasn't just a question of what was presented on the walls, but how it was presented. He was able to achieve something in Munich that he had been denied in Berlin: a rearrangement of the collection so that it was hung less densely, and, in his words, 'every single work is able to lead its own life'.

New museums sprang up. When the Mannheim Kunsthalle opened in 1909, the director Fritz Wichert took an imaginative if controversial step in mounting as one of his first exhibitions a show of works borrowed from dealers, even labelling some of them with their price. The relationship between the museum and the art market was still not fully understood at the beginning of the twentieth century. The realisation gradually dawned on museum directors that once they start buying art for their institutions – or condoning its exhibition in their premises – they become arbiters of value. This is particularly so with contemporary art. Like it or not, their choices impact the market. Museum curators may consider themselves simple unbiased art historians trying to present a balanced picture of how and why the art of the past – and the present – took the form it did, but in making acquisitions or mounting exhibitions they are implicitly privileging the work of the painter concerned, having an effect on its commercial value. These were issues brought into sharper focus for the first time in the early twentieth century.

In 1910 the director of the Bremen Kunsthalle, Gustav Pauli, bought van Gogh's *Poppies in a Field*. It was the first work by the artist to enter a public museum anywhere in Europe. It was testament to the exceptionally far-sighted generation of young museum directors that it should happen in Germany. Jens Thiis, recently installed as the first director of the National Gallery in Oslo, was a remarkably far-sighted runner-up in the van Gogh stakes. That summer he ventured to Paris on a buying trip. He found a Cézanne he very much liked at 30,000 francs, but it was snatched from under his nose by Hugo von Tschudi for Munich. Informed rumour had it that von Tschudi often bought without having the funds at his disposal, confident that once he got the picture to Munich he would find a rich patron to finance the deal. Thiis decided to risk the same strategy: when Bernheim-Jeune obligingly came up with another Cézanne still life at 25,000 francs, Thiis added to his check-out basket a van Gogh self-portrait from the dealer Blot for 10,000. He took both back to Oslo, plus a Delacroix at 10,000. He didn't have the funds to pay for them all but decided to wing it. In the end, by a mixture of wheedling rich patrons (of which there were fewer in Oslo than in Munich) and loans from charitable funds, he managed to keep the Cézanne and the van Gogh, but he had to send the Delacroix back unfinanced. He spoke of sleepless nights.

Swarzenski was also negotiating to buy a van Gogh for Frankfurt, and secured the outstanding *Portrait of Dr Gachet* in 1911. At this juncture Germany led the world in public acquisition of modern art. But the more modern the art, the greater the risk to the museum, as Franz Marc recognised ruefully writing in the *Blaue Reiter Almanac* in 1912. The authorities regarded old master purchases for public collections as much safer because they represented investment in considerable financial assets. Unlike the buying of a Picasso or a Matisse, 'the acquisition of a Rubens or a Raphael ... could certainly be considered a contribution to the nation's *material* worth'.

Still, there were missteps in the pursuit of national glory through the acquisition of the great art of the past. The German government continued its strategy of throwing money at the Berlin Museum in order to build a collection that asserted German pre-eminence on the international stage. Italian Renaissance art was of course the supreme investment area for achieving this, at least in the eyes of the kaiser and his right-hand man Dr Bode. But even the greatest experts err. In 1909 it was discovered that the wax bust of Flora, bought by Bode with German government money for £9,000 as a Leonardo, was not what it purported to be. In the words of Reitlinger, it was revealed that 'Flora had been acquired by the first vendor in Southampton for 35 shillings and that, being hollow, she contained part of the quilted early Victorian waistcoat of her maker, Richard Cockle Lucas'. It was an embarrassment for Bode, and the source of considerable mirthful schadenfreude in London.

But mistakes occurred in London, too. On 26 August 1909 Lord Crawford writes in his diary:

> I see Ribblesdale is appointed trustee of the National Gallery and Edgar Vincent as well, the number being increased accordingly. Both are good fellows however, and neither of them could pass an elementary examination as to the authorship of a dozen masterpieces in the collection. There is humour in the selection of Ribblesdale. He is Mrs Asquith's brother-in-law – and thinking he would like the trusteeship, made an application to the premier. Asquith, always ready to honour his relations ... gladly consented and gave the necessary instructions. The Treasury as usual blundered and appointed instead of Lord Ribblesdale an equally good fellow, equally incompetent, called Lord Redesdale. Tableau. However Asquith solemnly increases the number of trustees and Ribblesdale's ambition is realised.[42]

It is a revealing insight into the appointment of those entrusted with the governing of Britain's greatest museum of visual art. Five years later Redesdale, unencumbered by any sort of connoisseurship, had made the most of his chance elevation and become chairman of the board of trustees. In that role he was able to voice his immortal rejection of the Lane bequest of French Impressionists, at that point being offered to London: 'I should as soon expect to hear of a Mormon service being conducted in St Paul's Cathedral as to see an exhibition of the modern French art-rebels in the sacred precincts of Trafalgar Square.'

But in 1909 the National Gallery was more immediately exercised by another major old master from a long-established British collection, which was apparently about to leave the country. This time it was a very fine Holbein, *Portrait of Christina of Denmark*, being offered for sale by the Duke of Norfolk. There was considerable public outcry at its coming on the market at all. In press and parliament the view was sanctimoniously expressed that old families should hold in trust great works of art, not make money from them. The duke countered that it was only the direst financial pressure that had forced his hand, precipitated by Lloyd George's 'People's Budget' and consequent increased taxation. This time it was Colnaghi's who were charged with its sale. They were asking £72,000, considerably more than the £45,000 that had saved the *Rokeby Venus*, but old master prices in these fevered years were spiralling upwards.

Once again, it was clear that there was no shortage of rich Americans lining up to pay the price. Time was short: Colnaghi's drummed regretful fingers. The chairman of the National Art Collection Fund was at a loss to know where to turn. The king was not inclined to step in this time. A princess of Denmark was a less attractive proposition than the *Rokeby Venus*, not least because she had her clothes on. Then an extraordinary thing happened. The chairman of the NACF received a letter out of the blue from a mysterious lady writing from a spa in Germany. She offered to donate £40,000, which – after Colnaghi magnanimously knocked £2,000 off the price – was enough to save the portrait for the nation. It later emerged that the sum of money volunteered by this public-spirited British widow amounted to a third of her wealth. Very few people spend that proportion of their assets on a single work of art. She is one of the unsung heroines of British heritage.

It was hard enough to save for the nation major old masters being sold by private collectors without losing the most important work already held in your national collection. But that's exactly what the Louvre managed to do early in the morning of Monday 21 August 1911, when the *Mona Lisa* was stolen. The theft was carried out with disconcerting ease by a thirty-year-old Italian called Vincenzo Perruggia, a painter and decorator who had been working in the museum and secreted himself in the building overnight, capitalising on the fact that the Louvre was closed on Mondays. He removed the painting from its frame and took it away wrapped under his coat. There was hand-wringing in the press: 'Will we ever see her smile again?' wondered the *Petit Parisien*. France was in a state of mourning. French ownership of the most famous painting in the world had been a source of national pride and international status. Losing it was a disaster. Heads had to roll, and the director of the Musées Nationaux, Théophile Homolle, was peremptorily sacked. But the picture itself had vanished.

Huge press interest in the theft continued throughout September. Picasso, remembering the Iberian statuettes that Pieret had stolen for him in 1907, panicked and got Apollinaire to return them to a police station. Apollinaire was arrested on suspicion of stealing the *Mona Lisa* and spent some days in police custody, which didn't improve his relations with Picasso. Meanwhile various living artists were asked their opinion of Leonardo's masterpiece in the *Grande Revue*. Van Dongen was subversively modernist in his verdict: 'Everything eventually comes to an end so why miss her? In any case she had no eyebrows and a peculiar smile. She must have had bad teeth to smile so tightly.' And meanwhile the painting itself stayed undetected, hidden in a box under the stove in Peruggia's lodgings in Paris.

It was not till 29 November 1913 that an antique dealer in Florence, Alfredo Geri, received a letter signed 'Leonardo'. The writer, proposing himself as a patriot motivated by the desire to return to Italy an Italian treasure stolen by a foreign power, offered to bring home the *Mona Lisa*. All he asked was 500,000 lire to cover expenses. Advised by the curator of the Uffizi in whom he confided, Geri encouraged 'Leonardo' to bring the work to Florence. When 'Leonardo' (none other than Vincenzo Perruggia) turned up at Florence railway station, he was relieved of the large box he was carrying and arrested. The box was opened and the painting it contained was authenticated. Here was another opportunity for the politicising of a work of art, art politics at the highest level. Some in Italy – D'Annunzio among them – advocated hanging on to the most famous painting in the world on the grounds that it was an Italian national treasure. But diplomatic wheels turned, and an amicable understanding was reached with France. The picture was exhibited in Florence, Rome and Milan before being returned in triumph to Paris, in time for extensive New Year celebrations. Alfredo Geri at least pocketed the 25,000 francs that was on offer from Les Amis du Louvre as a reward for the painting's return. Perruggia spent nine months in jail.

In Britain the suffragettes were waking up to the idea that art had an emblematic significance, particularly when it belonged to the nation. Up until now the militant women campaigning for their rights, both social and political, had confined their actions to assaults on buildings – breaking the windows in department stores, and setting fire to empty properties – but their efforts had not got them very far. They had suffered imprisonment, and when they extended their protests to hunger strikes in jail, they were punished with forcible feeding. In 1914 they turned their attention to works of art in public collections. Mary Richardson, a young woman who had arrived in London from her native Canada and espoused the suffragette cause, had been outraged to discover that she had received the same sentence at Bow Street for breaking a few panes of glass as a man had received

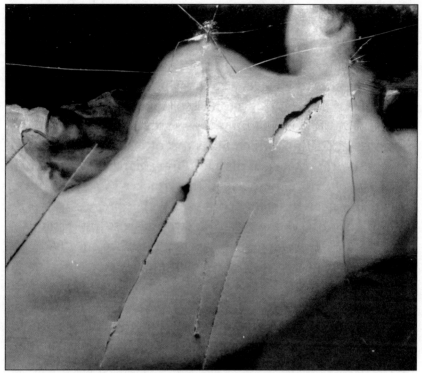

119. Not a Fontana: the suffragette attack on *The Rokeby Venus*

for criminally assaulting a child of eleven. Now she wanted to do something 'to stir the public sufficiently – even if they were but stirred to anger'.

So on 10 March she went out and bought a small axe which she secreted up the sleeve of her jacket and set off for the National Gallery. The painting she had selected to attack was *The Rokeby Venus*. Her first blow merely broke the protective glass on the picture, but she managed to get in several more slashes before she was restrained and arrested. In a much later interview she recalled 'I didn't like the way men visitors to the gallery gaped at it all day'. Immediately after her arrest a statement was issued on her behalf through the Women's Social and Political Union in which she said: 'I have tried to destroy the picture of the most beautiful woman in mythological history as a protest against the Government destroying Mrs Pankhurst, who is the most beautiful character in modern history.'

Reactions were grave. As a consequence of the attack, the National Gallery was closed to the public, as were the Wallace Collection, the Tate Gallery, the National Portrait Gallery, the Guildhall Art Gallery, Hampton Court and Windsor Castle. The artist Charles Ricketts in his diary ascribed the outrage to 'the spread of education, which leads too often to an exaggerated sense of the importance of the ego'. On 25 March, having thought about it a bit more, he decided the attack was a symptom of 'decivilizing change, latent about us, which expresses itself especially in uncouth sabotage, Suffragette and post-Impressionism, Cubist and Futurist tendencies'. When the Velasquez had been bought for the nation in 1906, *The Times* had waxed lyrical about what it represented:

> The picture which is in perfect condition is neither idealistic nor passionate, but absolutely natural and absolutely pure. We may indeed echo the words of an eminent critic and say that she is the Goddess of Youth and Health, the embodiment of elastic strength and vitality – of the perfection of Womanhood at the moment when it passes from the bud to the flower.[43]

Now, as the nation surveyed it in its damaged state, the sense of outrage was intensified by (a) the sum of taxpayers' money that had been recently spent on it, (b) its status as a national treasure and token of British power and (c) its shocking impact as a symbol of the right sort of womanhood outraged by the wrong sort of womanhood.

Suffragette attacks on works of art proliferated that summer. On 22 May Bellini's *Agony in the Garden* was vandalised, also in the National Gallery. When told the news, Ricketts 'had to sit down, as my knees began to shake'. The same month Sargent's portrait of *Henry James*, on exhibition in the Royal Academy summer show, was mutilated by another suffragette. The *Rokeby Venus*, whose subject matter was redolent of male exploitation of the female sex, made an obvious target; it is less easy to say what drew this female protestor to this particular picture of a leading American writer by a leading American painter. Perhaps it was just that they were both men. Or perhaps she was mesmerised by Henry James's plaid waistcoat, in the memorable words of Edmund Gosse 'heaving like a sea in a storm'.

On 21 August 1914 Charles Ricketts' soul was offered some balm when he was shown by the director of the National Gallery, Charles Holroyd, the repaired *Rokeby Venus*. Knees no longer shaking, he recorded that the Velasquez was 'very well restored and looking exceedingly well under a new coat of varnish'. Wyndham Lewis's Vorticist journal *Blast* also has a word of rather patronising advice for suffragettes that summer: 'IN DESTRUCTION, AS IN OTHER THINGS, stick to what you understand ... LEAVE WORKS OF ART ALONE, YOU MIGHT SOME DAY DESTROY A GOOD PICTURE BY ACCIDENT.' But at the end there is a more encouraging note: 'WE ADMIRE YOUR ENERGY. YOU AND ARTISTS ARE THE ONLY THINGS LEFT IN ENGLAND WITH A LITTLE LIFE IN THEM.'

Among the Russian establishment – those who made the decisions about what constituted Russian cultural heritage – there was confidence that the old order would go on for ever. Yes, there had been recent political and social upheaval, but it would take more than a few strikes and demonstrations to undermine a hierarchical system that had been in place for centuries. A 'small' fancy dress ball, given at home by Countess Kleinmichel in St Petersburg in 1914, was attended by 300 guests. They were all entertained to dinner and then danced on, oblivious. Indeed such was the confidence of the tsar this year that he did something rather extravagant: brushing aside the competition of Duveen, who thought he had a deal at £200,000, he bought Leon Benois's Leonardo for the Hermitage Museum. Advised by his curator Ernst Friedrich von Liphart, he paid £310,000 for it.

120. Leonardo, *The Benois Madonna*

There is something about works by Leonardo that makes potentates lose their heads when offered the chance to acquire one. £310,000 was a staggering amount of money, far and away the highest price ever paid for a painting; it was a statement of misplaced confidence in the long-term future of the Russian monarchy, and an assertion of Russian cultural might. It dwarfed Edward VII's contribution to the acquisition of the *Rokeby Venus* for the National Gallery, and even the kaiser's determined financial support for the Berlin museums. Had the tsar known that within four years the entire regime would have been overthrown and he and his family would be facing execution by firing squad, he might not have been so profligate. Or then again, perhaps he would. It was indeed a last spasm of the old order.

Finale: August 1914 – Art Suspended

On 4 August 1914, war was declared. Britain, France and Russia lined up on one side against Germany and the Austro-Hungarian Empire on the other. Spain, Italy, Holland and Belgium watched anxiously from the sidelines. Despite the fire-power and financial might that the combatants could draw upon – or perhaps because of it – the smart money was on a brief conflict. Those whose memories stretched back to 1870 and the Franco-Prussian War assumed that this one, too, would be over fairly quickly. Winners and losers would emerge, reparations would be paid, some boundaries might be marginally redrawn; then life would go on as before. The troops would be home by Christmas. Meanwhile for many young men across Europe joining up was a bit of an adventure, a diversion, a novel and exciting interlude in their lives.

A large number of the great artists of modernism were born in the 1880s, which meant that in 1914 they were the perfect age to be called up for military service. In France many modernists, despite their earlier anarchist sympathies, answered the call of la Patrie. Braque, Léger and Derain immediately reported for duty to their units. Picasso, disqualified from fighting because of his Spanish nationality, was cunning enough to make a quick round trip to Paris in the last week of July to withdraw from the bank his entire savings: 100,000 gold francs. On 2 August he was back in Avignon, in time to stash his money under his mattress and then bid farewell to Braque and Derain at the railway station as they set off to fight. He later reported to Kahnweiler, 'I never saw them again.'

Picasso was melodramatising for effect, but there was a sense in which he was right. After the war – which no one suspected was going to last four years – no one was the same. The extended conflict came as a massive caesura to all modern art. Artists disappeared into the military and stopped painting. Foreign artists had to leave Paris and, even if not compelled to join up in their countries of origin, found themselves cut off from the font of modernist inspiration.

So the dispersal began: artistic Paris was full of enemy aliens who had to abandon their studios and make a dash for it at the outbreak of war. They headed for the Gare du Nord and boarded the train for neutral Brussels, from where it was possible to catch last-minute services to eastern Europe. Emile Filla and Georges Kars, for instance, got back to Prague, where Kars immediately joined up and served in the Austrian army. But Kupka did not move quickly enough and was held in an internment camp for foreign nationals. Chagall had been enjoying a successful exhibition at Der Sturm Gallery in Berlin that summer; but there was no way back to Paris and he had to make the journey home to Russia and Vitebsk. One by one they withdrew: de Chirico went back to Italy, Mondrian to Holland; and rather than return to Paris, the Delaunays, who were holidaying on the French Atlantic coast, hurried on to exile in Spain.

Planned international exhibitions were abruptly cancelled. Works of art whose mobility had facilitated avant-garde artistic progress, creating a few years of unprecedented cross-fertilisation and experiment, stayed where they were. Freight trains, earlier in the year packed with modernist art en route from one show to another, were now only deployed for the movement of armaments and war materiel. Vinnen got his wish: no more French pictures would arrive in Germany. And no more Germans would arrive in Paris to buy them.

International hostilities affected those artists who stayed on in France, like Picasso, in subtler ways too. It is true that Picasso had just about reached the end of his intense initial engagement with Cubism. But his break with the style may have been accelerated by the perception in war-fevered Paris that it had Germanic associations. Partly this was because of the nationality of the unfortunate Kahnweiler, the impresario of the movement. Kahnweiler found himself stranded on holiday in Switzerland when war broke out. As a German national there was no way back for him to France. Within months his entire stock – of largely Cubist paintings – had been confiscated by the French state. He never managed to reclaim it. On the other side of the divide, Sarah and Michael Stein had similar problems. They had lent nineteen paintings from their collection in Paris to Galerie Gurlitt in Berlin for an exhibition. They, too, were confiscated, this time by the German authorities.

With Kahnweiler exiled and inaccessible in Switzerland, Juan Gris, who depended for survival on his monthly stipend from the dealer, found he had no money to live on. Matisse had got to know Gris in Collioure and arranged for Gertrude Stein to come to his financial rescue. Then Matisse found he had his own troubles to contend with. On 2 November Shchukin telegraphed him from Moscow to say that the banks were no longer allowing international transfers of money. It was the end of their artistic relationship. Three years later the Russian revolution would put a permanent stop to one of the most glorious collaborations between a patron and a painter in the history of art, a collaboration that enabled Matisse to achieve the artistic high point of his career. He would never do anything quite as good again.

The heroes of the Academic Salon sprang into action at war's declaration. What was called for was Patriotic Painting. Patriotic Painting meant the deployment of Allegory. Allegory meant the excuse to paint nubile young women in the personification of National Virtues. So Guillaume Seignac rushed out a composition in late 1914 called *La Belgique, la France, et l'Angleterre devant l'invasion l'Allemande*, calculated to rouse patriotic feeling to a high pitch of intensity. Three young women draped in their national flags (flags made of sufficiently thin material to allow full play to the breasts and thighs beneath) pose nervously

121. Guillaume Seignac, *La Belgique, la France et
l'Angleterre devant l'invasion Allemande*, 1914

in a stormy landscape, clinging together for mutual protection while Belgium brandishes a sword a bit like an umbrella. The threatening personification of L'Allemagne is no doubt lurking just out of picture, some ghastly Teutonic harpy too hideous for the artist to depict.

On the German and Austrian side there was a similar patriotic eagerness to join up, even among the modernists. Marc and Macke were early recruits; Max Beckmann too. Even Kirchner volunteered, as a driver supplying the artillery, in the hope that he would thus avoid the worse fate of being posted to the front as an infantryman; but by the end of 1915 he had been invalided out, his nerves in tatters. Further east, Larionov was conscripted into the Russian army in August 1914; he was lucky enough to be wounded almost immediately and discharged from the army as a result of his injuries. He was thus able to move to Switzerland with Gontcharova in 1915. The same year Kokoschka, encouraged by Alma Mahler to join up, reached the front and sustained a serious wound almost immediately. He returned to Vienna for treatment to find that Alma had done her bit for the war effort by running off with Walter Gropius. Even Schiele was called up in the end; the Austrian military authorities took one look at him and sensibly gave him a job minding the stores.

In Britain there was a robust military tradition among artists. There had even been a regiment called the Artists' Rifles formed in the nineteenth century by enthusiastic 'brothers of the brush'. But would the twentieth-century avant-garde turn out to be a more neurasthenic bunch, choosing service away from the front line in units like the mobile laundry? Some, like Mark Gertler, preferred not to get involved in the war, telling Dora Carrington that 'the best way we can help is to *paint*'. But others joined up immediately. Wyndham Lewis, for instance, became a bombardier. He rather enjoyed the anonymity of soldiering after the intensity of Vorticism. '"Bombardier" was after all a romantic incognito', he wrote later. 'The brief spell of sudden celebrity became a dream I had dreamt, of no particular moment.' He made a reassessment of German modern art in the light of hostilities; the Germans, Lewis decided, should just concentrate on their woodcuts. Woodcuts were 'where the Germans are best, disciplined, blunt, thick, and brutal, with a black simple skeleton of organic emotion'. Gaudier-Brzeska also went to fight in the trenches, having enlisted with the French army. In a letter home from the front he wrote that he had stolen a Mauser rifle from the Germans. The more he looked at it, the less he liked its 'powerful IMAGE of brutality', so he broke off its butt and carved it into a design that 'got its effect from A VERY SIMPLE COMPOSITION OF LINES AND PLANES'. Not long after this last defiant act of sculptural creativity he was dead, killed at Neuville St Vaast on 5 June 1915.

For the Italian Futurists the outbreak of war came as a welcome opportunity to put into practice the bellicose theories they had espoused with such passion in peacetime. But to their frustration the Italian government initially remained neutral; only in May 1915 did they come into the war on the side of the Allies. Marinetti, Boccioni and Russolo all joined up. What could be more glorious than death in war, 'the sole hygiene of the world' as Marinetti had called it? Indeed Boccioni did become a fatal casualty of the combat in 1916. The irony was, however, that his death took place not gloriously on the battlefield but prosaically in the barracks as result of a fall from his horse.

August Macke, although he had set off dutifully for the front, did not go into combat with any great relish or optimism. He grasped immediately what war meant for the progress of modern art. On 7 August he wrote to his publisher in Munich, 'Who knows how long art will be "suspended"?' One of his last works before the suspension took hold was the haunting *Farewell. Street with People at Dusk, Mobilisation*. There is an isolation and an anxiety to the darkened figures, in poignant contrast to the vivid colours of the Tunisian studies that he had made earlier the same summer. On 9 September he was writing to his wife from the western front: 'The din of the guns rages from morning to night. It is all so ghastly I would rather not write to you about it.' And he added: 'You're gone before you know it.' These were prophetic words. The fighting was particularly intense along this front, and on 26 September Macke was killed in Champagne near Perthes-les-Hurlus.

Franz Marc, on the other hand, took a much more positive line: 'I am not angry at this war,' he declared as he set out to join his unit. 'I am grateful for it, from the bottom of my heart. There was no other avenue to the time of the spirit; it was the only way of cleansing the Augean stables of the old Europe.' His first experience of the front, in September 1914, did not deter him: 'There is something unspeakably impressive and mystical about these artillery battles,' he wrote on 6 September. But at the end of the month Macke's death dealt Marc's enthusiasm for warfare a massive blow. He wrote to his wife about the Francophile Macke being killed by a French bullet in France, the country whose art he loved. Here indeed was an irony to ponder.

On 11 October 1914 Max Beckmann wrote lyrically of war in his diary:

> Outside the wonderfully grand sound of battle. I went out past hordes of wounded and exhausted soldiers that came from the battlefield and listened to this unique, horridly grand music. It's as if the gates to eternity are being ripped open when one of these great salvoes echoes towards you. Everything suggests space, distance, infinity to you. I wish I could paint this sound. Oh, this immensity and terribly beautiful profundity! Hordes of people, 'soldiers' moved in constant columns toward the centre of this melody, toward the determination of their fates.[44]

In a letter to Kandinsky in October, Marc was still talking about 'the salutary, if horrible, path to our goals' that the war represented. Kandinsky, in exile in Switzerland, disagreed with him: he felt 'the price of this kind of cleansing' was 'appalling'. Gradually, in the time that remained to him, Marc was worn down. He got to Verdun in 1916 and wrote to his wife that for days on end he had seen 'nothing but the most appalling things the human mind can imagine'. On 4 March 1916, on a reconnaissance near Braquis not far from Verdun, Marc was hit in the temple by shrapnel and killed.

In retrospect, Vlaminck blamed the war on the artistic preoccupation with science in general and on Cubism in particular: 'Science gives me a toothache. I am ignorant of mathematics, the fourth dimension, the golden section. For me the "Cubist uniform" is very militaristic. Madmen scare me. The reasoned, mathematical, Cubist and Scientific madness of 4 August 1914 has cruelly demonstrated to us the falsity of the result.' On the other hand it is also arguable that war was facilitated by the reverse of science, by the artistic embrace of instinct at the expense of reason. It fostered the Nietzschean belief that the natural state of man is to struggle – with his demons, with his passions, with his fellow men – and that there is something glorious about that struggle. Under this scheme of things the greatest art is born of ordeal; and war is the greatest ordeal of all. Or you could just stick with Klee's succinct verdict on the fighting: 'The whole business had as much sense to it as a wad of dung on a shoe-heel.'

Wherever blame is apportioned, there is no denying the tragedy that unfolded when artistic avant-gardes became military ones. It could have been a random shot from Léger that killed Macke, or from Marc that killed Gaudier-Brzeska. Those whose paintings a few months earlier had hung side by side in international exhibitions of European modernism were now armed with guns and told to take aim at each other. So some died. Others survived. But even the survivors, in most cases, died a kind of death as artists once the first shots in the war were fired, because the caesura in their lives that four and a quarter years of fighting and killing imposed meant they would never be as good afterwards as they had been before.

This decline in the post-war oeuvres of Balla, Severini, Chagall, Léger, Delaunay, de Chirico, Kirchner, Heckel, Wyndham Lewis, van Dongen, Vlaminck and Derain – and many others – is an uncomfortable truth that is not always acknowledged. Strictly speaking it is not the art historian's job to say if the art of an artist or period is any good, only to establish how and why it took the form it did. Art historians are people who know a lot about art but don't know what they like. Quality judgements are the territory of the art critic. But they are also a function of the art market. Every time a painting sells for a particular sum of money, a judgement about its quality is being made, and also one about its historical importance, an assessment of where it stands in relation to the oeuvre of the artist, and where the artist stands in relation to other artists. Opinions are fed into the mix by dealers, collectors, critics, academics and the general public. Together these various elements of art historical interpretation, aesthetic preference, cultural and social aspiration, commercial promotion and popular taste form an aggregated perception of relative merit that finds its ultimate expression in price. Take three paintings illustrated in this book, all sold in the same recent phase of the market (2016–20). The first is the Cubist portrait by Picasso, *Tête de Fernande* of 1909 (p. 251), which realised £46 million; the second, Boccioni's *Testa+Luce+ Ambiente* of 1912 (p. 286) made £12 million; and the third, Metzinger's *Cyclist* of 1912 (p. 193), sold for £2.6 million, These results tell us three things: that within the oeuvre of Picasso the *Tête de Fernande* is a major painting; that as a work in its own right it is significantly more important than the Metzinger or the Boccioni; and that Picasso's Cubism is to be rated many times higher than that of the Salon Cubists and several times higher than Italian Futurism's attempt to 'improve' Cubism in 1912.

This is not to argue that the art market is infallible as a measure of artistic quality. Its assessment of the value of contemporary art, for example, is open to distortion and revision. But with the art of the past, what the market prioritises, the hierarchy that price reflects, is often illuminating. There is an approximation of truth to its verdicts. What does it reveal about the artists who were in their youthful creative prime in 1905–14? Even if they went on to survive the Great War, the highest prices achieved in the twenty-first century have almost invariably been paid for their pre-First World War works. Post 1918, the market judges the quality and innovation of what they produced to have been in decline, and therefore pays less for it.

One of the few exceptions to this melancholy statistic is Picasso. He went on reinventing himself for six more decades, so it is probably for the best that he wasn't run over by a bus in 1905. Nonetheless, even in his extraordinary career, the ten years before the First World War still stand out as enduringly formative, the most important phase of his artistic life. In the intensity of their invention, imagination and daring, the years 1905–14 were a unique decade for everyone in the art world, unprecedented before and unrepeated since.

Endnotes

1. M. Vlaminck, *Dangerous Corner* (trans. M. Ross), London 1961.
2. Ibid.
3. P. Léautaud, *Journal of a Man of Letters* (trans. G. Sainsbury), London 1960.
4. *The Apocalyptic Landscapes of Ludwig Meidner*, Exhibition Catalogue, Los Angeles and Berlin 1989–90.
5. F. Gilot and C. Lake, *Life with Picasso*, London 1990.
6. B. Fulda and A. Soika, *Max Pechstein: The Rise and Fall of Expressionism*, New York 2012.
7. F. Nietzsche, *Twilight of the Gods* (trans. D. Large), Oxford 1998.
8. *Brücke: The Birth of Expressionism*, Exhibition Catalogue, Neue Galerie, New York 2009.
9. *Egon Schiele*, Exhibition Catalogue, Louis Vuitton Museum, Paris 2018.
10. M. McCully (ed.), *Loving Picasso: the Private Journal of Fernande Olivier*, New York 2001.
11. A. Muhlstein, *The Pen and the Brush*, New York 2017.
12. J. Bowlt (ed.), *Russian Art of the Avant-Garde: Theory and Criticism, 1902–1934*, New York 1976.
13. G. de Chirico, *Meditations of a Painter* (trans. J. T. Solby), New York 1955.
14. *Letters of Fritz Gartz and Giorgio de Chirico 1912–14*, de Chirico Foundation Journal no. 7/8, 2008.
15. P. Read, *Picasso and Apollinaire: The Persistence of Memory*, California 2008.
16. G. de Chirico, *Meditations of a Painter*, op. cit.
17. *Boccioni*, Exhibition Catalogue, Metropolitan Museum, New York 1988.
18. B. C. Buenger (ed.), *Max Beckmann: Self-Portrait in Words*, Chicago 1997.
19. H. Kollwitz (ed.), *The Diary and Letters of Kaethe Kollwitz*, Evanston 1988.
20. P. Assouline, *An Artful Life: A Biography of D. H. Kahnweiler*, New York 1990.
21. V Woolf, *Roger Fry*, London 1940.
22. A. Bennett, *The Journals*, London 1932.
23. A. Bennett, op. cit.
24. E. Marsh, *A Number of People*, London 1939.
25. F. Spalding, *Duncan Grant*, London 1997.
26. *Brucke: The Birth of Expressionism*, Exhibition Catalogue, op. cit.
27. *August Macke and Franz Marc, An Artist Friendship*, Exhibition Catalogue, Bonn and Munich 2014–15.
28. W. Kandinsky, *Reminiscences*, Munich 1913.
29. *Kasimir Malevich, Works from the Russian Museum*, Exhibition Catalogue, Amsterdam 1988.
30. R. Herbert (ed.), *Modern Artists on Art*, New Jersey 1964.
31. G. Burgess, 'The Wild Men of Paris', in *Architectural Record*, New York 1910.
32. P. Assouline, *An Artful Life*, op. cit.
33. F. Gilot and C. Lake, *Life with Picasso*, op. cit.
34. A. Danchev (ed.), *100 Artists' Manifestos*, London 2011.

35. C. Nevinson, *Paint and Prejudice*, London 1937.
36. M. McCully (ed.), *Loving Picasso: the Private Journal of Fernande Olivier*, op. cit.
37. E. Nolde, *Jahre der Kampfe 1902–14*, Berlin 1934.
38. A. Hoberg, *Wassily Kandinsky and Gabriele Münter, Letters and Reminiscences 1902–1914*, London 2005.
39. M. Semenova, *The Collector: The Story of Sergei Shchukin*, Yale 2018.
40. C. Vanderbilt, *The Glitter and the Gold*, London 1952.
41. A. Gide, *The Journals, 1889–1913* (ed. J. O'Brien), London 1947.
42. D. Lindsay (Earl of Crawford), *The Crawford Papers, 1892–1940*, Manchester 1984.
43. L. Nead, *The Female Nude: Art, Obscenity and Sexuality*, London 1992.
44. B. C. Buenger (ed.), *Max Beckmann: Self-Portrait in Words*, op. cit.

Selected Bibliography

In addition to the numbered endnotes above, which refer to key quotations in the text, the bibliography below directs the reader to the sources I have consulted in the writing of each chapter. Such is the quantity of material published on the art of the years 1905–14 that it is impossible to offer a comprehensive bibliography of this extraordinary decade, let alone read it all, so what follows is inevitably selective. But the challenge of writing this book has been made easier by the fact that two of the artists central to the story, Picasso and Matisse, are the subjects of outstanding modern biographies, by John Richardson and Hilary Spurling respectively. All students of the period are in their debt.

Introduction: A TUMULTUOUS DECADE

G. Busch and L. von Reinken (eds), *Paula Modersohn-Becker: the Letters and Journals*, New York 1983.

R. Shattock, *The Banquet Years*, London 1959.

P. Klee, *The Diaries, 1898–1918*, London 1965.

P. Weiss, *Kandinsky in Munich: The Formative Jugendstil Years*, Princeton 1979.

Kandinsky: The Path to Abstraction, Exhibition Catalogue, Tate Modern, 2006.

Part I: RELEASING CONTROL

1. Basic Instinct

S. Prideaux, *I Am Dynamite: A Life of Friedrich Nietzsche*, London 2018.

J. Whitebrook, *Freud, An Intellectual Biography*, Cambridge 2017.

F. Carco, *From Montmartre to the Latin Quarters* (trans. M. Boyd), London 1929.

E. Nolde, *Jahre der Kampfe 1902–14*, Berlin 1934.

Modigliani, Exhibition Catalogue, Tate Modern, 2017–18.

J. Farrington, *Wyndham Lewis*, London 1980.

Kokoschka: People and Animals, Exhibition Catalogue, Rotterdam 2013.

C. Butler, *Early Modernism: Literature, Music and Painting in Europe, 1900–1916*, Oxford 1994.

H. Spurling, *The Unknown Matisse (1869–1908)*, London 1998; and *Matisse the Master (1909–54)*, London 2005.

P. Read, *Apollinaire and Cubism*, Forest Row 2002.

H. Bergson, *Creative Evolution*, New York 2003.

L. Folgarait, *Painting 1909: Pablo Picasso, Gertrude Stein, Henri Bergson, Comics, Albert Einstein and Anarchy*, Yale 2017.

Juan Gris, Exhibition Catalogue, Whitechapel Art Gallery, London 1992.

2. The Guiding Lights: Van Gogh – Gauguin – Cézanne

H. B. Chipp, *Theories of Modern Art*, California 1968.

P. Léautaud, *Journal of a Man of Letters* (trans. G. Sainsbury), London 1960.

Expressionism in Germany and France, Exhibition Catalogue, Los Angeles 2014.

Sonderbund 1912 – Mission Moderne, Exhibition Catalogue, Cologne 2012.

Brucke: The Birth of Expressionism,
Exhibition Catalogue, Neue Galerie,
New York 2009.

J. Richardson, *A Life of Picasso: The Prodigy,*
1881–1906, London 1991; and *The Painter*
of Modern Life, 1907–17, London 1996.

3. Colour and Fauvism

H. Spurling, *The Unknown Matisse,* op. cit.

H. B. Chipp, *Theories,* op. cit.

J. Renard, *Journal 1887–1910* (ed. J. Barnes),
London 2020.

A. Gide, *The Journals, 1889–1913*
(ed. J. O'Brien), London 1947.

André Derain, Exhibition Catalogue,
Hermitage Museum Lausanne 2003.

Scandinavian Modernism, Exhibition
Catalogue, Copenhagen, Oslo,
Stockholm 1989.

4. Expressionism and Angst

R. Stang, *Edvard Munch, The Man and the*
Artist, London 1979.

P. Vergo, *Art in Vienna, 1898–1918,* London
1975.

J. Lloyd, *German Expressionism: Primitivism*
and Modernity, Yale 1991.

S. E. Bronner and D. Kelner (eds), *Passion*
and Rebellion: the Expressionist Heritage,
London 1983.

The Apocalyptic Landscapes of Ludwig
Meidner, Exhibition Catalogue,
Los Angeles and Berlin 1989–90.

5. Primitivism: The Wisdom of Savages

H. B. Chipp, *Theories,* op. cit.

J. Richardson, *Picasso: The Painter of Modern*
Life, op. cit.

V. Bell, *Selected Letters of Vanessa Bell*
(ed. R. Marler), New York 1993.

Emil Nolde, Exhibition Catalogue, Louisiana
and Frankfurt 2014.

E. Sprigge, *Gertrude Stein,* London 1957.

B. Fulda and A. Soika, *Max Pechstein: The*
Rise and Fall of Expressionism, New York
2012.

J. Lloyd, *German Expressionism: Primitivism*
and Modernity, op. cit.

E. L. Kirchner: The Dresden and Berlin Years,
Exhibition Catalogue, London Royal
Academy 2003.

Brücke: The Birth of Expressionism,
Exhibition Catalogue, op. cit.

D. Gordon, *Expressionism: Art and Idea,*
Yale 1987.

6. Sex and Sublimation: Exciting the
Whole Machine

B. Fulda and A. Soika, *Max Pechstein,* op. cit.

P. Klee, *The Diaries, 1898–1918,* op. cit.

H. B. Chipp, *Theories,* op. cit.

J. Renoir, *Renoir, My Father,* London 1964.

G. Melly, *Don't Tell Sybil,* London 1997.

S. Freud, *Complete Psychological Works* (trans.
J. Strachey), London 1953–74.

M. Seymour, *Ottoline Morrell: Life on the*
Grand Scale, London 1993.

Brücke: The Birth of Expressionism,
Exhibition Catalogue, op. cit.

H. S. Ede, *Savage Messiah: Gaudier-Brzeska,*
London 1971.

A. Danchev (ed.), *100 Artists' Manifestos,*
London 2011.

A. Comini, *Egon Schiele's Portraits,*
California 1974.

7. Anarchism

M. Macmillan, *The War that Ended Peace,*
London 2013.

P. Leighten, *Re-Ordering the Universe: Picasso*
and Anarchism, 1897–1914, Princeton 1989.

M. McCully (ed.), *Loving Picasso: the Private*
Journal of Fernande Olivier, New York
2001.

A. Muhlstein, *The Pen and the Brush,* New
York 2017.

R. Shattock, *The Banquet Years,* op. cit.

J. Richardson, *A Life of Picasso: Prodigy,*
op. cit.

P. Vergo, *Art in Vienna,* op. cit.

All Eyes on Kees Van Dongen, Exhibition
Catalogue, Rotterdam 2010–11.

8. Violence, War and Guns

P. Blom, *The Vertigo Years,* London 2008.

A. Danchev (ed.), *Manifestos,* op.cit.

S. Prideaux, *Edvard Munch: Behind the*
Scream, Yale 2005.

L. M. Easton (ed.), *Journey to the Abyss: Diaries of Count Harry Kessler*, New York 2011.

9. Journeys Inwards: The Symbolist Strand

Ferdinand Hodler, View to Infinity, Exhibition Catalogue, Neue Galerie New York 2012.

A. Weidinger, *Gustav Klimt*, London 2007.

Vallotton, Idyll on the Edge, Exhibition Catalogue, Zurich 2007.

P. Read, *Picasso and Apollinaire, The Persistence of Memory*, California 2008.

V. Noel-Johnson (ed.), *Giorgio de Chirico: The Changing Face of Metaphysical Art*, Genoa 2019.

De Chirico, Exhibition Catalogue, Museum of Modern Art, New York 1982.

Part II: PARIS, CAPITAL OF THE MODERN ART WORLD

10. The Artistic Mecca

Boccioni, Exhibition Catalogue, Metropolitan Museum, New York 1988.

11. Paris and Germany

Wyndham Lewis, *Tarr*, London 1916.

The Apocalyptic Landscapes of Ludwig Meidner, Exhibition Catalogue, op. cit.

B. C. Buenger (ed.), *Max Beckmann: Self-Portrait in Words*, Chicago 1997.

Brücke: The Birth of Expressionism, Exhibition Catalogue, op. cit.

August Macke and Franz Marc, An Artist Friendship, Exhibition Catalogue, Bonn and Munich 2014–15.

H. Kollwitz (ed.), *The Diary and Letters of Kaethe Kollwitz*, Evanston 1988.

Robert Delaunay: 1906–1914 de l'impressionisme à l'abstraction, Exhibition Catalogue, Pompidou, Paris 1999.

P. Paret, *The Berlin Secession: Modernism and its Enemies in Imperial Germany*, Harvard 1980.

P. Assouline, *An Artful Life: A Biography of D. H. Kahnweiler*, New York 1990.

Expressionism in Germany and France, Exhibition Catalogue, op. cit.

12. Paris and London

P. Levy (ed.), *The Letters of Lytton Strachey*, New York 2005.

K. Flint, *Impressionists in England*, London 1984.

F. Rutter, *Art in my Time*, London 1933.

André Derain: The London Paintings, Exhibition Catalogue, Courtauld Institute, London 2005–6.

I. Dunlop, *The Shock of the New*, London 1972.

D. Sutton (ed.), *Letters of Roger Fry*, London 1972.

A. Bennett, *The Journals*, London 1932.

Modern Art In Britain, 1910–1914, Exhibition Catalogue, Barbican London, 1997.

M. A. Caws and S. B. Wright, *Bloomsbury and France*, Oxford 2000.

13. Paris and Russia

B. W. Kean, *French Painters, Russian Collectors: The Merchant Patrons of Modern Art in Pre-Revolutionary Russia*, London 1994.

M. Semenova, *The Collector: The Story of Sergei Shchukin*, Yale 2018.

Malevich, Exhibition Catalogue, Tate Modern 2014.

From Russia, French and Russian Master Paintings 1870–1925, Exhibition Catalogue, London Royal Academy, 2007–8.

14. Paris and the Rest of Europe

Scandinavian Modernism, Exhibition Catalogue 1989, op. cit.

K. L. Carter and S. Walker (eds), *Foreign Artists and Communities in Modern Paris*, Farnham (Surrey) 2015.

E. Clegg, *Art, Design and Architecture in Central Europe, 1890–1920*, Yale 2006.

P. Wittlich, *Czech Modern Painters, 1888–1918*, Prague 2012.

Czech Cubism 1910–1925, Exhibition Catalogue, Prague 1991.

Futurism, Exhibition Catalogue, Tate Modern 2009.

Piet Mondrian, Exhibition Catalogue, The Hague and Washington 1994–5.

I. Dunlop, *The Shock of the New*, op. cit.

Part III : LOSING CONTROL

15. Trouble with Women

G. B. Shaw, *Man and Superman*, London 1907.

Modigliani and his Models, Exhibition Catalogue, London Royal Academy 2006.

Modigliani and the Artists of Montparnasse, Exhibition Catalogue, New York 2002–3.

B. Fulda and A. Soika, *Max Pechstein*, op. cit.

R. Stang, *Edvard Munch, The Man and the Artist*, op. cit.

O. Kokoschka, *Letters 1905–1976* (trans. M Whittall), London 1992.

K. L. Carter and S. Walker (eds), *Foreign Artists*, op. cit.

S. Tretter, *Gustav Klimt: Atelier Feldmuhlgasse 1911–1918*, Vienna 2014.

P. Vergo, *Art in Vienna*, op. cit.

A. Comini, *Egon Schiele's Portraits*, op. cit.

A. Weidinger, *Kokoschka and Alma Mahler*, Munich 1996.

16. Descent into Madness: The Case of Edvard Munch

P. E. Tojner, *Munch in his Own Words*, London 2001.

S. Prideaux, *Munch*, op. cit.

H. Spurling, *Matisse the Master*, op. cit.

17. Altered States: Drugs and Alcohol

A. Hayter, *Opium and the Romantic Imagination*, London 1968.

M. McCully (ed.), *Loving Picasso*, op. cit

18. Alienation from the Public

J. J. Sheehan, *Museums in the German Art World*, Oxford 2000.

Emil Nolde, Exhibition Catalogue, Louisiana and Frankfurt, op. cit.

P. Vergo, *Art in Vienna*, op. cit.

R. Corbett, *You Must Change Your Life: the Story of Rainer Maria Rilke and Auguste Rodin*, New York 2016.

19. Suicide, Death, Morbidity

J. Richardson, *A Life of Picasso; Prodigy*, op. cit.

G. Severini, *The Life of a Painter* (trans. J. Franchini), Princeton 1983.

J. Lloyd, I. Pfeiffer and R. Coffer, *Richard Gerstl*, Chicago 2017.

W. Rothenstein, *Men and Memories, 1900–1922*, London 1932.

Egon Schiele: The Radical Nude, Exhibition Catalogue, London Courtauld Gallery, 2014–15.

Egon Schiele, Exhibition Catalogue, Louis Vuiton Museum, Paris 2018.

Egon Schiele, Love and Death, Exhibition Catalogue, Van Gogh Museum, Amsterdam 2005.

H. J. Muller, *The Rudolf Staechelin Collection*, Basel 1991.

Kokoschka: People and Animals, Exhibition Catalogue, op. cit.

Ferdinand Hodler, View to Infinity, Exhibition Catalogue, op. cit.

20. Studio Gruffness and the Rewriting of History

Brucke: The Birth of Expressionism, Exhibition Catalogue, op. cit.

Futurism, Exhibition Catalogue, Tate Modern, op. cit.

André Derain, Exhibition Catalogue, Lausanne, op. cit.

B. Fulda and A. Soika, *Max Pechstein*, op. cit.

C. Butler, *Early Modernism*, op. cit.

E. Grisebach, *Ernst Ludwig Kirchner*, Bern 2014.

H. Spurling, *Matisse the Master*, op. cit.

Part IV: BEYOND INSTINCT

22. Supermen

August Macke and Franz Marc, An Artist Friendship, Exhibition Catalogue, Bonn and Munich 2014–15.

Mikhail Larionov: Pastels, Gouaches, Exhibition Catalogue, Galerie Aronowitsch, 1987.

P. Read, *Apollinaire and Cubism*, op. cit.

J. Richardson, *Picasso, Painter of Modern Life*, op. cit.

Robert Delaunay: 1906–1914, Exhibition Catalogue Paris, op. cit.

R. Shattock, *The Banquet Years*, op. cit.

J. Golding, *Cubism, A History and an Analysis 1907–1914*, London 1959.

R. Humphreys, *Wyndham Lewis*, London 2004.

E. L. Kirchner: The Dresden and Berlin Years, Exhibition Catalogue, London Royal Academy 2003.

C. Baudelaire, *The Painter of Modern Life*, London 2010.

23. Abstraction

C. Butler, *Early Modernism*, op. cit.

K. L. Carter and S. Walker (eds), *Foreign Artists*, op. cit.

J. Golding, *Cubism*, op. cit.

Robert Delaunay: 1906–1914, Exhibition Catalogue Paris, op. cit.

C. Green, *Léger and the Avant-Garde*, Yale 1976.

Kandinsky: The Path to Abstraction, Exhibition catalogue, op. cit.

Kandinsky: A Retrospective, Exhibition Catalogue, Pompidou, Paris and Milwaukee, 2014.

Malevich, Exhibition Catalogue, Tate Modern, op. cit.

Kasimir Malevich, Works from the Russian Museum, Exhibition Catalogue, Amsterdam 1988.

R. Herbert (ed.), *Modern Artists on Art*, New Jersey 1964.

M. Perloff, *The Futurist Moment*, Chicago 1986.

Mikhail Larionov: Pastels, Gouaches, Exhibition Catalogue 1987, op. cit.

Storm women. Woman Artists of the Avant Garde in Berlin, 1910–1932, Exhibition Catalogue, Frankfurt 2015–16.

W. K. Rose (ed.), *The Letters of Wyndham Lewis*, London 1963.

Hilma af Klint: Paintings for the Future, Exhibition Catalogue, Guggenheim, New York 2018–19.

24. The Blaue Reiter

K. Lankheit (ed.), *The Documents of Modern Art, The Blaue Reiter Almanac*, New York 1974.

August Macke and Franz Marc, An Artist Friendship, Exhibition Catalogue, op. cit.

A. Hoberg, *The Blaue Reiter in the Lembachhaus, Munich*, Munich 1989.

A. Hoberg, *Wassily Kandinsky and Gabriele Münter, Letters and Reminiscences 1902–1914*, London 2005.

C. Butler, *Early Modernism*, op. cit.

D. Gordon, *Expressionism: Art and Idea*, op. cit.

R. Corbett, *You Must Change Your Life*, op. cit.

H. B. Chipp, *Theories*, op. cit.

P. Blom, *The Vertigo Years*, op. cit.

25. Matisse: Beyond Fauvism

J. Richardson, *Picasso, Painter of Modern Life*, op. cit.

H. Spurling, *Matisse the Master*, op. cit.

C. Butler, *Early Modernism*, op. cit.

M. Semenova, *The Collector*, op. cit.

26. Picasso and Cubism

J. Richardson, *Picasso, Painter of Modern Life*, op. cit.

J. Golding, *Cubism*, op. cit.

P. Daix, *Picasso Life and Art*, London 1994.

M. McCully (ed.), *Loving Picasso*, op. cit.

H. B. Chipp, *Theories*, op. cit.

L. M. Easton, *Journey to the Abyss*, op. cit.

P. Leighten, *Re-Ordering the Universe*, op. cit.

P. Assouline, *Kahnweiler*, op. cit.

F. Gilot and C. Lake, *Life with Picasso*, London 1990.

Futurism, Exhibition Catalogue, Tate Modern, op. cit.

Marie Laurencin, Exhibition Catalogue, Giannada 1993.

C. Ambrosio, 'Cubism and the Fourth Dimension', *Interdisciplinary Science Reviews*, June–September 2016, pp. 202–21.

Cubism, The Leonard A. Lauder Collection, Exhibition Catalogue, Yale 2014.

The Cubist Cosmos from Picasso to Leger, Exhibition Catalogue, Basel 2019.

Alexander Archipenko, Space Encircled, Exhibition Catalogue, Eykyn and Maclean, London 2018.

H. Hess, *Lyonel Feininger*, New York 1961.

P. Read, *Picasso and Apollinaire*, op. cit.

J. Richardson, *Braque*, Penguin Modern
  Painters, London 1959.
Juan Gris, Exhibition Catalogue,
  Whitechapel Art Gallery, op. cit.

27. Futurism: Beautiful Ideas that Kill
G. Severini, *My Life*, op. cit.
M. Perloff, *The Futurist Moment*, op. cit.
Boccioni, Exhibition Catalogue,
  Metropolitan Museum, New York,
  op. cit.
Futurism, Exhibition Catalogue, Tate
  Modern, op. cit.
*Italian Futurism 1909–44, Reconstructing
  the Universe*, Exhibition Catalogue,
  Guggenheim New York 2014.
H. B. Chipp, *Theories*, op. cit.
*The Apocalyptic Landscapes of Ludwig
  Meidner*, Exhibition Catalogue, op. cit.
H. Hess, *Feininger*, op. cit.
*From Russia, French and Russian Master
  Paintings 1870–1925*, Exhibition Catalogue,
  op. cit.
C. Nevinson, *Paint and Prejudice*, London
  1937
J. Farrington, *Wyndham Lewis*, op. cit.
M. Antliff and S W Klein (eds), *Vorticism:
  New Perspectives*, Oxford 2013.

**28. Pioneers of Modernism: Dealers and
Collectors of New Art**

Dealers in New Art
P. Durand-Ruel, *Memoirs of the First
  Impressionist Art Dealer*, Paris 2014.
J. Richardson, *Picasso, Painter of Modern Life*,
  op. cit.
H. Spurling, *Matisse the Master*, op. cit.
M. McCully (ed.), *Loving Picasso*, op. cit.
P. Assouline, *Kahnweiler*, op. cit.
S. Koldehoff and C. Stolwijk, *The
  Thannhauser Gallery: Marketing Van Gogh*,
  Amsterdam 2017.
J. Halperin, *Felix Feneon*, Yale 1989.
Félix Fénéon, Exhibition Catalogue, Musée
  de l'Orangerie, Paris 2019.
R. Jensen, *Marketing Modernism in Fin-de-
  Siecle Europe*, Princeton 1994.

M. Fitzgerald, *Making Modernism: Picasso
  and the Creation of the Market for
  Twentieth-Century Art*, California 1996.
F. Illies, *1913: The Year Before the Storm*,
  London 2013.

Collectors of New Art
The Steins Collect, Exhibition Catalogue,
  Paris and New York 2012.
E. Hemingway, *A Moveable Feast*, London
  1964.
J. Richardson, *Picasso, Painter of Modern Life*,
  op. cit.
E. Nolde, *Jahre der Kampfe 1902–14*, op. cit.
H. Spurling, *Matisse the Master*, op. cit.
The Shchukin Collection, Exhibition
  Catalogue, Louis Vuitton Foundation,
  Paris 2017.
M. Semenova, *The Collector*, op. cit.
B. W. Kean, *French Painters, Russian
  Collectors*, op. cit.
A. Hoberg, *Wassily Kandinsky and Gabriele
  Munter*, op. cit.
P. Assouline, *Kahnweiler*, op. cit.
G. Severini, *My Life*, op. cit.
C. Saltzman, *Portrait of Dr Gachet*, New
  York 1998.
R. Corbett, *You Must Change Your Life*,
  op. cit.

Part V: KEEPING CONTROL

**29. Call the Police: Academicism and
  Conservative Taste**
Brücke: The Birth of Expressionism,
  Exhibition Catalogue, op. cit.
Ferdinand Hodler, View to Infinity, Exhibition
  Catalogue, op. cit.
P. Paret, *The Berlin Secession*, op. cit.
B. Fulda and A. Soika, *Max Pechstein*, op. cit.
A. Comini, *Egon Schiele's Portraits*, op. cit.
Kees Van Dongen, *Exhibition Catalogue*,
  Martigny 2002.
I. Dunlop, *The Shock of the New*, op. cit.

**30. Wriggle-and-Chiffon: Fashionable
  Portraitists**
W. R. Sickert, *A Free House!*, London 1947.
K. Lankheit (ed.), *The Documents of Modern
  Art, The Blaue Reiter Almanac*, op. cit.

P. and F. Dini, *Boldini Catalogo Ragionato*, Turin 2007.

V. Doria, *Boldini: Unpublished Work*, Bologna 1982.

T. Fairbrother, *John Singer Sargent: The Sensualist*, Yale 2000.

D. Lindsay (Earl of Crawford), *The Crawford Papers*, Manchester 1986.

C. Vanderbilt, *The Glitter and the Gold*, London 1952.

B. Pons-Sorolla and M. Lopez Fernandez, *Sorolla and the Paris Years*, New York 2016.

A. Weidinger, *Gustav Klimt*, op. cit.

L. M. Easton, *Journey to the Abyss*, op. cit.

31. Railroads and Rembrandts: Dealers and Collectors of Old Art

A. Gide, *The Journals 1889–1913*, op. cit.

M. Secrest, *Duveen: A Life in Art*, New York 2004.

G. Agnew, *Agnew's, 1817–1967*, London 1967.

H. James, *The Outcry*, London 1911.

D. Sutton (ed.), *Letters of Roger Fry*, op. cit.

B. Dawson (ed.), *Hugh Lane, Founder of a Gallery of Modern Art for Ireland*, London 2008.

G. Reitlinger, *The Economics of Taste*, London 1961.

32. Heritage, Museums and National Collections

J. Ridley, *Bertie: A Life of Edward VII*, London 2012.

J. J. Sheehan, *Museums in the German Art World*, op. cit.

A. Callu, *La Réunion des Musées Nationaux, 1870–1940*, Paris 1994.

Expressionism in Germany and France, Exhibition Catalogue, op. cit.

R. Jensen, *Marketing Modernism*, op. cit.

C. Saltzman, *Portrait of Dr Gachet*, op. cit.

N. Messel, *The Impressionist Trail*, Oslo 2019.

A. Poole, *Stewards of the Nation's Art: Contested Cultural Authority, 1890–1939*, Toronto 2010.

K. Lankheit (ed.), *The Documents of Modern Art, The Blaue Reiter Almanac*, op. cit.

G. Reitlinger, *The Economics of Taste*, op. cit.

D. Lindsay (Earl of Crawford), *The Crawford Papers*, op. cit.

D. Sassoon, *Mona Lisa: The History of the World's Most Famous Painting*, London 2001.

C. Saumerez-Smith, *The National Gallery: A Short History*, London 2009.

Mary R. Richardson, *Laugh a Defiance*, London 1953.

C. Ricketts, *Self Portrait, Letters and Journals*, London 1939.

M. Macmillan, *The War that Ended Peace*, op. cit.

Finale: August 1914 – Art Suspended

J. Richardson, *Picasso, Painter of Modern Life*, op. cit.

P. Assouline, *Kahnweiler*, op. cit.

K. L. Carter and S. Walker (eds), *Foreign Artists*, op. cit.

August Macke and Franz Marc, An Artist Friendship, Exhibition Catalogue, op. cit.

N. Carrington (ed.), *Selected Letters of Mark Gertler*, London 1965.

Wyndham Lewis, *Blasting and Bombardiering*, London 1937.

B. C. Buenger (ed.), *Max Beckmann, Self-Portrait in Words*, op. cit.

P. Klee, *The Diaries, 1898–1918*, op. cit.

H. B. Chipp, *Theories*, op. cit.

Acknowledgements

After a lifetime in the art world I am aware of the huge number of collectors, dealers, critics, historians, museum curators and auction house colleagues who have helped me write this book, too many to be able to mention them all here. But I would particularly like to thank Teresa Bimler and Thomas Boyd-Bowman at Sotheby's, and Olivier Camu at Christie's; James Stourton; Georg von Opel; Barry Donahue; Andrew Franklin; the ever-helpful staff of the London Library; and my wife Angélique for her unflagging intelligent support. I am also grateful – in this one small respect – to the coronavirus, which by precipitating repeated lockdowns at least created ideal conditions for writers to get on with their job.

List of Illustrations

64. Léger, *Contraste de Formes*. Digital image: © 2021 The Museum of Modern Art, New York/Scala, Florence © ADAGP, Paris and DACS, London 2021 p. 200

65. Kandinsky, *Bild mit weissen Linien*. Photo: Sothebys p. 201

66. Malevich, *Black Square*. Photo: © Bridgeman Images p. 203

67. Larionov, *Rayonist Composition*. Photo: Sothebys p. 205

68. Mondrian, *Composition*. Sothebys p. 206

69. Hilma af Klint, *Sjustjärnen*. Photo: © Heritage Images / Fine Art Images / akg-images p. 208

70. Kandinsky, *Landscape with a Green House*. Photo: Sothebys p. 213

71. Kandinsky, *Autumn Landscape*. Photo: © Fine Art Images / Bridgeman Images p. 215

72. Marc, *Deer in the Monastery Garden*. Photo: © Artothek / Bridgeman Images p. 220

73. Wilhelm Kuhnert, *Grollende Löwen*. Photo: Sothebys p. 220

74. Macke, *Figures in the Park*. Photo: Sothebys p. 222

75. Klee, *Tunisian Landscape*. Photo: Sothebys p. 223

76. Matisse, *Blue Nude*, 1907. Photo: Mitro Hood, The Baltimore Museum of Art: The Cone Collection, formed by Dr Claribel Cone and Miss Etta Cone of Baltimore, MA, BMA 1950.228 © Succession H. Matisse / DACS p. 227

77. Matisse, *The Dance*. Photo: © The State Hermitage Museum / Vladimir Terebenin © Succession H. Matisse/ DACS p. 230

78. Matisse, *Window*. Photoer: Philippe Migeat. Paris, Musee National d'Art Moderne – Centre Pompidou. © 2021. RMN-Grand Palais /Dist. Photo SCALA, Florence © Succession H. Matisse/ DACS p. 235

79. Picasso, *Les Demoiselles d'Avignon*. Photo: © Succession Picasso/DACS, London 2021 / Bridgeman Images p. 239

80. Braque, *Large Nude*. Photo: Bridgeman Images © ADAGP, Paris and DACS, London 2021 p. 244

81. Léon Comerre, *Lola and the Swan*. Photo: Sothebys p. 245

82. Picasso, *Dryad*. Photo: Sothebys© Succession Picasso/DACS, London 2021 p. 245

83. Braque, *Cubist Landscape*. Photo: Bridgeman Images © ADAGP, Paris and DACS, London 2021 p. 247

84. Picasso, *Tête de Fernande*. Photo: Photo: Sothebys © Succession Picasso/DACS, London 2021 p. 251

85. Braque, *Woman with Mandolin*. Photo: akg-images / André Held © ADAGP, Paris and DACS, London 2021 p. 255

86. Léger, *Nudes in the Forest*. Photo: Raffaello Bencini / Bridgeman Images © ADAGP, Paris and DACS, London 2021 p. 256

87. Le Fauconnier, *Abondance*. Photo: © Kunstmuseum den Haag / Bridgeman Images p. 257

88. Braque, *Le Portugais*. Photo: akg-images © ADAGP, Paris and DACS, London 2021 p. 260

89. Marie Laurencin in Picasso's studio. Image RMN-GP. Paris, Musee Picasso. © 2021. RMN-Grand Palais /Dist. Photo SCALA, Florence © Succession Picasso/DACS, London 2021 p. 262

90. Braque, *Violin*. Photo: Bridgeman Images © ADAGP, Paris and DACS, London 2021 p. 266

91. Picasso, *Guitar*. © 2021. Digital image, The Museum of Modern Art, New York/Scala, Florence © Succession Picasso/DACS, London 2021 p. 266

92. Gris, *Landscape at Ceret*. Photo: Sothebys p. 272

93. Boccioni, *The City Rises*. Photo: © Bridgeman Images p. 278

While every effort has been made to
contact copyright-holders of illustrations,
the author and publishers would be
grateful for information about any
illustrations where they have been unable
to trace them, and would be glad to make
amendments in further editions.

Index